AMONG THE
FANS

AMONG THE FANS

From Ashes to the arrows,
a year of watching the watchers

PATRICK COLLINS

WISDEN SPORTS WRITING

Published by Wisden Sports Writing and John Wisden and Co.
Imprints of Bloomsbury Publishing Plc
50 Bedford Square
London WC1B 3DP
www.wisden.com
www.bloomsbury.com

First published 2011
Reprinted 2011

ISBN 978 1 4081 3041 4

A CIP catalogue record for this book is available from the British Library

Edited by Matthew Engel
Commissioned by Charlotte Atyeo
Designed by James Watson

This book is produced using paper that is made from wood grown in
managed, sustainable forests. It is natural, renewable and recyclable.
The logging and manufacturing process conform to the environmental
regulations of the country of origin.

Typeset in 10pt Haarlemmer MT by seagulls.net
Printed and bound in Great Britain by Clays Ltd, St Ives plc

CONTENTS

To Julie, with love and thanks.

PROLOGUE
Setting Out: The Three-Legged Dog

Some time ago, in the course of a column, I made some faintly uncharitable observations about Bolton Wanderers and the way their followers tolerated their ponderous tactics. A few days later, I was taken to task by a reader, Mr Ray Heaton. He pointed out that football supporters are allocated a club at birth, and that fate had given him Bolton. He said he was born just four miles from the old ground at Burnden Park, and therefore Bolton was his team. Then he added something rather poignant. 'Supporting them is a bit like having a three-legged dog,' he said. 'You wish it had all four, but you still love it.'

Many of us understand precisely what he means; indeed, we're perversely proud of our predicament. We respect fate's allocation, because loyalty is what we do best. It is not a choice, but a condition. And this, in a sense, gives the club a free ride. It may be over-priced and under-performing, plagued by incompetents on the field and buffoons in the boardroom. It matters not. We are not about to desert to Old Trafford or Stamford Bridge, for we are stuck with our shop-soiled inheritance, our three-legged dog.

For the moment at least, football is confident of our loyalty, but what of the wider world of sport? How does it treat the people who fill its seats, acclaim its heroes and pay its bills? And how do those people feel about their treatment? In more than 40 years of writing about sport, I have frequently attempted to interpret the emotions of the crowd. It is a great impertinence since, unlike me, they have made some sacrifice to be present. They have paid their own entrance fees, travel costs and food bills.

And so, seeking to atone, I spent a sporting year watching the watchers: observing the ways and enjoying the company of the people who make our sports both possible and pleasurable. I went armed with a whole variety of questions: What are they doing there? What are they given? How do they behave? Are they there to see, or to be seen? What do they eat? How much do they drink? How do they react to miserable defeat and heart-lifting triumph? How has it changed? How much does it cost? How much does it mean?

The journey ranged widely, from Wembley to Wimbledon and from Cape Town to Cheltenham, with memorable excursions to a Test match at Adelaide and a greyhound meeting at Crayford. And it began on a springtime Sunday, in a green and pleasant corner of rural England...

'Do it right, Rosie!'

CHAPTER 1
POINT-TO-POINT IN SUSSEX

Buckholt Farm lies off Watermill Lane, in the village of Catsfield in the county of Sussex. 'Back of beyond,' says my local adviser. 'D'you have a satnav? You'll need it.'

In fact, on this sunlit Sunday in early spring, the route is splendidly simple: a prolonged bounce down a bumpy track, skirting the potholes and following the 'Vote Conservative' placards. Around the last bend is a large field. And in that field, some 5,000 people have gathered to enjoy the finest entertainment that the East Sussex and Romney Marsh Hunt can offer.

At a glance, the Catsfield point-to-point might be a crowd scene from an Ealing comedy, with Stanley Holloway as the loud-checked, deep-satchelled bookie and Alec Guinness in half-a-dozen deft disguises. The cast is familiar, an assembly of rosy-cheeked children, twinkling barmaids, solicitous vets, a wide-shouldered farrier and an elderly gent perched plumply on his shooting stick, mopping his brow with a spotted handkerchief. The colours are vivid, from the shimmering silks of the jockeys to the bright brush of green on the April branches. It is how a fanciful expatriate might remember rural England.

Point-to-point is defined as steeplechasing for amateurs. Like so many apparently English pastimes, the steeplechase was born in Ireland, in County Cork, in the year of 1752, when Edmund Blake challenged his neighbour, Cornelius O'Callaghan, to race for four and a half miles across the hedges, stone walls and fields of north Cork between St John's Church, Buttevant, and St Mary's Church, Doneraile. It was, in effect, a race between church steeples, and Mr Blake is said to have won his wager, a cask of wine. By contrast, victory at Catsfield merits no more than a token cheque and a round of applause.

At a glance, the Catsfield point-to-point might be a crowd scene from an Ealing comedy

The course is officially described as: 'an undulating long narrow oval, with bends at both ends on higher ground; fences inviting'. That term 'inviting' is one of racing's little jokes, for the birch barricades, almost 5 feet high, litter the field like a batch of health warnings. Yet the tone is light, warm, even jolly, for which much credit must go to the resident announcer, who features on the official racecard as John Ball CBE.

His is the first voice we hear, declaring the results of the pony races, which have been sponsored by a local prep school ('Happy children,' boasts the advertisement, 'hundred-acre grounds … Small classes: max – 18'). The ponies and their young riders have been out hunting together on at least four occasions during the current season, emphasising the link between hunting and racing. The trophies are presented in front of the weighing room, as Ball's voice, seething with static, barks: 'First: Oliver Beswick. Well *done*, Oliver! Second: Lucinda Beswick. Please put your hands together for Lucinda!' Up step the bonny Beswicks, to loud hurrahs. The vanquished loiter in the background, pluckily clapping. Poor Scarlett, unhappy Archie. One day their names will surely resound around Catsfield, but not yet.

Since the event is being staged by the East Sussex and Romney Marsh, there is a parade of hounds, a yapping, scampering, clamorous affair, which reinforces whichever hunting prejudice one happens to hold. The horses are toweringly, tail-flappingly imperious, likewise the huntsmen. The hounds are playful and yet, in the name of sport, patently capable of tearing limb from limb any fox that lacks the speed or guile to evade their attentions. Familiar with the spectacle, the locals give it scarcely a glance.

The roots of the sport lie deep in the hunting field, and each horse needs a current certificate from a registered hunt. Where there is hunting, then politics is never more than a furlong behind. For some, it is merely a matter for mischievous debate, like wheel clamping or Daylight Saving Time. One old lag of my acquaintance has evolved his own hunting policy: 'In town, I'm pro; in the country, I'm anti. I find it livens things up,' he says. But for others, it is real and terribly earnest. When Parliament banned hunting with dogs, the East Sussex and Romney Marsh was one of the most reluctant hunts in all of England to comply with the new rules. The traditional denouement has been swept away, yet people still follow in large numbers, and appear to love it no less, even if they remain unreconciled. Parliament has spoken explicitly on this question, yet there remains a feeling of victimisation.

Alongside advertisements for the Cherry Tree Pet Crematorium ('We Care Because You Care') and a personal trainer from Hailsham who specialises in weight reduction ('What have you got to lose?'), the racecard carries a full-page appeal from the Countryside Alliance, with an exhortation to 'Scrap the Act'. '2010 will be a defining year for the countryside,' runs the message. 'If you believe in liberty and tolerance then the Alliance is an organisation you should support.' I point out the page to the old chap with spotted handkerchief and shooting stick. Did he not think that this sort of thing might cause offence? 'To whom?' he asks. 'Well, to people who struggle to see the Countryside Alliance as the natural defenders of liberty and tolerance,' I suggest. He nods, indulgently. 'I quite see what you mean,' he concedes. 'But I don't think we need take it too seriously, do you?' Mercifully, he refrains from patting me on the head.

The locals swallow their first drinks of the afternoon before paying a precautionary visit to the bank of portable loos, close by the bookmakers' pitches. A country ritual is being observed, as a 30-yard queue quickly forms: polite, chatty, impeccably discreet. When they reach the head of the queue, they bow their heads, waiting for the sound of a green plastic door being unbolted. Nobody looks up at the person emerging.

Across the field, the multitude is preparing for the first race of this Sunday afternoon. There will be no cavalry charge, since it has attracted just two runners: Mr Tee Pee, owned and ridden by Matt Braxton, and Soldershire, ridden by Rose Grissell, who also trains both horses. Like all six races of the afternoon, it is contested over two circuits, three miles and eighteen fences. With the sadism of their calling, the bookmakers are offering 25–1 for 'no finishers'. Despite the slender entry, the race holds the hope of enthralling sport. Matt is an estate agent in his late thirties; a shy, affable man, belatedly converted to the thrill of guiding large horses over 'inviting' fences. Rose is 25, slim and patently capable. She is the daughter of a racing family. Her father, Gardie, is the secretary of the meeting; her sister, Hannah, will be riding later in the afternoon. And her mother, Diana, was once a trailblazer for women jockeys and now looks after a string of horses in the area, including Mr Tee Pee. It is an enduring wonder of the horsey world that everybody involved appears to be inter-related.

The punters take sides. Rosie springs aboard Soldershire. An intense, middle-aged woman approaches the horse, peers up at its rider and hisses, enigmatically: 'Do it right, Rosie!' As they canter to the start, the announcer intrudes with a piece of breaking news: 'A chocolate Labrador, who answers to the name of Biscuit, is missing. He has a blue collar. His owner would dearly love to have him back.' As we scan the crowd for the errant Biscuit, the starter sends the horses away, and suddenly the point-to-point ceases to be a gentle rite of spring and becomes an occasion of authentic, exhilarating competition. This is patently not the Cheltenham Gold Cup, with its tensions and pressures, heaving grandstands and jostling fields. But it is a distant, recognisable cousin. It is a race in which decisions are made, fences are flown and genuine excitement is generated. For fence upon fence, the outcome is in doubt. Then Soldershire starts to falter, two or three jumps are untidily negotiated, Matt drives his horse on, and the gallant Rosie goes crashing out through the wing of the penultimate fence.

Matt comes home in triumph, to win £100 and various cups. Rosie returns on the back of a quad bike to a small, sympathetic cheer from the popular side. In the reassuring bulletin of the race commentator, she is 'none the worse'. True, she will be plagued by aching bones and a fat lip when she goes to work in the City next morning, but she seems unconcerned. The crowds buzz, the way that real sports crowds do.

Along with the meeting and the greeting, the drinking and the gambling, this is what brought them to Catsfield: the sheer excitement of watching fine horses and bold riders in honest competition. And after that first bout of action, the watchers are clearly contented. Some study the card, others simply socialise. Around the paddock, owners and trainers gather in sagacious conclave, swapping murmurs, tapping noses. There are ladies of a certain age, with ash-blonde hair and jaunty trilbies and gold at ear and throat and voices made husky by Silk Cut and gin. And there are men with binoculars and brick-red faces and the kind of flat caps that confer an air of mysterious authority.

... this is what brought them to Catsfield: the sheer excitement of watching fine horses and bold riders in honest competition

Over on the rails, two elderly couples meet by chance. The men twitch their eyebrows in vague recognition; the women smile politely. One of the men explains himself: 'We haven't actually met, but we live just up the road from you,' he says. 'We're the ones with the egg-table outside.' He turns to his wife: 'Your pocket-money, isn't it my dear?' She smiles again, and nods brightly. Then she points to the other man. 'I know you, don't I?' she says. 'I see you every morning, when I'm mucking out.' More smiles, everyone nods, and they all move on.

The horses for the next race are circling the paddock. They are led by stable girls who cling to the reins and stride out strongly. Shy, embarrassed, yet fiercely proud of their charges, the girls pat their hair and tilt their heads and pretend not to notice their friends who stand and wave. A mother leads her toddler to the rails. She points across the paddock. 'Look at the horses, Alice,' she says. 'Aren't they beautiful!' And, of course, they are.

This race has seven runners, which is surprising given its exclusive terms of entry. As the racecard has it: 'For horses owned by current Members of the South East Hunts Club; to be ridden by current Members who, prior to 27 November 2009, have not won more than three races under the Rules of any recognised Racing Authority (Point-to-Points included)'. Rose of the fat lip rides again, rather more successfully. Despite the odd adventure – 'Oh dear, he made an absolute Horlicks of that one!' gasps the commentator – she brings her steaming beast home in second place, behind the 6–4 favourite.

The bookmakers pay out with barely adequate grace from their thin line of pitches by the paddock. One of them sits on a stool, yawning in the sun. I inquire about trade: 'Rubbish,' he says. 'Total rubbish. If I wanted to get rich, I wouldn't come to Catsfield.' He is wearing a singlet, as if he had dressed absent-mindedly. 'I suppose everyone's made that joke about the bookie losing his shirt,' I remark. 'No,' he says. 'You're the first.'

In fact, those bookmakers are a relatively minor sideshow. For one thing, even the biggest bets tend to be modest: 'hundreds rather than thousands,' I am told. And for another, the real interest lies in watching the horses move and work. This is not Royal Ascot, with its charmless cast of City touts applying the techniques of the FTSE to the vagaries of the formbook, and Essex girls teetering on stilettos and falling off barstools. This is a place to see rather than to be seen. It is a place where the sport holds sway.

Yet the sideshows do rather well. Across the racecourse, the action is brisk in the village of tents. For these patrons, the afternoon is less a point-to-point meeting, more a country fair. The Dinky Donuts are flying off the stall, similarly the Sweets 'U' Like. The Pimm's tent sells out soon after the third race, and even the 'Ranch and Adventure Holidays in the USA' tent is attracting the curious. I find myself wondering who turns up at the Catsfield point-to-point and says: 'That reminds me: I really must book a ranch holiday in Arizona.'

In the small fairground, loud with the shrieks of ecstatic toddlers, a small boy sits astride a mechanical bucking bronco. He is wearing an uncertain smile and an England football shirt, with 'Lampard' on the back. The iron horse jerks sluggishly backwards and forwards, and the child clings on, fearfully. His friends harangue the operator: 'Turn it up! Turn it up!' 'Don't you bloody dare!' yells Lampard's mother. The operator grins slowly, relishing his power.

Here there are a few shaven heads, some vaguely irascible dogs and a Chelsea away shirt. There is a stout lady in a rashly cropped top, with a gold ring glittering from her navel and a horse's head tattooed on her bicep: the head large, the bicep ample. There are giggling girls and jostling boys and winter-white arms which have not seen the sun in half a year. There is a constant, bubbling stream of lager, yet no disruptive louts, and unpredictable eruptions of laughter, growing louder and livelier with the afternoon. For those of us whose sporting experience normally encompasses large stadiums and teeming crowds, there is an unusual sound in the air. It is the sound of people enjoying themselves.

Like many an English village, Catsfield is content with its own company. Unlike most villages in the area, it survived the Norman invasion, and it seems to have been keeping its head down ever since. There *... there is an unusual sound* was a small flurry in 1791, when the *in the air. It is the sound of* Princesse de Lamballe, one of Marie *people enjoying themselves* Antoinette's ladies at court, arrived at Catsfield Place bearing a consignment of the queen's jewels, having smuggled them out of France. She returned soon after, and was executed in Paris a year later. Contact with the outside world is now maintained by those commuters who drive the three miles down the B2204 to catch the London train at Battle. Their journeys seem to be regarded as a regrettable necessity, and they are not greatly envied by those they leave behind.

There is another crackle of static. John Ball CBE is clearing his throat. 'On behalf of the East Sussex and Romney Marsh, I should like to thank Vanessa de Quincy for organising the raffle,' he says. 'Prizes may be collected from the secretary's tent'. The prizes include 'a child's toy,' 'a screwdriver set' and, most intriguingly, 'a voucher for a chocolate and almond torte'. Vanessa has done her work well.

Beyond the winning post, the occupants of the £25 car park are preparing their picnics. The entrance fees are nicely calculated: £5 for patrons arriving on foot, £10 for a car and its driver, £25 for a car with several passengers. The cost of running the meeting is approximately £15,000, with rent, insurance and the building of the jumps the biggest items of expenditure. Around 300 free tickets are distributed to farmers over whose land the hunt operates, and another fifty to the owners of the horses entered. Profits are shared with other hunts in the South-East, so that those who suffer small attendances as a result of bad weather can top up their funds from successful meetings.

None of which matters a jot to the hedonists of the £25 car park. They gather at the rear of their Jeeps and Range Rovers like worshippers at wayside pulpits. Tablecloths are spread upon tailgates and swiftly covered in flans and fudge, puds and pies, chocolate cake and home-made biscuits. The wine is plentiful, the conversation engagingly indiscreet. Matt Braxton has received a glitter of silver trophies for winning the opening race. They now stand on the bonnet of the family 4x4, next to a month-old copy of *Farmers Weekly*.

Matt's wrist is heavily strapped, having broken a bone in a recent fall. 'Nothing serious,' he insists. 'Not the sort of thing real riders have to put up with.' Like so many of his calling, his modesty is instinctive. He gives all the credit to the horse: 'my feller' did this; 'my feller' jumped that. It is not an affectation, he sees himself not as a driver, but a passenger. In the entire panoply of sport, perhaps only professional boxers bring the same kind of understated courage to their task.

People approach him with congratulations. He thanks them and changes the subject. After the third such encounter, he seems blushingly embarrassed. 'Look, I ride perhaps three times a week,' he says. 'I love it. I wish I'd taken it up much earlier. I ought to do more, but there's no time. So I am what I am. Nobody's ever going to mistake me for A.P. McCoy.' He cites the great jockey as a club leg-spinner might speak of Warne.

More wine is taken, more pies devoured. The sun burns still more brightly, and people tell each other how lucky we've been with the weather. A tall, middle-aged man approaches our group, lightly waving a careless hand and greeting people by their first names. He has short, tightly curled hair, and suede boots and a green, exquisitely tailored jacket of the kind seen only at rural racecourses and country christenings. He might easily be another estate agent, save for the large blue rosette on his elegant chest. In fact, he is Greg Barker, the sitting member for Bexhill and Battle, and he is here to remind us that the General Election is little more than two weeks away.

He does this quite gently, by talking about anything but politics. Instead, he discusses the hunt: 'Greg hunts quite a lot,' I am informed. And he recalls his salad days, when he dabbled in point-to-pointing: 'I felt really rather nostalgic for a while today,' he says. 'Until I saw poor Rose go flying.' He pulls a 'hey, that's not for me' face. A lady of mature years joins the group. She takes in the happy scene with a broad sweep of an arm and attempts to convey the sheer inclusiveness of the great assembly: 'Everybody's here,' she says. 'From the top to the bottom of society, the top to the bottom of income.' The elected representative of this democratic throng forces a tight little smile. In Cameron's brave new dawn, I sense it isn't quite how Greg would have expressed himself.

I ask about his majority in Bexhill. He enters all the usual caveats about boundary changes and the size of the turnout, before admitting to 13,500. 'Not a marginal, then?' I suggest. He shrugs, modestly. So I inquire about the progress of the national campaign and he switches to auto-pilot: 'Labour's sunk, finished, that much we do know … we must leave nothing to chance … work for every vote … ballot box is the only poll that matters …' He pauses, suddenly suspicious at my interest. We are introduced. 'Patrick's from the *Mail on Sunday*,' says one gentleman, helpfully. The smile vanishes; bonhomie dies. Moments later, Greg is at the heart of a different gathering, several yards away. He leaves behind a brief, faintly awkward silence, ultimately broken by the mature lady. 'Haven't we been so lucky with the weather!' she says.

Later that evening, I check out the bashful canvasser. The first relevant cutting is dated May 2009, and it is taken from the *Mail on Sunday*. It begins: 'Millionaire Tory MP Greg Barker pocketed £320,000 in just over two years from buying and selling a flat he bought with the help of expenses. The Shadow Climate Change Minister owned the home in Pimlico, near the Houses of Parliament, for 27 months before selling it and moving back to his old address. Last month the *Mail on Sunday* revealed that Mr Barker had claimed £43,000 in second-home allowances while insisting the constituency house where his estranged wife lives is his main residence – even though he left her for a gay lover in 2007.' All news to me, of course, since they don't trust the sports desk with that sort of stuff. As I could have explained, if only he'd asked.

A man of many parts, Greg later declared a financial interest in a company that produces 'ethical caviar' in Latvia, thereby earning the nickname of 'the sturgeon-general'. It all seemed a touch exotic for East Sussex, but the electors of Bexhill and Battle were clearly unconcerned. They would ultimately return him with a majority of 12,880, and he became Minister for Energy and Climate Change in the Coalition Government.

Meanwhile, back at Catsfield, they are working through their picnics while they await a renewal of the action. A distant shout breaks across the musky afternoon, indicating that another race is under way. A barefoot child with a chocolate-smeared face goes skipping through the chattering crowd. 'Come away from the rails, Evie,' calls her mother. 'Rose'll be coming by soon'. There is a thunder of hooves and Rose comes crashing past on a large chestnut. It is impossible to watch these mighty animals launch themselves at the fences without fearing for horse and rider. The risks are daunting, the consequences potentially appalling. The racecard contains a terse explanation of the flags on the course: 'Orange – Veterinary Surgeon Needed, Red and White Chequer – Doctor Needed, White – Ambulance Needed'. Yet the jockeys are at ease with their skills, and dangers are seriously assessed and soberly accepted.

In fairness, sobriety is not universally observed. I meet an unsteady lady of middle years who seems to have supped her way around the point-to-point venues of south-east England. She speaks of these places with the befuddled awe that a seasoned swiller might reserve for Bordeaux. 'Aldington. Bloody Aldington! What a night we had there! And Penshurst! Amazing! Have you ever been to Penshurst? Well, you should. As for Godstone: just sensational! Honestly, I can't remember a thing! Not a thing! It's just one big, sort of, blank!' Later, I look up Godstone. It is the home of something called the Mid-Surrey Farmers Drag. Small wonder that her memory let her down.

The Grissell stable has seven runners, but Matt Braxton remains its only winner. Neither Rose nor her sister Hannah can add to the total, and their disappointment mirrors the intensity of their effort. Hannah is 26, blonde and striking. She works for Racing Enterprises Limited, part of the Racing for Change movement which, commendably if belatedly, aims to promote British horseracing by making it more consumer-friendly. Racing can be an insular sport, a sport which claims you at birth and holds you for life but discourages interlopers. In search of productive ideas, Hannah started to look more closely at other sports. She was surprised by the results. 'I went to my first-ever football match last year,' she says, 'Wolverhampton against Wigan. This chap I was with thought it was a good date. Do you know, I found myself getting angry with the Wigan fans. Really angry! Wolves weren't playing very well, and Wigan were sort of gloating. And the more they gloated, the angrier I became. Can you believe it! But it was very useful. I now understand what gets into people when they watch other sports. You see, I'd always sort of assumed that everyone reacted like racing people.'

The sun beams on, undaunted. The weather has indeed been kind. The programme announces that: 'tractors are available for free towing at owner's risk'. Those supportive tractors will not be required. More pints are pulled. Small rivers of strong drink slide down dusty throats. Nobody misbehaves. At the open ditch, a stout little man assesses his next bet. He is wearing a white T-shirt with a drawing of a large crustacean across his chest. It bears the motto: 'Prawn Star'. It seems a slight joke to carry through a warm April afternoon, yet people smile as they pass him by. Across at the tents, a younger man, tall and thin and pushing a pushchair, wears a blue T-shirt with the faintly implausible slogan: 'I Don't Carry a Weapon – I am One'. Once again, we smile. He seems strangely miffed.

Some of the punters start to leave just before the last race, hoping to beat the Catsfield rush hour. They depart reluctantly down the same bumpy track; inch upon inch, tyres stirring the dust. From time to time they run over one of the fallen Tory placards, soliciting votes for Greg. Not everybody approves of such intrusive advertising. 'I'm quite sure they don't pay a penny,' one of the organisers tells me. 'They just stick them up on the basis that no one will bother to take them down. Bloody cheek in my view.'

Owners, trainers, jockeys and honoured guests all gather at the pub to reflect and gossip and analyse the day. Hannah Grissell leaves at 7.30p.m.: 'I have to do the horses,' she explains. 'All the girls get the weekend off, you see. Someone's got to cover.' Her mother, Diana, returns rather later. 'She came staggering in at one this morning,' reported her daughter next day. 'Well, perhaps not exactly staggering,' she added, loyally.

So a splendid time was had by all, and I recalled the reaction of Sheena, Matt Braxton's mother, as she surveyed the cavalcade. 'D'you know,' she said, 'I really think this is England at its very best.' I suspect she meant rural England, which remains a touch hierarchical for a town dweller's taste. But if she was marginally mistaken, then it was an innocent mistake. Because the overwhelming and totally unexpected impression was of a genuine anxiety to please, to entertain, to communicate the joy of a sport which is brave, uncomplicated, demanding and thrilling. It is a sport that succeeds in that rare trick of uniting performers and spectators and bringing out the best in both.

> 'D'you know,' she said, 'I really think this is England at its very best'

Sure, there is a natural allegiance to the tradition of the hunt and the ethos of the countryside, but that Countryside Alliance advertisement is a passing aberration. Because, by and large, there is no concerted attempt to convert doubters. Familiar attitudes may be struck, stances adopted, scripts scrupulously obeyed. Yet underlying all this is an abiding courtesy. Liberty and tolerance, you see. In this crowded field in Sussex, people may believe what they choose to believe. Provided they don't frighten the horses.

They came, they saw, they crumpled

CHAPTER 2
THE WORLD CUP
IN SOUTH AFRICA

Early evening on Long Street, and the England fans outside The Dubliner have been drinking through the drowsy afternoon.

The city of Cape Town has thrown itself at this World Cup, and the English have been made especially welcome. A board by the pub's main entrance bears the message: 'The Dubliner Says Good Luck England', which may be one of the more unlikely sentences in the language, but sets an agreeable tone.

And the English have made themselves at home. Flags of St George are hung around the door, festooned with place names: Babbacombe, Leighton Buzzard, Sutton-in-Craven. Two men dressed as Crusaders lean against a wall. They are carrying cardboard swords and pints of lager and staring at a large screen that is showing the closing stages of Greece versus Nigeria. And then the singing begins.

It is the usual stuff at first: 'Football's Coming Home', 'England Till I Die' and the dreary, obligatory 'Ing-er-lernd! Ing-er-lernd! Ing-er-lernd!' But then, emboldened by booze, the tone changes. Someone deep in the crowd starts to yell 'No surrender to the IRA!' The befuddled chant is taken up with belligerence. A young woman clambers on to a man's shoulders, swaying and slurring. Across the way, two men climb up on tables. Together, arms outspread, they persuade the group to sing 'Ten German Bombers'. It is a xenophobic dirge about the 'RAF of England', and it involves a number of young people drunkenly wallowing in the heroism of their great-grandfathers. Across the courtyard, a group of bewildered Algerians is watching the capers. Tomorrow, they will be supporting their lightly regarded team against England. Tonight, they are mixing with fellow fans.

Those of us who have observed these events down the decades start to settle our bills in the adjoining bars. We know precisely what lies in store. We can measure the script in a sequence of sounds. Threats will be bellowed at the Algerian 'intruders', followed by screeching insults. There will be the tinkling smash of breaking beer glasses, the anguished screams, the implosion of shattering shop windows. Then, in predictable succession, the clatter of running feet, the howling of police sirens and the hissing of tear gas. And yet, the very last thing that any of us had expected actually comes to pass. Nothing happens. Nothing!

On the eve of an England football match, Cape Town is curiously, eerily, satisfyingly silent

The singing subsides, the young woman slides off her friend's shoulders and buries her nose in yet another drink, the Algerian fans move on, Greece score a late goal against Nigeria which turns out to be the winner, and the bulk of the England supporters go shuffling away to search for restaurant tables. I find myself recalling a much-loved journalistic colleague, a man of red-top renown, who would travel to World Cups with a pre-packed story which started: 'Gun-toting cops threw a ring of steel around this frightened city last night, as rioting fans dragged the name of English football through the gutters of …' Conflict was his stock-in-trade. He would not have appreciated this outbreak of pacifism. But something is changing; a strange civility is emerging. On the eve of an England football match, Cape Town is curiously, eerily, satisfyingly silent.

Those England supporters have travelled far and paid dearly for their place in Africa's winter sunshine. Most have attended England's opening game in Rustenburg. A strange town, one that deters visitors by its remote location and paucity of hotels. It was built upon the site of an old Boer settlement, sustained by a platinum mine, and it boasts the Royal Bafokeng Stadium in which England drew 1–1 with the USA. The local people were charm personified, but only FIFA could explain why such a place was thought appropriate for a World Cup match.

Thomas Cook had offered that match for £2,699 per person, including flights, a match ticket and four nights' hotel. The Algeria game was priced at £2,600 per person, with one more night's stay. Keith Prowse advertised a package that involved all three England group games, in Rustenburg, Cape Town and Port Elizabeth, for £4,495. And it sold out. This was partly due to that passing spasm of self-delusion which afflicts the English at major international football tournaments. At such times, history holds no lessons and form has no meaning. And at such times, it is traditional to blame the media for overstating the English case. In fact, I detected a rare caution in most of the punditry. Sure, there was a feeling that if Fabio Capello, England's Italian manager, could evolve an effective system and Wayne Rooney, his outstanding talent, could reproduce the form he regularly reveals in the English Premier League, then good things might happen. But, by and large, expectations were held comfortably in check.

I say this as one who was embedded with Ally's Army when Scotland attempted to win the 1978 World Cup in Argentina. Try as it may, English football has never approached those heights of premature euphoria. That memorable campaign was led by the estimable Ally MacLeod, a man whose mission in life was the liberation of expectations. Ally thrived on hyperbole and regarded self-effacement as a sign of weakness. There was no point in skulking off to South America with cautious hopes of moderate progress. No, his team would travel with chests thrust out and heads full of dreams. Before they left Glasgow, they arranged a little local farewell at Hampden Park; just Ally, the players, and perhaps 50,000 tartan-wearing, flag-waving, anthem-bawling supporters who had popped in to wish the lads well. Somebody asked what he planned to do after the World Cup. 'Retain it!' said Ally. The more prudent footballers and fans could recognise the potential pitfalls, and even as they flaunted their Saltires, their fingers were tightly crossed. But they were in a small minority. For the most part, it was pints of hubris all round, and who do we fancy meeting in the final?

By contrast, the English expedition to South Africa was a circumspect affair. Results had been encouraging and qualification a sure-footed process. The notion that this was a 'golden generation' of footballers had been quietly jettisoned after quarter-final eliminations in the 2002 and 2006 World Cup finals and the failure to qualify for the finals of Euro 2008.

The sight of Green turning and scrambling to redeem his mistake ... instantly became one of the defining images of England's World Cup

True, a few small seeds of baseless optimism were sown in the early stages of that opening match, when England gained a lead and proceeded to play with vigorous cohesion. But they were trampled into the dust when the goalkeeper Robert Green allowed the softest of shots to squirm through his grasp. The sight of Green turning and scrambling to redeem his mistake, like a deranged batsman trying to repair his broken stumps, instantly became one of the defining images of England's World Cup.

So even limited aspirations were reassessed, and yet the fans trekked on to Cape Town, confident of enjoying some undemanding target practice before facing the challenges that lay beyond the group stage. Football rarely plans its schedules with fans in mind, but this time FIFA had excelled itself. After the Rustenburg excursion, England's followers were required to make the 900-mile trip to the Cape. Flights were the obvious yet most expensive option. Other choices involved a 17-hour drive or a 27-hour train journey. England bring with them vast numbers of fans, who are diligently courted by all manner of businesses. Prominent among these are the hotels, many of which insisted upon a minimum of four nights' stay at extortionate rates. And so, rather than adopt the civilised course of playing all group matches within the same area, the cash cow was moved around this enormous country. The decision – as is the case with all such decisions – was taken by people who themselves drift luxuriously from city to city, blissfully free from stress, expense or the smallest inconvenience.

That said there is little doubt that English spirits have been lifted by this glittering city. The journey was onerous, but after the damp gloom of Rustenburg, Cape Town has the dazzling glare and warmth of a film set. On this, the morning of the match, all the visual clichés are unfolding. Table Mountain is grandly looming. The promenaders are drifting along the Victoria and Alfred Waterfront, past the statues of Nelson Mandela and Desmond Tutu, F.W. de Klerk and Walter Sisulu, the founding fathers of the modern nation. Across the bay, shimmering in soft focus, lies Robben Island, the place where great men were incarcerated.

Football rarely plans its schedules with fans in mind, but this time FIFA had excelled itself

At such a time, with the world in town, it is well to be reminded how things used to be in these parts. I speak with no special authority, because the people running the place would never let me in. Like many other journalists, I would apply for a visa and they would consult some of the things I had written about their apartheid system. They would then decide that we weren't likely to get along, and so they would refuse my request. Not in so many words, nothing so crude; instead, they would offer a visa which expired an hour after arrival in South Africa. A subtle soul was brother Boer.

In fairness to FIFA, a phrase that tends to stick in the keyboard, they were always on the side of the angels in this matter. Along with the International Olympic Committee (IOC), they swiftly and decisively expelled South Africa from international competition. Other sports were infinitely more selfish, cricket and rugby being prime examples. But FIFA and the IOC remained both staunch and principled on this, the most critical of issues. To be here today is to understand how momentous was FIFA's decision to entrust this tournament to Africa. Like the Olympics, the World Cup has the power to enthuse and enthral the host nation. I recall especially the eruption of joy that swept across the England of 1966, the delirium of Argentina in 1978 and that astonishing summer evening in Paris in 1998, when a beguiling French team paraded the trophy through the broad avenues of the capital.

On each of these occasions, the hosts were celebrating proudly emotional victories. In South Africa's case, the pride and the emotion stem from its joy in becoming the first nation on this continent to stage the global festival. The excitement of what they are undertaking seems to seize the entire country. A few hours before the opening ceremony, I stopped at a tollbooth on a lonely stretch of the road to Rustenburg. A young lad is employed to wave down the cars and collect handfuls of rand. It is a dull, repetitive chore, but this day was different. On this bright winter morning, he was beaming fit to burst and chanting a little verse: 'It's here! It's here! You can feel it! You can feeeel it! Today, it's here!' And I found myself praying that the event would be worthy of his energy and pride.

Of course, the country has its dreams, and these were most vividly articulated in the pages of the Sowetan newspaper. On the day of the opening ceremony, a stirring editorial on the front page assured the men of Bafana Bafana, the team of South Africa, that in the demanding days ahead they would not stand alone. 'We are behind you and there is no shred of doubt in our minds that you will make us proud. We will call your names with *amour propre* throughout the spectacular ... Bafana Bafana in our homes, at taxi ranks, shopping malls, on the streets ... Bafana Bafana everywhere across the country ... Your names were also heard in neighbouring countries, and how proud we are to be associated with you ... Madiba [Mandela] will also wave his magic wand to ensure that you fare well in this historic World Cup. Once again, we are firmly behind you and nothing will sway our attention from you.'

South Africa drew with Mexico that afternoon, an ideal result, in that it served to restrain unreasonable expectations while averting the disappointment of defeat. For the English supporters in Cape Town today, anything less than conclusive victory is unthinkable. Six days of reflection have helped some of the fans rationalise the draw with America. It was the first game, and the lads were finding their feet, and we're traditionally poor starters and anyway, it was a big price to pay for one goalkeeping error. More than once the phrase was heard: 'The World Cup starts here'. It sounded like one of those cheery maxims one finds in Christmas crackers.

The restaurants along the Waterfront are starting to fill with early lunch guests. The English are still coming to terms with the happy reality that, while common caution is plainly required, South Africa is not a war zone. Alarming stories of routine atrocities had been circulating for months, causing a good number of potential travellers to call off their trips. One bunch of London chancers promoted a tasteful line of stab-vests. They cost £50, carried the cross of St George and were said to protect the security-conscious fan from stabs, cuts, slashes and blows from sharp-edged or spiked weapons.

'We feel the stab vests are a form of insurance, in that if something happens you are covered,' said a representative of the firm. 'We certainly don't want to offend South Africa,' he added, sensitively. Members of the media were also instructed in the hazards they might encounter. I attended one intensive briefing from a former Metropolitan policeman, who urged ceaseless vigilance from the moment we stepped off the plane. The advice which made the deepest impression was: when picking up a hire car, always drive at least twice around the first roundabout you encounter upon leaving the airport. 'And for why?' he asked, rhetorically. 'Just in case they're following you.' Even without knowing who 'they' were, I felt like George Smiley. As we were leaving the briefing, a foreign correspondent, a man who has spent much of his professional life in a flak jacket, said: 'What did you make of that?' Searching for a response, I said I thought it had been very ... well ... instructive. He frowned. 'Bit *de trop*, I reckon,' he said. 'We're not going to bloody Baghdad, are we?'

I suspect that some of my fellow diners in the excellent fish restaurant had attended similar briefings. You could sense it in the way they would periodically tap every pocket while silently mouthing a checklist: 'Passport ... credit cards ... match tickets ... cash.' They were corporates, for the most part; middle-aged managers who had pulled rank and sent their resentful underlings to that marketing conference at the NEC, or young thrusters being treated to a vision of how things might be if only they would promise to give the company at least 22 hours a day.

Across the centre aisle, two men in their early fifties are weighing the relative merits of the sole and the kingklip while discussing England's likely team this evening. Clearly, they have been disillusioned by the USA game, and their mood is unforgiving. One reads the list of names from the morning paper, the other offers a thumbnail assessment.

'Johnson.'

'Rubbish!'

'Terry.'

'Crap!'

'Lampard.'

'Carthorse!'

'Lennon.'

'Who?'

'Lennon.'

'Like I said: Who?'

'Good job it's Algeria, then,' says the first man.

'Correct,' says his laconic friend.

Eight men sit at the long table on my left; all young, all wearing approved brands of 'smart casual'. Most of them drink water, some refer to a game called 'footy', a few strike bets over the first England scorer. In a corner of the restaurant, a television is showing the Germany vs Serbia match from Port Elizabeth. One of the men has been following its progress. 'What are the Germans like?' asks a colleague. He thinks for a moment: 'Efficient,' he says. All defer to the man at the head of the table, perhaps five years older and possibly two executive grades higher. They nod at his observations, laugh at his small jokes and praise his choice of lunch venue. Suddenly, the senior man picks up a spoon and clinks it against the side of his glass, requesting attention. 'Guys,' he says, 'here's to Game Day Two.' They all appear to understand this curious terminology, as they raise their glasses, toast 'Game Day Two,' and toss back their water.

I am musing on this change in the character of the English follower, when the ghost of football past appears on the terrace overlooking the sea. An exceedingly fat man, stripped to the waist, is bawling a familiar chant: 'Ing-er-lernd! Ing-er-lernd! Ing-er-lernd!' He is carrying a bottle of Castle lager, and as he sings he does a little boob-bobbling, sweat-dripping dance. The diners ignore him, but three Japanese ladies pause to take pictures. He rewards them all with an enveloping cuddle, and I wonder how they will explain him when they get back to Osaka.

By now most of the restaurant is watching the single television. There is a small cheer as a German player is sent off. A louder cheer as Serbia score: 'Come on you Ser-erbs!' A roar of relief as the Germans miss a penalty, and a bellow of acclaim as the Serbs win 1–0. The table of young execs is applauding, arms above their heads. All the English are smiling, instinctively delighted by Germany's misfortune. They sense this could turn into a rather good day.

All the English are smiling, instinctively delighted by Germany's misfortune. They sense this could turn into a rather good day

The afternoon is blessedly free from incident. This was once the time when security forces began to twitch, when drink took its hold and a herd of timid young men became artificially bold. Everybody has a theory about the reasons for the change: recession has whittled down the travelling numbers and police intelligence has halted known hooligans at the airports. Mark Perryman, a leading figure in the organised fans' movement, believes: 'There's been a real sea change. We've always had a few idiots, but they no longer run the show. People have learned that it's much more fun to be loved than to be loathed.' All of which sounds a little like wishful thinking, until you experience Cape Town.

There is a light police presence, one more in tune with a rugby international than with the most important football match the England team has played for at least four years. In a turning off Dock Road, a group of Zulu dancers are performing to a throbbing barrage of drums. Several white-shirted fans are watching intently, alongside a small bunch of Algerians. One dancer, clearly the star, flings himself into a

'There's been a real sea change … People have learned that it's much more fun to be loved than to be loathed'

violently dramatic finale, arms shooting, legs pumping. An English fan, entranced by the spectacle, punches his fist into his palm. He searches for an appropriate response to the frenzied gyrations. 'Go'rn my son!' he yells. It is a good moment. Once, not long ago, it would have been quite different.

By now, the bulk of the fans are on the move from Grand Parade in the city centre. They walk along a secure route, a mile long, to the Green Point Stadium below Signal Hill. As is the case so often in this country, the liberal conscience is hopelessly torn. A South African World Cup is a declaration of national self-confidence. The tournament has provided a considerable amount of employment and, in time, it should increase tourism and promote inward investment. But the cost is daunting. Ten stadiums are being used in nine host cities. Five are newly built and five existing grounds have been upgraded. The construction and infrastructure costs have exceeded £3 billion. Green Point has cost around £450 million, and in order to build it an 18,000-seat football stadium was demolished. After the World Cup, its capacity will be reduced from around 70,000 to 55,000, with little prospect of being regularly filled. Similar stories are told around the country. Should they have seized the chance to stage such a competition? Or should they have spent £3 billion on the multitude of humanitarian problems afflicting the country? The choice was theirs to make and, as an independent nation, they made it. I doubt it was an easy decision.

The fans are halted three times before entry: first for a visual ticket check, then for a bag and body search, and finally for a barcode ticket reading at the turnstiles. Those carrying flags are required to unfurl them: partly to root out any obscene or unseemly messages, but largely to make quite certain that no unofficial sponsor is being given free exposure. They endure these minor inconveniences quite cheerfully.

The actual number of England fans inside Green Point is unclear. The English FA has sold 7,000 tickets and a similar number have purchased seats from FIFA. Others have obtained tickets through various channels, and the large corporate presence is overwhelmingly English. Already, a disappointment of the tournament is the relatively small number of local people attending matches. The organisers have attempted to attract them with cheaper tickets, but even a rate of £14 for these group games is too great a slice from the average wage. Those who do come tend to arrive with a vuvuzela. The plastic horn, 2 feet long, emits a sustained, monotone blast of sound with the capacity to damage the hearing and destroy the concentration. Bishop Tutu has defended the instrument on the grounds that it is 'part of our culture'. Perhaps so, but the noise is mindless, tuneless, relentless. Above all, it is totally divorced from anything that is happening on the pitch. It highlights nothing, celebrates nothing and is incapable of discerning between the sublime and the mundane. One colleague, desperately seeking positives, had argued that at least it might obliterate the sound of that dreadful English band which ceaselessly and artlessly pumps out 'The Great Escape'.

In fact, the vuvuzelas are relatively muted this evening, in keeping with the tenor of the game. Algeria are neat, bright and tidy. Although physically limited, they embody the old virtues; they pass and they run, they seek space and they use it, they know precisely what they intend to do with the ball before they receive it. It makes for a pleasing fluency, a style that belies their lowly international station. Although incapable of inflicting serious damage, they can make indifferent sides look extremely ordinary. And, at the moment, England are looking a good deal less than ordinary.

The English fans seem bewildered. From time to time they manage a swift burst of 'God Save The Queen', as if blind patriotism might be the missing ingredient. But their team is just too poor to be true. The central defenders, John Terry and Jamie Carragher, are being run ragged by the nimble Algerians. Terry, who had been stripped of the captaincy by Fabio Capello after his latest bout of shoddy behaviour, is playing like a man who is ageing rapidly and gracelessly. Carragher is in the side after a phone call from the manager caused him to reconsider his decision to retire from the international game. Watching his performance this evening, how Capello must wish that

The English fans seem bewildered ... their team is just too poor to be true

Carragher had been otherwise engaged when he made the call. Frank Lampard was indifferent against the Americans, tonight he is far worse, a frowning irrelevance incapable of altering the trend of events. Likewise Steven Gerrard, who scrambles England's first shot on goal after 29 minutes and 39 seconds. Wayne Rooney is flinging poisonous sideways looks at the wretched Lampard. Aaron Lennon is still playing like 'Who?'

The fans are increasingly perplexed. They had travelled more in expectation than in mere hope. The USA was one thing, but Algeria are the team beaten by Slovenia. How can the representatives of the self-proclaimed best 'league in the world' struggle against this side? Another desperate burst of 'The Queen', which withers and dies as Gareth Barry plays a pass directly into touch. At half-time, the stadium seems full of Englishmen with frantic points to make. Of course it may yet come right. Three or four second-half goals, and it will be one of those 'We were never really worried' games. And England could quite easily knock in three or four against this lot, couldn't they? The question is asked without conviction. Because the one England player capable of running riot against Algeria is the player who appears to be suffering most of all.

Rooney is the man most fans secretly wish they could be. He's the lad who performs like the best kid in the street, the one who is still out there volleying a ball against the wall when night has fallen and his mother is calling and his tea is spoiled. His bulk of a body belies a wonderfully balletic touch, his appetite for unselfish work would shame half of his fellow pros, his courage is far beyond question. But, most of all, he has a hunger. Rooney wants to be the best, he wants to demonstrate just why he is the best, he wants to assert his God-given talent on the grandest stages. In short, he wants to be the kind of player he always dreamed of becoming. And he seemed to be on the brink of delivering that dream, until he came to Africa.

So the fans settle to the second half, yelling encouragement, trusting that noise and commitment will carry them through their difficulties. But as the game progresses, the fervour dwindles. There is no response, no reaction from England's players. Lampard's shoulders are visibly sagging. Gerrard, who has played like an accident waiting to happen, comes to the touchline to speak to Capello. Shaun Wright-Phillips is brought on, prompting the observation that if he's the answer then we should consider changing the question. And Rooney just gets worse: dropping deeper and deeper, proving less and less productive, growing more and more frustrated.

With 5 minutes remaining, and the cause moving beyond hope, the mood in the stadium changes. Tolerance has run its course, replaced by a swelling anger. These people have travelled a long way. Some have made great sacrifices; most have suffered genuine discomfort. They can cope with failure, since it is a regular visitor. But this is of a different order. There is a shabby ineptitude about this performance, along with an acceptance that hints at indifference. Of course the players must be disappointed, but none of them seems heartbroken, merely peeved. And so the jeers begin, rolling down the slopes of the Green Point as the final whistle announces the sterile draw. High in the grandstand, I try to recall a more abject English result … '1066,' suggests my helpful neighbour. We are still smiling at the daft quip, when an image of Rooney pops up on the screen by the seat. His head is lowered and he is striding purposefully towards the dressing room when he hears the abuse. Briefly, his irritation spills over, and he turns to sneer at the attendant camera. The scene is played again, then again on the media screens. Slowly, we become aware of his words: 'Nice to see your own fans booing you,' he is saying. 'That's what loyal support is.'

I try to recall a more abject English result … '1066,' suggests my helpful neighbour

It could be dismissed as a trite little moan. Footballers dislike criticism and, having experienced very little in his career, Rooney finds it difficult to accept. But this was something quite different. Effectively, he was saying that fans are here simply to encourage, to sympathise and to endorse whatever performance England's players choose to give, no matter how dire. Any other emotion will be construed as an impertinence. For they are props, extras, people with no claim to an opinion, especially one that is unfavourable. Their function is to pay, to approve and then to fade from both sight and mind until it is time to pay once more. It was an astonishingly revealing remark.

In times gone by, the travelling public would have been unaware of this arrogant outburst for several days. No longer. Back home, friends and families are watching the broadcast. Seconds later, they are jabbing at mobile phones. Long before the stadium has emptied, there are few English fans who have not been informed of and affronted by Rooney's contemptuous reaction. The more thoughtful had always suspected that their affection was not reciprocated by England's players. Sure, they would acknowledge their presence at the end of a game, usually at the behest of the manager. They would wave and smile, and if things had gone especially well, one or two might even throw their shirt or their shin pads into the crowd. It was the equivalent of a pat on the head. The idea that these people had views or opinions never seemed to cross their minds. As for the notion that those opinions might be hostile, even scathing…

It was as if all the submerged resentment was surging to the surface. How dare they take us for fools! How dare they demand docile approval for such floundering incompetence! These are people who feast on flattery, who surround themselves with courtiers and sycophants telling them only what their egos wish to hear. Well, tonight they must prepare themselves for some angry candour. Already the vox pops are under way, television and radio reporters moving among the fans for initial reactions. And already the 'pampered prima donnas' cliché is being dusted down and trotted out in dozens of snatched interviews. When results are good, questions of lifestyle and salary are rarely raised. Yet they lurk unacknowledged in the dark depths, part of that submerged resentment. Even the game's most star-struck followers believe that footballers earn too much, far too easily. They resent the crassly conspicuous consumption, the louche lifestyles, the preening vulgarity, the armour-plated sense of entitlement. They deplore the fact that a man like Terry is paid £125,000 a week, around five times the annual salary of the average British worker. They recall that just a few months earlier, Ian Wright, the father of Wright-Phillips, had accused Manchester City of 'mugging

Even the game's most star-struck followers believe that footballers earn too much, far too easily

off' his son for refusing to increase his weekly wage of £60,000. Now many of us find the modern City difficult to love, but the attempt to brand them as flint-hearted mill owners for daring to offer £3 million a year was fatuous even by the standards of Ian Wright. By coincidence, £60,000 was precisely the wage that Ashley Cole was seeking from Arsenal some years ago. When they offered £55,000, he declared that he was so insulted he almost crashed his car. The public have yet to forgive him for that squalid little outburst. Indeed, it is brought up again this evening as the jeers continue to resound around Green Point.

And then there is Rooney. Shortly before the start of the tournament, I had searched for players who had been equally indispensable to English ambitions. I could offer only three contenders: Paul Gascoigne at Italia 90, Bryan Robson in Mexico in 1986, and Bobby Charlton in the golden year of 1966. Nobody argued with the contention, because that was the kind of company Rooney was keeping. All has changed. The ball, which used to obey his every whim, now bounces capriciously off knees and boots. His finishing lacks all conviction, his combative instincts have dimmed and his air of passionate intensity has evaporated. He plays like a Wayne Rooney impersonator, a shambling parody of the player he used to be. He is 24 years old, and he looks like an athlete in steep decline. So reduced is his status that we were starting to feel sorry for the bewildered young man until, in that instant of foolish truculence, he turned on the fans.

Rooney's bewilderment is shared by his manager. Fabio Capello is under pressure from both fans and media, and for the moment he has no answers. He moves from interview to interview deep inside the stadium. Everybody asks about Rooney. Will he be dropped for the third match? A week ago, such a question would have been inconceivable. Yet this evening, Capello treats it seriously. He gives it some thought: 'It's not a problem of his fitness, but of his mind,' he says. 'At the moment, Rooney isn't Rooney.' He is asked loaded question about his training methods. He gives a weary smile: 'That is the way I train my teams,' he says. 'It is the way I have always trained them.' He does not add, although he could, that in the course of a glittering career, he has been used to working with rather more promising material. One of Capello's fellow-countrymen says he has never seen the coach so depressed. 'All these hostile questions,' he says. 'They're still in the competition. England didn't lose, did they? He looks like the world is against him.'

Once again, I remember Argentina 1978, and the great Ally MacLeod. Having lost to Peru in the opening match, Scotland played Iran in the second game, having promised to rectify matters. They drew 1–1, and the team bus was besieged by a furious platoon of the Tartan Army. Next morning, we drove 20 miles or so from the city of Cordoba to a desolate hotel in the middle of nowhere. And there, in a place called Alta Gracia, we found Ally, sitting on a stiff-backed chair in the centre of an empty lawn. Lost in gloom, he seemed unaware of our arrival. Then he started to muse aloud about Scotland's situation. I vaguely remember a line about the darkest hour being just before the dawn. Suddenly, a small dog came trotting across the grass and stopped at Ally's chair. 'Here he is,' said Ally, a smile breaking through. 'Here he is, my only friend in South America.' He reached down to stroke his chum, and the dog snarled and snapped at his outstretched hand. With his media minders, his FA functionaries and his security detail, Capello will never be so perilously exposed, but at the moment he looks just as lonely as poor Ally MacLeod on that distant morning in Alta Gracia.

His Algerian counterpart, Rabah Saadane, is cheerfully answering every enquiry. 'I thought England would be better,' he says. 'I don't know what happened. It's up to their coach to draw the necessary conclusions.' It is pointed out that Algeria had lost five of their previous six matches. 'I said we'd improve,' he replies, casually. An insistent English reporter makes one more effort to elicit a newsworthy quote. What did he really, really think of that England performance? Rabah Saadane understands this media game, and so he does his best to keep the smile from his face. 'They were not at their best,' he says. 'England didn't have their day. *C'est dommage.*' It is neat, curt and rather appealing. Just like his football team.

The English fans are now retreating: some to the Waterfront, others along the 'secure route' into the centre of town. Historically, this is the time when bad things happened. People suddenly realised how much this has cost them, how great were their expectations, how miserable was the team's performance. They would mull things over for perhaps 5 or 10 minutes before taking the aggressive option, whereupon the world would go mad. The major tragedies have been exhaustively documented, but the ones that linger most poignantly are the small, individual sadnesses.

I remember an evening in Turin when the England supporters had conformed to their Neanderthal image and the consequences had followed their familiar course. Leaving the stadium late that night, a colleague and I stumbled over a fair-haired young man slumped at the kerbside. He was perhaps 16 years old, he was English, and he was distressed. Leaving the stadium an hour earlier, he had become separated from his friends. A small band of Italian thugs had spotted him and, as they rushed past, one had run a knife across the lad's back. 'Is it bad?' he asked us. 'Tell me the truth. Is it bad?' He turned his back to us, and we saw the white shirt of England, darkly stained by his blood. My colleague hurried off to search for police and an ambulance, while I stayed with the boy. He began to cry, softly. He said his mother would be worried. She had told him that football was dangerous, and she'd let him come only when he had begged and pleaded. Then one of his lost friends turned up, the ambulance arrived, a siren sounded through the empty streets. We were bitterly sad for the boy, yet not surprised. This was the risk that people ran when they travelled abroad to watch England play football.

Tonight is different; hearteningly, mercifully different. English disappointment is as keen as ever, as is the feeling that 'proper' football teams shouldn't draw with sides like Algeria. But the small, wholly unthreatening, number of Algerians in Cape Town will celebrate the point in peace. If there is English anger, and there is a good deal, then it is directed at the people they feel have let them down. These are the people who live in drives as long as a well-struck six-iron. They are people who have come to understand such things as offshore accounts, private jets, corporate boxes and the favoured guest areas of trendily trashy nightclubs. They have more money than they can comfortably handle. Thus, they can park in bays for the disabled at their local fast food store and settle the fine with a bundle of notes rather than move the car. They can eat in exotic restaurants and cultivate the companionship of minor show business figures. And they can hire rapacious agents and high-profile lawyers to protect their image rights, enforce their privacy and injunct those scurrilous characters who might want to throw a little light on their social activities.

If there is English anger, and there is a good deal, then it is directed at the people they feel have let them down

The fans are aware of all these things, and they have started to shrink from the players' crass acquisitiveness, their reluctance to act from anything other than selfish motives. If England should ultimately fail in this World Cup, and all the signs are suggesting that they will, then the fans will be inconsolable. The players, for the most part, will make appropriate noises, tell themselves that it just wasn't meant to be, and before the week is out they will be adorning the private beaches of Barbados or the velvet-roped VIP areas of the finest Las Vegas casinos. The supporters used to love them through the good times and, more frequently, the bad. Even today, they want to believe that the people playing for England are the heirs to Moore and the Charltons, to Banks and Ball and Hurst and the iconic Nobby. This is why they have travelled so far and spent so freely. Seduced by the canard that the game they watch every Super Sunday is actually the best in the world, they wanted to be here when Football Came Home. And now that sharp-elbowed reality has come bustling in, they feel rather silly.

They never quite believed the ancients when they spoke of the days when a Dixie Dean or a Tommy Lawton would arrive in Lime Street on a tram, en route to Goodison. But they revered the tales of the Sixties, when the heroes were recognisably frail and human. Jimmy Greaves of Tottenham Hotspur and England once told me of the days when footballers earned £60 a week and mixed freely with their public: 'We'd go in the Bell and Hare after matches,' he said. 'Load of players, few fans, bunch of press lads. All in the back room of the pub. We'd have a good few drinks, knowing the fans'd be no trouble and the press wouldn't turn us over. Sometimes we'd stay there till gone nine o'clock. We knew how to live, eh?'

Greaves was as greatly loved as he was lavishly gifted. He was a man, like Bobby Charlton or Jimmy Armfield, of whom it was said: 'He's never forgotten himself'. His flaws and foibles were of no account, because he was one of their own and, as such, they would follow him to the ends of the earth. As for this lot, well, they have followed them to the ends of the earth, and they wonder why they bothered. By now, Ashley Cole's latest reflection has become common knowledge. 'It could have been worse,' he said. 'But we pick ourselves up and get ready for Wednesday [against Slovenia], which is a big game for us now. We'll have to play a bit better than we did today.' They boggle at his nerve. How much worse could it have been? And do they really think they can get away with playing 'a bit better'? Like Rooney before him, he was adding insult to injury.

The bars at the Waterfront are solidly packed an hour after the match. The Dubliner, that 'Genuine Irish Music Pub' with branches in Gothenburg, Stockholm, Copenhagen, Cape Town, is pumping out pints of Guinness, as if it will help the fans forget. I hear no attempt to excuse or justify the England performance, just condemnation and scorn. I meet Dave from Birmingham, an optimist who, together with his cousin, has spent £11,500 on a 'Follow England to the World Cup Final' package. The trip lasts for 33 nights and includes tickets for the USA, Algeria and Slovenia matches, plus the round of 16, quarter-final, semi and final. 'It was a sort of declaration of confidence in England,' says Dave, 'although, tell the truth, I was never really that confident.' He pauses, significantly. 'I'm a bleeding sight less confident now.'

One or two diehards try to get a song going, but they have no real heart for it. Most are quietly anxious about the Slovenia match. Dave from Birmingham stares into his beer and quietly articulates his concern. 'We're England, and we're worried about playing Slovenia. I mean, Slovenia! I don't know anyone who's ever been there. And we're worried! And what's worse, we've got every reason to be worried. That's what it's come to.' There is talk of sacking Capello while there's still time, of bringing in an English manager, someone with 'a bit of passion'. Empty rhetoric, a trite solution to an enduringly complex problem.

Minds turn to the next journey. Port Elizabeth is an hour's flight, or an eight-hour drive along 480 miles of the Garden Route, through some of the most glorious scenery that this land can offer. Hedonists can opt for the Blue Train, which goes the pretty way, takes 40 hours and costs up to £1,022. I sense that the England fans are in no mood to relish the landscape. Because something important happened in Green Point stadium tonight, something that will not be erased by fawning explanations or gushing apologies or contrived public relations gestures.

There was something in the body language which suggested that, deep down, too many English players didn't care enough. At least, not in the way they care when they play for United or Chelsea or Liverpool or one of those teams in 'the greatest league in the world'. For some of those young men, playing for England had become a chore, an optional extra, something which will come in useful when their agent negotiates the next commercial endorsement. The fans sensed that hint of indifference, that feeling that it won't be the end of the world if they are eliminated. The training camp is said to be spartan, tedious, not at all what they are used to. There is mumbling discontent with Capello's methods, the kind of mumbling which never surfaced when England were qualifying with such ease. Perhaps it is best to call it a day. After all, there's another World Cup coming along in four years.

The fans, who live in a different world, seemed shocked by their own suspicions. Slovenia is just five days away, and they are dreading what might lie in store for their team. Dave and his friends file out of The Dubliner. The bar is open until 2a.m., but they haven't the heart for drinking. They make arrangements for tomorrow, when they will set off for the next town. From time to time they begin to sift through the embers of the match, but the task is too painful, the subject quickly changed. From time to time they mention Wayne Rooney, usually with a sad shake of the head. They worshipped him, they thought he was different from the others, they even thought he might win them the World Cup. And they were wrong.

There was something in the body language which suggested that, deep down, too many English players didn't care enough

They will cheer for Rooney and England when they reach Port Elizabeth, and they will hope and pray that their journey still has some way to run. But the mood has subtly changed; the atmosphere has altered. For this was the night when their team, their England, performed with a shrug of the shoulders, and a kid from Croxteth flung their loyalty back in their face. They may cheer, but they will not forget.

Three days before the Slovenia match, John Terry made a crude, self-serving attempt to usurp Capello's authority by questioning both his strategy and his selections. 'I'm doing it for my country,' said Terry. 'If it upsets him [Capello] then I'm on the verge of just saying: "You know what? So what. I'm here to win it for England … I was born to do stuff like this."' It was quickly established that the former captain enjoyed no support among the players, and within 24 hours the manager had secured a public apology.

England beat Slovenia by a single goal and qualified for the last 16, where they would play Germany in Bloemfontein. Germany won 4–1, with all the ease that score suggests, and England went home. In the outcry that followed, widespread demands were made for Capello's head. One contribution came from the Wigan chairman Dave Whelan. He had a solution: 'We've gotta get real now,' he said. 'We get an English manager and we get real about it … Let's get the Premier League in there, get an English manager. England throughout.' At the time, the Wigan club website listed 34 first-team players, of whom 11 were English. The manager was Roberto Martinez, a Spaniard.

Sir Dave Richards, chairman of the Premier League and formerly chairman of Club England, the body that oversees England teams at every level, helpfully announced that Capello would 'benefit from his first international tournament experience'. He did not mention that with compensation figures of up to £12 million being mooted, Capello was far too expensive to sack.

A leading travel agent removed from its website an advertisement placed some months earlier, which read: 'England's quarter-final, from £3,550 per person – with an official match ticket, and four nights at the three-star Westford in Sandton, Johannesburg, this is the ideal base for England's quarter-final match.'

In March 2011, to general amazement, Capello made the discredited Terry his captain once again. And Wayne Rooney was the victim of a tabloid sting operation which revealed, among other things, that he considered £200 a reasonable price to pay for 20 cigarettes in five-star Manchester hotels. His form did not instantly improve, but he managed to secure from Manchester United a new contract, which paid him £200,000 per week, or £10 million a year. During the protracted negotiations, Rooney succeeded in alienating many United fans. They accused him of disloyalty.

An apology from the pits of the world

CHAPTER 3

TENNIS AT WIMBLEDON

It is the second day of the Wimbledon fortnight. The sun is streaming, the crowds are shuffling, and on the outside courts, the pressure is taking its toll. An off-duty line-judge is lighting a cigarette.

We know he is a line-judge because he is wearing the uniform of his calling: a preppy jacket with piping at collar and pockets, a striped shirt with stiff white collar and club tie, cream trousers with matching sneakers, and a white cap, worn at a jaunty angle. The fantasy fostered by Ralph Lauren is of Jay Gatsby, staring across Long Island Sound and dreaming of his darling Daisy. Reality is a stout, middle-aged official, sucking at a Silk Cut in the alley off Court 11.

I make a note of the cameo, with just a touch of gleeful censure. For this is my first day at Wimbledon in 13 years. I used to come regularly, but with increasing reluctance. Then I stopped. Nothing dramatic, just a growing feeling that the people running the tournament believed that the public was lucky to be there. And the public, incredibly, appeared to agree with them. It was a place in which fawning deference mingled with simple silliness, where minor royals outranked major sporting talents, and where the audience giggled fit to burst whenever they heard the cry 'Come on Tim!' It was the giggle that drove me away. A place which giggled like that could have nothing in common with grown-up sport. And so we separated: I to

... the audience giggled fit to burst whenever they heard the cry 'Come on Tim!' seek sporting alternatives, Wimbledon to carry on giggling.

Wimbledon did not suffer from my absence. In truth, it didn't even notice. It just continued to grow bigger, more popular, more deeply embedded in the English summer scene. Sure, some malcontents thought it strange that the nation which staged the richest tennis tournament on earth could not discover a man or woman capable of winning it, but most saw it as lovable eccentricity: 'Look at us! Honestly, aren't we hopeless!'

Yet amid all the frivolity, the rumours were telling interesting tales. The old place, they insisted, was changing. It was less smug, less shrill. Deference was diminishing and visitors were no longer treated like trespassers to be prosecuted. As for the tennis, that was astonishing. No major sport had improved at such a breathless pace. Why, when people said they were going to Wimbledon to watch the tennis, quite a lot of them actually meant it. All in all, the event was a great deal better than ever before. My boycott was looking less like principled objection and more like churlish affectation with every passing year.

Which is why, on this bright and beautiful afternoon in June, I am scribbling notes in a smoky alley alongside Court 11. On the court itself, a Frenchman, Jeremy Chardy, is playing a Spaniard, Daniel Gimeno-Traver. Chardy is ranked 55 in the world; Gimeno-Traver is at 91. Neither is expected to feature in the second week of the Championships, and yet they are involved in a match whose pace and skill is beyond the comprehension of their modest audience. There are thumping serves, instinctive returns and more topspin than you'd find at a party conference. Half-volleys are picked up, flashing forehands are hunted down; rallies become small wars of attrition. It beggars belief that these men can play as well as this, and that others can play a great deal better.

As for the tennis, that was astonishing. No major sport had improved at such a breathless pace

Occasionally, their control betrays them and a ball goes soaring out of court, in the general direction of the Pimm's Bar. One is thrown back during a rally, provoking some confusion. The crowd laughs, in a Wimbledon-ish way. But mostly, they are engrossed in the contest, their spattering applause punctuating the thwack and thwock of the struggle. One matronly woman hurries off court at the end of the second set, jabbing at a mobile phone. 'Hi, sweetheart!' she says. 'How's things? Have you seen us on telly yet?' The answer sends a small cloud of disappointment scudding across her face.

Although the grounds accommodate around 40,000 people each day, the strolling is much easier than I recall. Rebuilding has been conducted on an epic scale, and yet, on the tea lawn to the east of Centre Court, space has been found for the bandstand. And it is being put to splendid use. Having enjoyed the Carousel String Quartet between 10.30a.m. and 1p.m., today's patrons are anticipating the Baseline Dixielanders from 6p.m. till 8p.m. tonight.

'Epic' truly is an accurate description of the work that has been undertaken. I find myself constantly consulting a map of the grounds, as old landmarks seem to have shifted. There are now courts where previously there were none. The museum is a wonder of innovation, a fascinating place to visit when the Championships have run their course. But what have they done to No. 1 Court? I don't recall it being just there. And what's that up there in the rafters above Centre Court, the thing that looks like a roof? Surely not? Wimbledon was always an elegant venue; an ivy-clad, green-painted establishment, with manicured lawns and bursting blooms.

'Epic' truly is an accurate description of the work that has been undertaken

But it was also crowded, uncomfortable, a place where people knew their place and were never allowed to forget it. I sense the change has been profound.

Inside the Church Road gate, a kilted man in a Jimmy wig, ginger and grotesque, stands gurning by the Fred Perry statue as his friend takes a picture. Fred, I fancy, would not have been amused. I once helped make a television documentary of Perry's life, built around the creation of the statue. Fred gave us several expansive interviews, full of forceful views and lusty anecdotes. His memory was extraordinary, so that some 50 years on he could recall pretty well every point of his three Wimbledon victories. And yet he repeatedly overlooked two of his four marriages. This presented certain chronological difficulties.

'And then, in 1941, you married ...' I would prompt.

'I did?' Fred would say.

'Well, well ...' and he would shake his head in mystification and change the subject.

But he loved his statue, and he was not overly distressed to be known as the last Briton to win the Gentlemen's Singles.

A Wimbledon champion of more recent vintage hurries past on his way to the Broadcast Centre. John McEnroe is wearing a jacket, tie and trainers. He has a peaked cap jammed on his head and an expression on his pugnaciously Irish face that discourages casual contact. I try to remember when I last saw him play here. I believe it was the late Seventies, early Eighties. The year of the fight.

They used to hold press conferences in a small, airless room beneath Centre Court. And when McEnroe was in the chair, they could have sold tickets. At that time, he was taking his tennis from the gods and his tantrums from the gutter. The tabloids called him 'Superbrat', and the soubriquet tended to stick, as such things do. He would be accompanied by a representative of the All England Club, an affable cove whose job was to weed out unsuitable questions. It was an unrewarding task. The American press gave him no trouble at all, with their detailed queries on the minutiae of McEnroe's latest match. He would snap out some surly responses, all the while glaring challengingly at Fleet Street's finest. The British news reporters, whose interests lay in a quite different direction, were up for the challenge.

A New York correspondent had just burbled through a turgid interrogation: 'Tell me, Jahn, when you played that backhand cross-court pass off a short ball at break point at 3–4 in the third, can you remember what was going through your mind?' McEnroe grunted an answer, whereupon one of Her Majesty's red-top representatives seized the microphone. 'John. Is it true you've broken up with your girlfriend? When did you tell her and how does she feel about it?' he inquired, smiling as he did so. It was the smile that did it. McEnroe exploded in a flurry of oaths. A glass of water flew through the air, a table went over, the New York scribbler insulted the chap from the red-top, and was immediately cuffed by that gentleman's colleague. The pair rolled around the floor, chairs shattered. McEnroe continued to bawl his protests, while his All England Club minder called the conference to a close, then scampered for cover. The whole affair was captured on closed-circuit cameras, and it led every evening news bulletin in Manhattan.

Ancient history, of course. Now the middle-aged man in the peaked cap strides unmolested along the South Concourse. Gone are the days of the long, frizzy hair and the red bandana and the attitude that epitomised everything that is wrong with modern youth (*Daily Telegraph: circa* 1980). Instead, we have a media lion who is bright, perceptive and amusing. Even the *Telegraph* might agree that J.P. McEnroe has made something of himself.

McEnroe is a genuine celebrity in a place where nostalgia rules and celebrities are in short supply. There is a Last Eight club close by Church Road. It is open to those who have reached the quarter-final of the Wimbledon singles or the semi-final of the doubles. Apparently, they sit around and talk about how much better things used to be, and occasionally a passing civilian will recognise them. Britain specialises in tennis players who find it desperately difficult to reach the last eight, but have no problem in remaining anonymous. Even in SW19, you rarely hear people say: 'Isn't that Mark Petchey?' or 'Look, everybody! It's Buster Mottram!' A few appear to recognise Andrew Castle from the breakfast television sofa, but he is scarcely under siege.

Tim is the exception. Timothy Henry Henman, the most enduring icon of Middle England. There is no anonymity for our Tim on Wimbledon's acres. People stop and stare. They bother him. They produce their phones and plead for pictures. They offer programmes and ask for autographs. They invoke or invent mutual acquaintances: 'We're great friends of the Randalls. D'you remember the Randalls? They remember you.' And he is patient with them; civil, going on charming. He never actually won Wimbledon, never even reached the final. He only ever encountered one of Kipling's

Timothy Henry Henman, the most enduring icon of Middle England

39

twin impostors, and it wasn't Triumph. And yet, in some curious fashion, that is part of his appeal. Even when he was at his absolute peak, Tim was always just one small step away from crushing disappointment. They know how that feels, and they love him for it. Hence the small corner of the All England Club lawns that is forever Henman.

Henman Hill, aka Aorangi Terrace, stands at the side of No. 1 Court. On this scorching afternoon the Hill is occupied by thousands of people, mostly women, mostly young, who are sprawled on the grass in the full sun. They are nibbling at picnics, drinking warm white wine and staring down at the vast screen on which matches are unfolding. Many of them appear to be answering questions from Fleet Street feature writers, who are desperately seeking authentic 'colour'. At around teatime, Andy Murray will play his first match of the Championships, against Jan Hajek of the Czech Republic. Most of the writers seem to be asking the tired old question about the name of the terrace: is it still Henman Hill, or may it now be called Murray Mount?

I meet a uniformed attendant, a man who will spend the next two weeks moving on people who wish to linger on the footpath to watch the televised tennis. 'Could you tell me,' I mumble, 'if this is still Henman Hill, or may it now be called Murray Mount?' He doesn't hesitate. 'Henman Hill, sir,' he says. 'Always Henman to me. Always will be. The other man's a newcomer. Only been here for, like, a couple of years, hasn't he? No question. Henman.' He pauses and smiles. 'But then,' he concedes, 'I s'pose I'm a bit of a traditionalist.' The 'traditionalist' can be no more than 17 years old. Wimbledon has that effect on people.

In truth, the Hill is a curious place. For one thing, it is remarkably uncomfortable, with its dusty, uneven, steeply angled surface. And, for another, the fuzzy screen is uncannily close to the source of the action; so close that we can hear the sound of ball on racquet; so close that, occasionally, a hoisted lob will pop up above the wall of the court. And yet you realise that almost all of these people would actually prefer to be here than inside. Because this is the place which attracts the cameras.

It is difficult to exaggerate the importance that Wimbledon fans attach to a television appearance. It is a harmless indulgence, yet they crave attention with the zeal of Big Brother housemates, and the Hill is their spiritual home. At some stage in most major matches, the BBC director will resort to the Hill shot. And the Hill is on full alert. There is a communal eruption when they see themselves on the big screen. Some have arrived in fancy dress with just this moment in mind: dresses made from the Union flag, or placards bearing the letters of their favoured player's name. One group of women – prominently placed having patiently queued – have Scottish Saltires painted on their cheeks, denoting their allegiance to Murray. The camera swoops and dwells for perhaps five seconds and, spotting themselves on the screen, they leap and yell and screech at their images. The camera moves on and, as one, they reach for their phones, asking the familiar question. Later, I hear them discussing the magical moment. Their accents are located perhaps 350 miles south of Murray's native Dunblane. In fact, the incident tends to illustrate just how the Hill feels about the young man. There is applause when he wins the first and second sets, a smattering of cheers when he secures the match. But not everybody claps or cheers, since old loyalties die hard. Even on the Hill, people repeatedly cite his absurdly misrepresented remark about supporting 'anyone but England' in international football tournaments. The quotation is brandished like a charge sheet. Once again, it's the Tim thing. I ask one of the Hill ladies about the 'anyone but' incident. 'Shouldn't have said it. Great mistake. Pretty disrespectful,' she replies, in purest Weybridge. I am tempted to mention the Saltire on her cheek, but I haven't the nerve.

It is difficult to exaggerate the importance that Wimbledon fans attach to a television appearance

Still, at least they are here for the tennis; others have different priorities. Today is Budget Day, and the Chancellor is appealing for personal and public sacrifice on a scale not seen in this country for some 80 years. His message has yet to reach this corner of south-west London. A notice near one of the gates points the way to 'Marquees 1–21', which conveys some idea of the scale of corporate entertaining during the Championships fortnight. Wimbledon may be one of the few British sporting institutions whose bars can unblinkingly offer a bottle of Lanson black label champagne for £57 and a magnum of the same for £110. But even this level of consumption pales in comparison with the depth of the corporate trough. It is reported, for instance, that the Royal Bank of Scotland (RBS) is enjoying the use of the luxurious Suite H, attached to No. 1 Court. Here RBS is entertaining selected staff and fortunate clients. RBS is 70 per cent State-owned following the Treasury bailout. It slashed around 15,000 jobs in the wake of its rescue, and British taxpayers are guaranteeing something in excess of £325 billion in toxic assets. With heroic indifference to public disfavour, it is paying £260,000 for the duration of the tournament.

A matter of yards from No. 1 Court, close by the summit of Henman Hill, a queue is forming as a rather more sympathetic financial transaction takes place. Here stands the Ticket Resale Office, the site of a thoroughly good idea. Across the grounds of the All-England Club, holders of tickets for the show courts place their unwanted tickets into red boxes for collection by Honorary Stewards. The resale begins after 3p.m., as the first few spectators start to drift away. The queue is long and agreeable. Small-talk is swapped and politeness reigns. Tickets cost £5 each, and all proceeds go to various charities, including SPARKS, the Dan Maskell Tennis Trust and other excellent causes. HSBC, the 'Official Bank of the Championships', has agreed to match the proceeds, which in 2009 came to £123,000. Somebody sat down, thought hard and came up with this quite brilliant notion.

The old Wimbledon used to take a perverse pride in the practice of queuing. It was one of the things that drove me away from the place. The queue would stretch from the main gate and along Church Road, with scores, hundreds, of people, all desperate to tell the nearest camera how many days they had been camped out, how many new friends they had made, what songs they had sung, what enormous fun it all was. This, it seemed to me, was not a gathering of tennis fans but the annual reunion of people who love queuing. As with so much at Wimbledon, things have changed. The campers no longer line the pavements in anything like the same numbers. Instead, there is a system of queue cards – 500 each for Centre, No. 1 and Court 2 – which are handed out in the evening and redeemed next morning for wristbands, enabling the queuers to purchase the appropriate tickets. The cards are numbered sequentially, so that people do not need to stay around all night but can complete their 'queuing' at home if they choose. Those who choose to stay tend to gather in the field across the way, where toilet facilities are provided. This is much less newsworthy but infinitely more civilised. Naturally, there are a few malcontents who yearn for the daft old days, but most recognise the sanity of the reform.

And so the day peters out. It is not an auspicious one for British tennis. All the women have gone and all the men, save Murray, have fallen. And the tournament is scarcely 30 hours old. Even by Britain's miserable standards, it is a spectacular cull. Murray is asked about it in his interview. He searches for words: 'Yeah, it's not great, is it?' he says, 'I mean, you know, I said obviously I'd like to see more British players playing in the tournament and more British wins. Yeah, it's not ideal ... it's not a great start.'

But since there were no expectations, there is little disappointment. These things happen, pretty well every year. In any case, while most countries have tennis players, the British have Wimbledon, and they love it. A small arcade houses a shop full of people forking out for all manner of Wimbledon souvenirs. There are teddy bears from £10 to £15, water bottles from £7 to £9, beach towels for £18. Who, I ask myself, really wants a Wimbledon beach towel? A long line of customers supplies the answer. A neighbouring stand is devoted to 'British Tennis'. A knot of Lawn Tennis Association (LTA) people stand chatting behind the counter. There is nobody in front. A notice on the stand announces: 'Davis Cup tickets on sale here'. Great Britain is to play Turkey at Eastbourne, and the fixture is being promoted on the dubious slogan: 'Blood, Sweatbands and Tears'. I stand and watch for 10 minutes. Not a single ticket is sold.

... while most countries have tennis players, the British have Wimbledon, and they love it

I wander back through the grounds. The place is still fetchingly green and, despite the commercial concessions and 40,000 visitors, almost country cute. I pass a restaurant and count 54 umpires and line-judges eating, drinking and gossiping. On Court 18, just behind the Broadcast Centre, a match between the French qualifier Nicolas Mahut and a large and relatively promising American named John Isner is beginning. Nobody seems especially interested, yet a kind of history is in the making.

Two days later, Isner overcame his French opponent. He took 11 hours and 5 minutes of play, stretched over three days, to win 70–68 in the final set. That set lasted 8 hours, 11 minutes and the contest was the longest in the history of tennis. Our old friend McEnroe said the protracted struggle had made him proud to be a part of his sport. He said: 'We often don't get the respect we deserve in tennis for the athletic demands it places on players, but this should push that respect way up.' And he added that, in his view, the match might well have shortened the careers of Isner and Mahut by six months. He placed the battle in its proper context. Isner was abruptly dismissed in the next round. His inability to stand unaided was seen as a factor in his defeat.

Today, eight days after my first visit, I am sitting by No. 1 Court, watching Rafael Nadal playing Robin Soderling of Sweden for a place in the semi-final. Once again, the pace and athleticism is stunning. I thought the last generation of players was pretty good, but this lot are playing a different game. Soderling is serving at 133mph, yet Nadal is not only getting a racquet to the missiles but actually directing his returns. Television is unable to capture the sheer violence of his game, the bewildering speed of thought, of foot, of reaction. Soderling is intimidating, his aces thud into the backcloth, causing the line-judge to leap aside. The official reacts with the brave little grin that says: 'I'm a good sport, me.' And the crowd stifles a snigger, guiltily praying that the next service ace will dislodge his white cap.

Yet if Soderling is a wonder, then Nadal is a force of nature. Standing 6 foot 1 inch and weighing around 190lbs, he has the neck and shoulders of a light-heavyweight contender. He goes about his work with the calculated ferocity which one recalls seeing in 'Marvelous' Marvin Hagler when he assaulted the heavy punchbag. And he has other virtues that set him apart. He has the imagination to envisage and enact a shot long before the possibilities had crossed anybody's mind. No matter how adverse the geometry, Nadal discovers solutions. In addition to that little lot, he is modest to a fault. With certain brash exceptions – Jimmy Connors, Andre Agassi – Wimbledon prizes modesty in its champions, and Nadal has the respectful bearing which endears him to all and sundry. Roger Federer is revered, and properly so, but if Nadal should reclaim his title, then the Wimbledon public will have no cause for complaint.

And yet, that public have by now been exposed to a week of patriotic optimism. Murray has advanced confidently into the last eight. The Queen, attending the Championships for the first time in 33 years, has watched one of his matches, and it seems that she might return should he reach the final. As one venerable member of the All England Club confides: 'We know it'll all end in tears. Always does. Nothing more certain. But it's really rather exciting while it lasts.'

'We know it'll all end in tears. Always does ... But it's really rather exciting while it lasts.'

And on this day, No. 1 Court is blissfully buzzing, for unlikely events are conspiring. The flickering courtside scoreboard tells us that Federer is losing on Centre to an unconsidered Czech named Tomas Berdych. Now they quite like Federer, so they refrain from clapping, as his plight grows increasingly desperate. Instead, they affect to cheer the plucky Berdych in his efforts to eliminate the favourite. Meanwhile, could you believe it, Nadal loses the first set! The significance is not lost on the banks of No. 1 Court. As the Spaniard prepares to serve in the second set, there is the usual jousting from opposing camps. 'C'mon Rafa!' comes a plea from one end. 'C'mon Robin!' squeaks a response from the other. There is a second of silence, before a throaty, fruity and possibly privately educated voice pipes up: 'Come on Murray!' The crowd bellows at this Wildean thrust. Ribs are tickled, eyes are dabbed, thighs are slapped. There is even a smattering of applause. We may imagine the wit in his pub in Barnes or possibly Kew this evening: 'Spur of the moment. Honest. It just came out. I was like: "Come on Murray!" And everyone just, like, collapsed. Awesome!'

The scoreboard announces that Federer is down 5–2 in the final set. 'Oooooh!' comes the gasp, and this time there is no attempt at impartiality. With Federer out of the way, Murray's chances would be enormously enhanced. Another flickering message. Federer is out of the way! Hope races around No. 1 Court with the speed of a plague. If only Nadal could somehow contrive to fritter the next two sets, then HM could book her seat for Sunday afternoon.

Nadal, however, is not the frittering kind. Erasing the opening set from his mind, he lifts his game to punishing heights, and pretty soon poor Soderling is finding it difficult to breathe. He seems to relish the respite of the changeovers, when ball girls stand behind the players, shielding them from the sun with umbrellas in the colours of the All England Club. Behind the girls loom two heavies in black suits. The likelihood of anyone in the patently peaceable assembly attempting to damage either contestant seems remote, yet the authorities recall the dreadful stabbing of Monica Seles in Hamburg in 1993, so the heavies are allotted their discouraging roles. Suburban Sopranos, they glare challengingly at all and sundry.

With Nadal leading 4–3 in the second set, a grey-haired man in blazer and club tie shuffles out of the grandstand. He looks just as you would expect Tim Henman's father to look: detached, discreet, a man not prey to unseemly passions. He knows precisely what lies in store for Soderling, and he is not wrong. Soderling misses a simple volley at break point in the third, and he slams his racquet down in a Swedish sort of rage. But he doesn't really mean it. He is about to meet his predicted fate, and he accepts his beating like one who knows it might have been a great deal worse.

I reflect that Wimbledon tantrums are not what they were in that golden age, when McEnroe could not only deliver a foot-stamping, eye-bulging eruption, but could decorate it with a string of memorable phrases. There are still gentlemen in England who think themselves accurs'd they were not there to hear: 'You cannot be serious! ... Chalk flew up! ... This is the pits of the world!'

The last truly memorable outburst came in 1995 and was the work of one Jeff Tarango, a journeyman from California. Goaded beyond endurance by the saloon bar subversives and primary school provocateurs on an outside court, he rounded upon his tormentors with a squeal of: 'Oh, shut up!' The umpire, whose skin was even thinner than Jeff's, deemed this nursery outburst an 'audible obscenity' and issued a code violation. Whereupon Jeff walked out, pouting his way off the court while Mrs Jeff, a French lady, slapped the umpire on the cheek while yelling: *'Je ne regrette rien!'* I promise I am not making this up. In the aftermath of this blissful farrago, a psychologist interpreted Jeff's performance as, yes, 'a cry for help'. You may not be entirely surprised to learn that Jeff is now employed as a pundit by BBC Radio 5 Live.

Anyway, while Nadal is dispensing of poor Soderling, Murray is starting his own quarter-final against Jo-Wilfried Tsonga of France. The players walk on to a thinly populated Centre Court, since the crowd has been held spellbound by Federer's defeat and is now answering various calls of nature. The chap compiling the point-by-point story for the BBC website makes a shocking discovery: 'I can't quite believe what we've seen at this Wimbledon,' he writes. 'I'm not just talking about Federer crashing out. I've just popped to the gentlemen's toilets on Centre, and there are ladies in there! Not at the urinals, not yet, but it's surely only a matter of time.' I doubt that many women would see the point of that joke, especially those who suffer similar indignity during theatre intervals. After all the reforms already undertaken, the provision of adequate toilet facilities for women might be next on the agenda of the All England Club Committee.

There are no such problems on the Hill. Sound of wind and sturdy of bladder, the extroverts work through their entire repertoire. And this time, the television cameras seem to linger longer on their caperings, as they wave and leap and grimace to the manner born. Three days earlier, the England football team was brusquely dismissed from the World Cup by Germany. This is some small chance to lift the national mood, to prove that the Brits at large are not entirely hopeless at sport. The chance is enthusiastically seized, and Murray comes through in style and comfort.

In fact, football's World Cup has proved a point of contention, with the All England Club refusing requests to show matches on the big screens 'out of courtesy to the players on court'. I find it impossible to question its stand. There is no shortage of chances to watch the World Cup; indeed, the entire nation is currently being force-fed a diet of football. This is a tennis tournament, and Wimbledon is quite properly standing up for itself.

Its success remains virtually undiminished. In 2010, despite general economic distress and a slightly reduced capacity, it will attract combined attendances of 489,946, the second highest in its history. As ever, tickets are desperately difficult to come by. Corporate seats aside, they are allocated to those who are successful in tennis club, LTA or public ballot, or those prepared to try their luck in the queues. The prices vary with the fare on offer, but, given the significance of the tournament, they are not unreasonable. On my first visit, a Centre Court seat would have cost £41, a seat for No. 1 Court £38 and a ground pass to the outside courts £20. On my second visit, eight days later, those prices were, respectively, £85, £72 and £17. The prize-money totals £13,725,000, with the men's and women's champions each receiving £1 million. And when all the costs are set against income from tickets, corporate entertaining and worldwide television receipts, Wimbledon is left with a profit of around £30 million, all of which is handed over to the LTA to blaze fresh trails of glory for British tennis. As Rex Bellamy, the eminent former lawn tennis correspondent of *The Times*, once observed: 'We know how to make money out of tennis players. If only we could make tennis players out of money.'

'We know how to make money out of tennis players. If only we could make tennis players out of money'

And yet, on this Wednesday evening at the end of June, there is more than a flicker of hope. Murray is being scrupulously prudent, watching every word of every interview, but his form is good, he senses the enormity of the stakes, and he knows that ultimate victory would transform his life. Sadly, that transformation will have to wait. On Friday, the nation will halt as he faces Nadal in the semi-final, but Nadal will overwhelm him in straight sets. The Spaniard will then proceed, in similar fashion, to batter poor Berdych in the final, and some will acclaim him the most accomplished champion that the tournament has ever known.

I am unqualified to assess his place in history, but I can report that his place of work has changed beyond recognition. Deference is indeed in retreat, and while giggling has not been completely eradicated, it doesn't seem to jar as once it did. The game itself, once an afterthought, has been restored to centre stage. Played to a quite staggering standard, tennis now reveals its finest colours. And, most importantly, the public are regarded as guests rather than interlopers.

One day, a Briton will take his or her place on the plinth alongside Perry and an ancient anomaly will be removed. But even that omission seems somehow less pressing. For too long, Wimbledon was part of 'The Season', a dreamy festival to set alongside Glyndebourne or the Chelsea Flower Show. Now it is a tennis tournament, possibly the best that the world has to offer. As one who rejected it for too many years, I sense I may owe it an apology.

CHAPTER 4
CRICKET AT CANTERBURY

On a windblown January morning in 2005, staff arrived at the St Lawrence Ground, Canterbury, to find a lime tree lying across the outfield at deep midwicket. In truth, they were somewhat slow to spot it. The head groundsman, Mike Grantham, later confessed: 'To be honest, I'd been out in the middle sweeping the square for about 20 minutes when I looked up and thought: "Something's missing".'

A committee member of Kent County Cricket Club said he much regretted the loss, since the tree had always seemed 'something of a fixture at Canterbury'. In fact, the lime had stood on that spot for almost 200 years, and the ground had been built around it. 'Something of a fixture' scarcely conveyed its antiquity. But this apparently cavalier attitude was explained by the fact that they had a replacement ready and waiting. Six years earlier, shrewdly foreseeing the demise of the tree, Kent had invited the cricket writer and broadcaster E.W. 'Jim' Swanton to plant a successor in another part of the ground. When the old lime snapped and fell, the understudy was lifted, transported and installed in its place; inside the boundary ropes, amid the ashes of generations of Kent members.

A visiting Australian professional declared himself bewildered when he arrived at the ground that summer. 'So this bloody great tree's been in everyone's way for 200 years. It does us all a favour and falls over. And you stick another big bastard in the same place. Sorry, I don't get it.' One can imagine the indulgent smiles and patronising shrugs that followed this little outburst. The fellow's an Australian; of course he doesn't 'get it'. He wouldn't 'get' the gentle quirks and fetching foibles of Kent cricket. And he certainly wouldn't 'get' Canterbury Festival Week.

Canterbury divides cricketing opinion. Some see it as a place for people who are still coming to terms with the death of King Edward VII, a theme park for vaguely distracted gentlefolk, who find the sport engaging but would really rather be pacifying America's North-West Frontier or civilising Australia's dusty outback. Others are seduced by the understated grandeur of the setting: the quaintly decorous pavilion, the lush, encircling trees, the low, staid stands named after Kentish heroes: Woolley, Ames, Cowdrey. And, in Canterbury Week, the marquees, jostling shoulder to billowing shoulder about the sightscreen, gurgling with strong drink and humming with gossip and goodwill. And never more than on Ladies' Day.

It is best to arrive early, not merely to watch the watchers, but to test the validity of Tom Cartwright's theory. Cartwright dealt in swing and seam, but the late England bowler was also a wonderfully perceptive observer of the rhythms and rituals of the game he loved so well. He was a shy man with the soul of a poet, and this was how he approached the day: 'If I go on to a ground in the morning, an hour before a game, it's the loveliest of times … There may be a mower still ticking and the groundsman marking the ends, but there's a silence as well. You can stand and think and listen. You've got the birds singing, the craftsman working, the smell of everything. That's something that makes cricket different from all the other games.'

'If I go on to a ground in the morning, an hour before a game, it's the loveliest of times …'

This, the second of the match, is a morning that Tom would have recognised, with sombre cloud to promote swing and brief, flickering shafts of sunshine to encourage spectating. The cars begin to occupy the space beyond the boundary, moderate of pace and bumping gently across the grass. They ought to be Hillmans and Humbers, but are mostly Toyotas and Hondas, of exceptionally low mileage and carefully driven by considerate owners. One such owner unwinds himself from his vehicle, clutching his back and staring hopefully at the sky. He has been dressed by Central Casting, in blazer and regimental tie, Viyella shirt, stout brogues and trousers of that shade of red which only men of a certain age and rank can carry off. A panama hat might complete the picture. He reaches in to the back seat, and pulls out a panama hat.

As he salutes chums and passing acquaintances, his wife excavates the car boot. She brings out a small trestle table, two fold-up chairs, a flask of tea, two cups, two paper plates, a packet of shortbread biscuits, a carton of milk and copies of the *Daily Telegraph* and the *Daily Mail*. She pours the tea, adds the milk, distributes the biscuits and hands her husband the *Telegraph* while she retains the *Mail*. They sit in their chairs, sipping tea, and she smoothes down her sensible skirt, kicks off her sensible shoes and primps the collar of her sensibly cut jacket. It is only then that I notice the object on her head. It is small and feathery and its colour may well be cerise. It is, I am informed, a 'fascinator', loosely defined as 'a stylish, hand-crafted cocktail hat'. By now, she too is nodding to friends, many of whom are wearing similar confections: bright, wispy, verging on the exotic. Just the thing for Ladies' Day.

The cricketers are sprinting and stretching … in preparation for the day ahead. Their efforts go largely unnoticed in the marquees

By now, the marquee guests are arriving. There are suited men, purposefully striding, and women tottering on precipitous heels, with hands clutching improbable hats. Tickets are offered, credentials examined. There are manly handshakes and fluttering air kisses. Trays of drinks appear and bashful banter is exchanged.

'Swift sharpener?'

'Ooooh! Too early for me.'

'Come on, just the one.'

'Go on, then. Twist my arm.'

Outside, a few yards away, the cricketers of Kent and Somerset are sprinting and stretching, darting and drilling in preparation for the day ahead. Their efforts go largely unnoticed in the marquees.

Canterbury is unique among the traditional cricket festivals, in that the event is staged at the county headquarters. It was founded in 1842 and has been played at the St Lawrence Ground since 1847. Gloucestershire's version is the Cheltenham Festival which, since it started some 30 years later, styles itself as 'the longest-running cricket festival on an out-ground in the world'. Yorkshire have been holding their end-of-season festival at Scarborough since 1876, and it counts among its landmarks W.G. Grace scoring 174 for a Gentlemen's XI in 1885, and Don Bradman taking 153 off Leveson-Gower's XI in his farewell innings in England in 1948. The festivals were designed as celebrations of cricket, social occasions which would bring together people who might be infrequent visitors to county grounds but who shared an interest in the game and the club. The decline in county attendances over recent years has been unhappily reflected in festival attendances, but they battle on in the hope that the sun will shine and that the public's disturbing obsession with football will show some signs of easing. And Canterbury is battling bravely against the prevailing tide.

On the two 'popular' sides of the ground, square of the wicket, Ladies' Day makes a more marginal impact. Here the audience is both overwhelmingly male and nearer 60 than 50. Many are tanned from countless days spent in the glare of the Kentish sun. They appear thoroughly knowledgeable about the game and the people who play it. A raffish few wear singlets, exposing patriotic tattoos. Some wear football shirts: Charlton Athletic, Gillingham, and one that puzzles me but turns out to be Real Zaragoza. The talk is of the old-timers, of Underwood, Denness, Leary, Woolmer. Every conversation touches on the nonpareil, Cowdrey. They do not forget the great ones in this corner of England. On the opening day of every festival, a large and respectful group lays a wreath at the memorial to Colin Blythe, a left-arm spin bowler for Kent and England, who died at Passchendaele in November 1917. He was 38 years old, played in 19 Tests and took a hundred wickets at a remarkable 18.63. His first-class career spanned 15 years, during which he took 2,503 wickets. He once took 17 wickets in a single day at Northampton, and they say that he did it all with style and grace and rare humility. There is something curiously affecting in remembering such a man.

Meanwhile, the moderns are being analysed. A small, slightly nerdish, clique sits by the scoreboard, swapping anecdotes about the

Kent team. Articulate men in late middle age, they use the players' first names, coyly, self-consciously: 'As Joe was saying … you know what Geraint's like … typical Rob, eh? Typical bloody Rob!' They make plans for next week, when they intend to watch a Kent Second Eleven match against the universities at Cambridge. In the course of their conversation, one man is asked: 'Coming on Saturday?' He shakes his head, regretfully. 'I was hoping to,' he says, 'but we have a family wedding and the wife's put her foot down.' I sense that the wedding in question might well be his daughter's.

The visitors, enjoying a vibrant season, have brought a fair smattering of followers. One young couple, part of a group down at deep extra-cover, drove up from Taunton at 6a.m. They covered the two hundred miles in something over four hours, and they will make the return journey this evening. By motorcycle. The Somerset supporters mingle easily with the home fans, swapping details of decent pubs and reasonable restaurants. 'It's nice and friendly, just the way football used to be,' one of them tells me. I'm not sure that English football was ever so nice or so friendly.

After a prosperous first day, Somerset's first innings ends this morning at 380. Kent then dwindle to a worrying 47 for three just before lunch, when Geraint Jones and Martin van Jaarsveld come together to confront the crisis. The ground falls quiet, an almost resigned silence. More than 30 years have passed since Kent last won the County Championship, and the tide shows no obvious signs of turning. Somebody sneezes loudly at the long-on boundary. 'Bless you,' calls a Somerset fielder. Such is the silence that everybody hears the remark, and some giggle. A small number desert the Woolley Stand and make an early run for refreshment, hurrying across to the Bat and Ball pub on the Old Dover Road. There they stand and stare incuriously into their pints to the background blather of Sky Sports News. One man, with hands like hams, delicately picks out the lettuce and tomato from his cheese sandwich. They shrug off their disappointing morning, and speak of football.

Back at the ground, the announcer is urging us to welcome the band of the Parachute Regiment. They drift to and fro across the outfield, pumping out standards like 'Soldiers Of The Queen', 'The Minstrel

Boy', and, as a concession to modernity, 'Puttin' On The Ritz', by Mr Irving Berlin. Toes are tapped, memories are jogged and there is spasmodic applause. As they troop away, the field is re-colonised by a babble of small children with bats and balls. The announcer is ready for them: 'We remind those on the outfield that you're very welcome to be out there, but NO hard balls are allowed,' he barks. The words 'health' and 'safety' come spitting from every stand.

Very little of this activity penetrates the various marquees, where lunch is the social event of the day. The most intriguing venue is the most enigmatic, the marquee occupied by the Band of Brothers. Founded in 1858 and described as 'a wandering cricket club which requires a territorial allegiance to Kent,' its title is apparently taken from 'a popular song of the Christy Minstrels'. It is, in fact, a rather disconcerting Confederate marching song:

> We are a band of brothers and native to the soil,
> Fighting for the property we gained by honest toil.

Its leader is called 'Chief', its members are known as 'Brethren', and it has exerted enormous influence on the policies and practices of Kent cricket down the generations. Any number of Kent captains, including the Cowdreys, have been members, but its leading light was Lord Harris. He played his first game for 'B.B.' in 1867 as a 16-year-old Etonian, and his last some 61 years later, when he took four wickets with his lobs. The official Band of Brothers history says of him: 'As the leader of B.B. (he would not take the title of Chief until after the death of the last Original Brother in 1919) his undeviating fairness and kindness inspired everyone's respect and affection, in spite of the utterly despotic rule which he exercised.'

A fascinating man was the Chief. He was the second man to captain England in a Test match and he captained Kent for 18 years, after which he was sent out to rule a chunk of India. When he left office, it was written: 'Never during the last hundred years has a Governor of Bombay been so sternly criticised and never has he met with such widespread unpopularity on account of his administration as Lord Harris.' He returned home to take up the Presidency of MCC.

Harris was a man who divided opinion, as did the late Jim Swanton, planter of lime trees and a towering influence on Kent cricket in general and the Band of Brothers in particular. Of Swanton it was said: 'His idea of democracy is to travel in the same car as his chauffeur.' An aristocrat by everything except birth, he acquired a repertoire of patrician airs which were so convincing they might almost have been authentic. As a young reporter, I once encountered him in a cloakroom, following a cricket dinner at the East India Club. He was in liverish mood.

'Did you hear what they did to signify that it was time to stop serving drinks?' he asked. I hadn't.

'They rang a bell!' he hissed. 'A bell!' He pulled on his overcoat, shaking his head. 'This place is becoming more and more like a … what's the word? It's becoming like a…'

'A pub?' I suggested.

'That's it!' said Swanton. 'It's becoming like a…' He struggled with the noun, but eventually it sullied his tongue. 'A pub,' he said.

I peep inside the marquee as lunch is served. There are three long tables: old men, old ladies, old money. A sizeable chunk of the county's wealth is gathered in discreet conclave over the soup course. No voice is raised; no infinitive is split. An air of Masonic complicity pervades the proceedings. People do not apply to join these exclusive Brethren; they are invited. Moreover, or so I am told, nobody is formally expelled from the Brotherhood. Instead, when the cricket fixtures are sent out in March, those who do not receive them may no longer call themselves members. I steal one more glance at the chattering assembly. They radiate assurance. For them, March holds no terrors.

Of Swanton it was said: 'His idea of democracy is to travel in the same car as his chauffeur'

Along the row stands a sign announcing 'Hopper's Tie Club (Members Only)'. Now this is cricket remembering its own. William 'Hopper' Levett was a gentleman farmer from Goudhurst who kept wicket for Kent for 17 seasons between 1930 and 1947. Overshadowed by his county colleague Les Ames, he nonetheless secured one England cap, at Calcutta in 1934, when he scored five and two not out, conceded 15 byes and held three catches. Himself an amateur, he was offended by the rule which dictated that Kent professionals could not wear the county tie, with white horses on a red background. He therefore designed a tie – barrels and hops on a blue background – to be worn by those who loved Kent cricket. The club is the result of his gesture, and the lunch seems appropriately agreeable.

Close by is the Lord Mayor of Canterbury's tent. The sign says so, as does the mayoral limousine, bearing the city's coat of arms and parked close by. As I pass, the great man emerges, plump and sombre-suited, mopping his brow. 'Warm in there,' he observes, to nobody in particular. Mercifully, he has remembered his pint.

Then there is the Old Stagers' marquee. Now this is the stuff of festival cricket. Created in 1842, the fifth year of Victoria's reign and the year in which it first graced Canterbury Week, the Old Stagers claims to be the oldest surviving amateur dramatic society in the world. Its literature observes that it is older than the Wimbledon Championships (1877), the Promenade Concerts (1895) and the modern Olympic Games (1896). With the exception of two world wars, these cricket-loving actors have appeared at every Canterbury Week since 1842. Traditionally, they conclude their stint with a satirical review in which they lampoon politicians, public figures and prevailing ideas 'with reverence for nothing save cricket and Canterbury'.

In August 1999, the journalist and former Cabinet Minister William 'Bill' Deedes wrote: 'Around this time of year, while the Second World War was on, I consoled myself by thinking that Canterbury Cricket Week, founded in 1842 with its tents and famous lime tree, unchanging in a changing world, was the sort of thing I was in business to preserve. Most of us had daydreams like that in those days. This year, I took a long look round the ground between the showers. Then I caught sight of a programme for the 149th season of the Old Stagers at Canterbury's Gulbenkian Theatre, which accompanies the week – they were playing Ronald Gow's version of the Sackville-West novel *The Edwardians*. And there was the lime tree. A dream come true.'

For Englishmen of Deedes' caste and generation, Canterbury Week represented an island of reassurance in an ocean of turbulence. Others are equally enthusiastic, if a touch less reverential. 'Get that down you,' the man in the CAMRA marquee advises me. 'Good stuff.

You'll like it.' It is, and I do. They are an eclectic bunch in this crowded tent: some are clearly devoted to the cause of real ale, some are merely circumventing the walk to the pub, while the gentleman in the doorway – bare-chested, wearing an outsize nappy and sucking a large dummy – is called Spencer and he is about to be married and today is his stag party. Spencer's friends, a dozen or so, have come dressed as women to mark Ladies' Day, which may explain that conversation behind the Ames Stand between a bewildered elderly member and a beefy siren in an ice-blue cocktail number. Yet this is Canterbury, where even cross-dressing extroverts have conformist hearts. Spencer apparently asked the Kent Committee to give permission for his friends to wear dresses, and after discussion – presumably under 'any other business' – permission was forthcoming. I would love to have heard Swanton's views on the matter.

The cricketers return after lunch, and for the first five or six overs their presence is scarcely noticed by the festival crowd. The Brothers are chattering over the cheese, the CAMRA crowd are bending companionable elbows, while in the Old Stagers' tent, the thespians all appear to be speaking at the same time. A waiter emerges to stack boxes of bottles. 'I don't know where they're putting it all,' he confides. The gentleman in the red trousers is sleeping soundly, panama balanced on the bridge of his nose and blazer draped across the back of his chair, while his wife dozes gently over her *Mail*. Down at long leg, a couple of Spencer's friends are balancing pints on preposterous bosoms while taking subtle, satirical swipes at their rural visitors: 'Ooooh, arrrr! Ooooh, arrrr!' The Garden of England mocking the cider county. Meanwhile, Jones and van Jaarsveld are building something substantial. With admirable application they battle through to tea, yet, once more, the attention of their audience is starting to wander.

The reason may be found in a marquee which stands apart from the rest. It is 'The Ladies' Arcade', a perfumed temple to the milliner's art. The place is a riot of fronds, feathers and fascinators. Some of them perch on petite stands, and are advertised for sale. I think of asking who comes to Canterbury to buy a hat, when the crowded tent is called to order. A woman of obvious authority places a finger to her lips.

'Shhhh!' she says. 'Judging is about to begin.'

'Of what?' I inquire.

'Of the Ladies' Hat Competition,' she says, with a combative glare.

What follows is a scene from a society wedding of the Fifties. Twelve ladies drift about the marquee, parading exotic hats and winsome smiles. One matronly soul, looking just like my mental picture of Jill Archer, with her headwear a symphony in saffron, flashes a beam at the trio of judges. They stare back impassively, scribbling small notes, offering no clues. All that is missing is music: Mantovani, perhaps, or a serene waltz from Victor Silvester and his Ballroom Orchestra. I ask the woman of authority if they hold this contest every year. 'Of course,' she says, 'what else should we do?' I suggest something cutting-edge: a cake-making contest, perhaps, or a competition involving jam. Her glare is incinerating. Somebody raps a spoon on a table, and the tent falls silent. The judges are ready and the ladies stand at centre stage, gathered for the verdict. Suddenly, a person in green chiffon, with blonde hair and a cheeky little pillbox hat, steps forward and flings out bare, brawny arms. 'Ladies, you all look stunning!' booms a rich baritone. One or two of the older contestants seem genuinely alarmed as another of Spencer's chums breaks cover.

The results are announced, in reverse order, and the winner is an elegant woman named Maggie, who smiles through her feathers and tries not to seem smug. Bouquets are presented, pictures are taken, and a man in a bowler hat appears at the entrance, beckoning the winners. Outside is a dray, with two large, snuffling horses. The triumphant Maggie leads out her runners-up, including a lady named Josie whose vivid yellow suit contrasts violently with the deepening dullness of the afternoon. A small crowd gathers to watch them helped aboard. The public address crackles out, with the announcer attempting to keep the whole ground abreast of events. His words are not well chosen: 'Across at the Ladies' Arcade, the winners are being mounted on the dray.' A Kent official shakes his head. 'Oh dear,' he murmurs. 'How very unfortunate.'

And off they go at a stately saunter; Maggie flaunting her flowers to the crowd, Josie waving in the manner of the late Queen Mother. The smiles are broad and the collective colours an assault on the senses as they come clattering around the boundary. A few years ago, it seems, one of the horses defecated quite spectacularly, causing the final session to be delayed for several minutes. This time, despite the fervent prayers of at least half the audience, they remain stubbornly continent. They disappear behind the Woolley Stand, the ritual complete. The applause fades and dies, while the announcer bids them a graceful farewell: 'Many thanks to all the ladies who wore their hats and brightened up Ladies' Day in Canterbury Week.'

'Many thanks to all the ladies who wore their hats and brightened up Ladies' Day in Canterbury Week'

It is easy to be seduced by the immutable charms of the festival. A few days earlier, the Kent chief executive Jamie Clifford cited this timeless quality as its most potent selling point. 'The great thing about Canterbury Week is that it doesn't change,' he said. 'It will be very much the same as it was 168 years ago … Certainly in cricket it is the oldest festival in the country and others are now following suit, Derbyshire just had their first, so we must be on to a good thing.' Well, perhaps. But if the charms are obvious, then so too are the dangers. The St Lawrence Ground can accommodate around 15,000 spectators, and on this festive day in August it seems scarcely more than a third full. There is too much space in the car parks, too much room at the bars. The queue for the ice-cream van is too short; too few people are browsing at the cricket book stall. In this of all weeks, the place should be crowded, bustling. Instead, there are clusters of vacant seats, each one a cause for anxiety and regret. Canterbury, as I said, is fighting its corner. But the struggle grows more difficult with each passing year.

A year earlier, following confident predictions that the club would break even, Kent declared a loss of £802,000, after losing some £700,000 in the previous year. Among various financial mishaps, the annual report cited the staging of two unsuccessful concerts. This gave the Kent chairman George Kennedy the chance to deliver a line which his predecessor Lord Harris was never required to utter: 'The Sugababes

61

were the wrong act. We got that wrong.' In fairness, his lordship was never called upon to advance several hundreds of thousands of pounds to keep his county afloat. But Kennedy's loan, along with loans from the England and Wales Cricket Board, helped stave off penury.

Although rates have been raised, membership is still something of a bargain given the amount of cricket on offer. Yearly fees start at £200, rising with optional extras like parking facilities, guests and so on, to £4,590 for life membership for under-21s, £3,930 for ages 22 to 40, £3,276 for 41 to 60 and £2,622 for age 61 and over. Such fees seem moderate when set against the £100 it costs for a Grand Stand seat at the Lord's Test against Pakistan. Yet costs, especially wage costs, are high. Kent report overseas players of moderate ability asking for £10,000 to £15,000 a week, the kind of salaries that are impossible to justify at a time of enforced austerity. English cricket relies on broadcasting deals for more than 80 per cent of its income, and the Sky television contract alone is worth some £300 million. Such is the prevalent short-termism of the English game, that an unseemly chunk of that Sky money is being used to pay those preposterous sums to jobbing mercenaries. It is generally accepted that such dependence upon satellite money is both perilous and unhealthy, but the game is running short of straws to grasp. Kent are not alone in their straitened circumstances, yet clearly their position is more exposed than most. Hence the concern: how long can a glorious anachronism like Canterbury Week survive? How long can past glories be preserved and an uncertain future be held at bay?

The task grows more demanding with every passing year. For instance, the Sky deal is distinctly double-edged. That sum of £300 million buys exclusivity, but it also denies a vast swathe of the sporting public the chance of watching the national summer sport. The coverage may be excellent, but the market is much smaller than that of free-to-air television. And the results of such exclusion are obvious: sure, the 2005 Ashes series was possibly the finest the game has ever known, but contrast the national reaction to England's victory in that series with the response to another English success at home in 2009. The first was shown on Channel Four, and was a widely shared phenomenon that provoked national euphoria. The second, shown on Sky, evoked little more than warm approval for a job well done. Every sport needs its heroes and, because of the nature of the game and the people who watch it, cricket needs them more than most. Yet the current heroes are operating behind a subscription barrier.

Certainly they are not playing in places like Canterbury, and the names of those stands illustrate the nature of the problem. Frank Woolley, Les Ames and Colin Cowdrey and were men of Kent who went off to perform stirring deeds for their and returned trailing clouds of glory. One week they would score a hundred off Australia, next week they would take guard at Canterbury. That link has been all but broken. In these days of central contracts, the England player places county cricket somewhere below Test matches, one-day games, guest appearances on *A Question of Sport* and long lunches with his agent on his list of priorities. The people who line the ropes at the St Lawrence Ground may stare long and hard at both Kent and the visitors, but the only instantly familiar figures will be Test players recovering from long-term injury or those who have served their international purpose. No grandstands will be named after this little lot.

Out there in the middle, Jones and van Jaarsveld continue to graft on a wicket growing increasingly placid. The Somerset fielders are anxious to convey a sense of urgent purpose; sprinting between overs and chirping confident encouragement, the way cricketers do when they are at their wits' end. Drink has taken a toll on the two stag party members at long leg. One is in lilac, the other in a shepherdess ensemble, complete with smock and bonnet. They sprawl across the benches, bawling at nobody in particular: 'You're not singing any more'. The Kent members ignore them and stare at the darkening clouds. Bad weather has cursed the country, disrupting the county programme, but so far Canterbury has been a blessed place. So far.

Then the rain begins: a shower, a squall, a downpour. Across the ground, I can see the man in red trousers thrusting fold-up chairs into the boot of his car. His wife is struggling with a trestle table, while her stylish, hand-crafted cocktail hat has lost the will to live, its wilting feathers slapping wetly at the back of her neck. The covers are being rushed to the square, propelled by groundstaff and supervised by umpires longing for the comfort of a dry dressing room. Already, a spluttering traffic jam is forming on the Old Dover Road.

And in front of the pavilion, lashed by rain, fuelled by drink and watched by the head-shaking members of Kent County Cricket Club, the friends of Spencer are doing a bold little hip-grinding, thigh-flashing dance. Ladies' Day has been transformed into *La Cage aux Folles*. And that ominous rumble, erupting just a dozen miles to the east from the medieval town of Sandwich, is not a summer storm. It is Jim Swanton, revolving in his grave.

'You make some noise and the boys perform'

CHAPTER 5
SPEEDWAY AT EASTBOURNE

On a bitterly cold evening in mid-September, 16 people are peering through a wire fence, watching a group of mechanics tune a batch of motorcycle engines.

The noise is acutely distressing: a shrill and violent screech, like a circular saw attacking a tin tray. The mechanics are clustered in oily confraternity: adjusting their earplugs, concentrating fiercely, ignoring the watchers. From time to time they run the backs of their hands across their damp noses, then, with a small sniff, they return to the innards of their engines and resume their revving.

The 16 outsiders, mostly men of middle age, continue to watch and listen. They have no earplugs. From time to time they detect a change in tone or volume, whereupon they nod knowingly, as if they had successfully interpreted a particularly intricate piece by Stockhausen. When they want to communicate with their neighbours, they shout through the din. Everyone uses brief sentences, since the pits do not encourage conversation.

I tug the sleeve of a watcher, a large man in a quilted anorak. 'What's happening?' I ask. He waves a hand at the pits. 'Listen,' he bawls. The din grows louder, so loud it is almost intolerable. 'There!' he yells, as if he has answered my question. I back away, bewildered. More people have arrived at the wire fence. Clearly, they are having the time of their lives. We are at Eastbourne Speedway, home of the Eastbourne 'Lifestyle' Eagles, and the first race is half an hour away.

I chose Eastbourne because it seemed the most unlikely town to house a speedway team. According to its official website, Eastbourne has long been known as 'The Empress of Watering Places', and while the borough council is anxious to throw off its dusty, fusty image, old perceptions die hard. For most of us, Eastbourne is tea dances and nursing homes and a bandstand which entertains holidaymakers with tribute concerts to Abba and the Beatles, along with a regular Sunday Night at the Proms: 'Wave your flag to all the traditional singalongs, including "Land Of Hope and Glory" and "Rule Britannia".' The town has never truly embraced the motorcycle, but if it had, then it would be ridden by a polite sort of chap who respects speed limits, remembers his hand signals and can recite by heart the Highway Code. Modernity is one thing, speedway quite another. Which is why the Eastbourne speedway track may be found a discreet distance from the town, some ten miles north of Beachy Head and the waving palms.

Arlington Stadium is humble, stark and set in a field off the A22. 'Stadium' may be pitching it a little high, since it resembles a small, unambitious, non-League football ground. Tonight, the Eagles will face the Wolverhampton Wolves, and most of the patrons have arrived up to an hour before the opening race, paying the £1 parking fee in the adjoining field. Their vehicles belie their sporting passion, being mostly family saloons or small, practical vans. A swift inspection reveals not a single motorcycle. I learn that speedway does not appeal to motorcyclists, since they find it difficult to identify with speedway bikes.

Most fans come from within a 30-mile radius, although some have made the journey from London. They buy adult tickets for £16, tickets for children for £8, or family tickets (two adults, two children) for £40. Speedway takes a proper pride in being a family sport: there is no chanting, no segregation of supporters and certainly no police presence, as there is never a hint of trouble. The fans appear marginally older than the average sports crowd, and they number just a few hundred shivering souls. They seem to be creatures of habit as they shuffle across the terracing with fold-up seats under their arms;

selecting familiar places, gathering in small groups and discussing the evening's prospects with apparent authority. Confident forecasts are made: 'I've got a real good feeling about tonight. And I'm not often wrong,' confides a lady wearing a blue Eagles jacket with matching bobble-hat. Absent friends are excused: 'He's pulled out. Liverpool's on telly.' The prevailing feeling is of controlled excitement and decent anticipation.

Some read the match-day programme (£2), in which one contributor bemoans the foreign domination of the domestic sport: 'There are just not enough young Brits in British speedway. A way must be found of solving the problem if Britain is once again to be a world speedway power.' *Speedway takes a proper pride in being a family sport…* The Eagles make his case by failing to field a single British rider this evening. Another writer opts for a lighter approach: 'I went into my local DIY shop and asked for some nails. "How long do you want them?" said the shop assistant. I said: "I want to keep them!"'

Some supporters unscrew steaming flasks and packets of sandwiches, while others, of a more adventurous nature, make for the fast food huts, where they find 'Cheese Burger, Egg Burger, Salad Burger or Burger', all at £3.20. Close by the mechanical bedlam of the pits is another hut, which serves as a bar and calls itself the 'Eagles' Nest'. It is empty, save for a couple of heroes in donkey jackets: sturdy fellows who scoff at the piercing cold and drink ice-cold lager from plastic beakers. Briefly, I wonder about the 'Lifestyle' section of the Eagles' name. It is not, as I had assumed, a gym-cum-salad bar, but one of the leading Renault dealerships in Kent and Sussex.

The loudspeaker is playing mood music: 'Come On Eileen' by Dexy's Midnight Runners. One little group, six strong, jigs absent-mindedly from foot to foot, clutching mugs of tea and staring at the empty track. I ask the lady in the bobble-hat what brings her out on such an evening. She replies with a slogan: 'Thursday night is Eagles night.' And she adds: 'I wouldn't want to be anywhere else in all of Sussex. Honest.'

Her passion summons echoes of an earlier age, and of that immediate post-war generation which set speedway alongside the cinema and football as the most popular entertainment in Britain, attracting crowds of 300,000 every week. In London alone, the fans could attend a meeting every weekday evening: Wimbledon (Monday), West Ham (Tuesday), New Cross (Wednesday), Wembley (Thursday) and Harringay (Friday). It was said that you could watch speedway each night in the course of a 20-mile trip around the London Underground. They were the days when football knew its place, when West Ham United FC made sure that their home games never clashed with West Ham speedway, for fear that their attendance would be affected. And the appetite for speedway endured down the decades. As late as 1981, the last World Final at Wembley drew a capacity crowd of 100,000 fans. Today, London does not possess a single speedway club, yet memories linger on. When West Ham's 80,000-capacity Custom House Stadium was demolished in the early Seventies, new housing estates were built. Their streets bear the names of some of the old stars, like 'Bluey' Wilkinson, Eric Chitty and Tommy Croombs; men whose skills found a national stage and a prodigious audience.

Times change, numbers diminish, but still there are those who cater for a devoted clientele. Near the stadium entrance, a few yards from a modest sign announcing 'Arlington Raceway – Europe's No. 1', one of the largest men in the South of England sits at a stall composed of three tables. He is tending the Track Shop, which sells the full range of Eagles merchandise: scarves, buttons, T-shirts, pins, posters, teddy bears, jackets, hats, caps, autograph books, pens, models and mugs. One shopper – an intense individual in his late forties, with narrow eyes and a three-day beard – paces in front of the stall. His cap is covered with speedway pins and badges, likewise the lapels of his jacket. He is peering at the bill of fare: pondering, wavering, silently debating. From time to time, he shakes his head abruptly and walks away, returning seconds later, more intense than ever. I consider asking him about his motives for coming out in the cold. Was there nowhere

Her passion summons echoes of an earlier age ... which set speedway alongside the cinema and football as the most popular entertainment in Britain

he would rather be on a Thursday night? But I suspect he would not welcome frivolous interruption.

By now, the music seems louder. People are stamping frozen feet to a blast of 'R-e-s-p-e-c-t' from the divine Aretha. The din from the pits seems more urgent as the first race draws near. I spot two riders limbering up. They are swinging their arms, more in token exertion than real exercise, but their billowing breath creates a cloud about their heads, as the night grows colder. Their racing leathers are covered in advertisements, not a single inch of space remains unsold. They are surprisingly small men, small as jockeys, with sharp features and serious eyes. At the edge of their gaze, at each end of the straight, hangs what appears to be a collection of lilos. They are the air fences which, inflated by portable generators, absorb the impact when a rider or a machine flies out of control. Acting like an airbag in a car, a fence is designed to save limbs and lives, to cushion a rider hitting the fence at 70mph. As an added precaution, riders wear a safety device on their wrists. In the event of a crash, the engine will cut out when the rider departs from the bike. This prevents the bike from taking off and roaring into the crowd. Even so, a precautionary private ambulance lurks close by for, while casualties are few, it remains a desperately dangerous sport. Just a week earlier, Adrian Rymel, a 34-year-old Czech rider, suffered a broken neck and a severely damaged spinal cord while riding for the Berwick Bandits team in Edinburgh.

I am studying a fence when I become aware of a figure in the middle of the arena. His name is Kevin Coombes; he is holding a hand microphone and is the track presenter, and he is ready for a hard night's work. Tonight's match involving the Eagles and Wolverhampton Wolves is essentially meaningless, since the Wolves have qualified for the end-of-season Elite League play-offs, while the Eagles are already out of the running. But 'meaningless' is not a word that Kevin recognises: 'Laydeez 'n' gennelmen, boyz 'n' girls,' he booms. 'It may be a dead rubber, but there's nothing dead when these sides go wheel to wheel in anger! Welcome to Sussex by the Sea!' A marching tune breaks out. It sounds familiar. Why, it's 'Sussex By The Sea'.

A couple of pick-up trucks, heavy with riders, start to circle the track on a lap of introduction. The riders wave, self-consciously.

The fans clap, approvingly. In front of me, a father nudges his young daughter: 'Don't just clap,' he orders. 'Scream!' She tries, really hard, but in her excitement all that emerges is a mild whinny. Crimson with embarrassment, she hides her face in her coat.

Kevin introduces the opposition, to magnanimous applause. He mentions Adam Skornicki 'from the land of Poland', and a Swedish gentleman named 'Fast' Freddie Lindgren. They sound ominously capable. Then the riders for the first heat take the track, showing off like mad, with much revving and the odd extravagant wheelie. The fans love it; roaring them on, singling out their favourites by name. A genuine tension is building and, attempting some small understanding of the occasion, I consult the beginners' guide to the sport, featured on the Eagles' website.

'The bikes have no brakes, have fixed gears, limited suspension and acceleration to match Formula 1 cars ... there are four riders on the track at a time, and the track is a skinny oval ... There are three tiers to the sport in Britain: the Elite League, Premier League and National League. The Eastbourne Eagles compete in the Elite League, the sport's top level, a league that involves some of the best riders from around the world.

'All British League matches see teams of seven riders compete over a 15-race formula to decide the match-winner. Each of these 15 races lasts four laps, and points are awarded on the basis of the rider's individual finishing position – three points to the winner, two to second place, one to third place, and nothing for last place. There are two riders from each of the two teams represented in each heat ... and their combined totals, called the "heat total", are used to complete the scoring for a meeting. After the 15 races, the team with the highest running score of "heat totals" added together is the winner ... the match announcer will keep you up to date throughout the meeting, and there are also plenty of friendly fans around who will help you if you ask.'

All true, especially the part about 'friendly fans'. Yet, helpful as it is, the outline does nothing to prepare me for the dramatic eruption of that opening race. The tapes are lowered across the track in the home straight, and the four riders move forward, nudging the starting gate with their front wheels. Two men, dressed in the style of baseball umpires, move among the riders to keep them in line. One of the umpires stands between the middle two riders with his arms extended, and there he will linger until the final few seconds, when a distant starter will press a button and the tapes will shoot up. After assessing my own options, I have elected to stand close to the start line, perhaps 10 feet from the rider in the outside lane. I am frankly surprised that nobody else has shown similar foresight.

The engines change pitch. There is a violent whine, followed by a demented roar as riders and machines scream into the first corner, where the race is effectively won or lost. A shower of cinders is thrown up, stinging my face, sticking to my coat, lodging in my hair. Beneath the clamour, I fancy I can hear the sound of mocking laughter. Later, I shall be told with much chuckling that it is 'a rite of passage', that you can always tell a newcomer to speedway by the cinders in their hair.

Everybody in speedway recites that statistic about motorbikes accelerating at the same speed as an F1 car, but it is impressive all the same. Then there is the deceleration of the communal slide into the corner. In the absence of brakes, the speed is manually controlled, with the left leg locked and stabilising, the right leg working the bike around the bend. The strength of the riders is remarkable, the valour quite extraordinary, with nobody yielding a yard. The bend negotiated, they tear up the straight at nerveless speed, close to 70mph, before preparing another slide into the corner. More noise, more chaos, more finely calculated courage.

There is a violent whine, followed by a demented roar as riders and machines scream into the first corner

'Fast Freddie' wins that first heat, covering the four laps in 56.2 seconds. The cognoscenti on the terraces analyse his performance, and the buzz of their conversation replaces the mechanical bedlam. There is the singular scent of ethanol in the air, the smell that symbolises speedway. The starters rake the shale, where the racing wheels have dug deep ruts as they surged away. A tractor appears, dragging a chain around the bends to smooth the surface. The breath returns, the heart stops pounding. And Kevin returns to the airwaves with a bubbly: 'Happy birthday to Alex for last Monday!'

I am beginning to see the point of Kevin's contribution. Most people take their sport from television, where an authoritative voice explains the story, unravels the technicalities and occasionally offers contentious opinions. Such a voice invites strong reaction, and already this evening I have heard Kevin described in sadly unflattering terms. But his skin is evidently thick, his zeal is infectious, and I sense that Arlington wouldn't be the same without him.

Like most fans, he is preoccupied with the following week's Knockout Cup quarter-final, the Eagles' last chance to take something from the season. 'Seven days' time, our date with destiny! Lakeside!' he bawls. I marvel at his ability to enthuse over a shopping centre in suburban Essex. Then I am made aware of the Lakeside Hammers, a speedway team that stands between Eastbourne and glory. Lakeside failed to make the Elite League play-offs, and Kevin understands their anguish. 'That's gotta hurt, hasn't it?' he muses. 'Gotta hurt.' All around the track, people are nodding sadistic agreement.

After the first three heats, Wolves lead by 11 points to 7. I meet a man who is swathed in a blue and yellow scarf and chomping on what might be a cheeseburger. I ask if he is worried about the score. He beams from behind his bun. 'Not a bit,' he assures me. 'We're the Eagles. I'm actually quietly confident.' As for Kevin, he is busily massaging one of the sponsors: 'Macey Industrial Fixings are proud to put their names to heat number four.' He too is clearly untroubled by the state of play; indeed, he might be said to be loudly optimistic as he seeks to instil some backbone into the home forces: 'We wish the lads all the best of Eastbourne luck' is his rallying cry.

The crowd may be modest, but it is growing louder with each race. The tempo is maintained as the races follow each other in rapid succession. One of the promoters, an amiable man with the curiously appropriate name of Trevor Geer, flits ceaselessly from pits to grandstand to trackside; organising, harrying, advising and encouraging with all the frantic energy of a former rider. Although I know nothing about speedway, I do know something about Trevor. Back in the Seventies, he was a very fine speedway rider, and he once had what was described as 'a coming together' with another rider at Eastbourne. A veteran observer of the sport recalled: 'It looked the most innocuous incident, but poor old Trev was screaming in agony. The primary chain had shed and sliced across his boot, taking his big toe off. The medics did their work quickly and managed to save the toe. But if you should meet him, don't mention it. He won't want to be reminded.'

Trevor bustles past yet again on one of his urgent missions. He calls back over his shoulder: 'Going quite well, isn't it?' I try not to stare at his feet. But Trevor is fine; it is the riders who cause concern. My attention is taken by three photographers on the crown of the first corner, popping away with vivid flashes. When men are suffering g-forces as they race into the bend – bikes bucking, legs stretching, bodies racked by conflicting strains – ordeal by camera seems an unnecessary imposition. I am alone in my concern. Nobody else is remotely bothered. 'Not a problem,' I am told. 'The riders know where the flashes are coming from. Now if the fans started using flashes, that's a different matter.'

In fact, the first fall of the night occurs in heat six. It is a straightforward slide. Everyone shrugs, the race is abandoned and the rider drives away in silence. Kevin fills the gap. 'Happy birthday to Sue,' he chirps. 'Sue Hobbs. Last Tuesday.'

Heat seven produces something more serious. The Wolves' rider Tai Woffinden's clutch drops. The bike rears and he loses control as he hurtles into the first bend. Lukas Dryml of the Eagles is struck by the careering machine, and for a few minutes the consequences are disturbing. Then, to relieved applause, Dryml climbs to his feet. Woffinden is disqualified and Dryml walks off, clutching his wrist. Kevin is philosophical: 'That's gotta hurt a little bit, hasn't it?' he remarks. And he adds: 'It's a funny old game.' The man is simply magnificent.

The interval is taken. 'Get yourself a coffee,' counsels Kevin. 'Getting a li'l bit chilly, innit?' The crowd takes him at his word, wandering off in search of sustenance. I meet Michelle and Emily, who are wearing jackets with the word 'Ambulance' stencilled across the shoulders. I assume they are nurses, but they refute the assumption. Michelle works for a pump manufacturer while Emily is a child-minder, and they are here to help the paramedics. Emily has left her husband and children waiting in the car while she carries out her duties. Michelle has been coming to Arlington since she was a small child: '35 years. Never got tired of it.' I inquire about accidents, but they are admirably phlegmatic. 'We had a nasty one the other week. Dislocated shoulder. And a cracked collarbone. Nasty.' But what was the worst? 'One rider got third-degree burns when his hand got trapped in his engine.' Nothing worse? 'Well, two years ago, one poor bloke had a heart attack. Just over there. By the food hut.' 'The one selling doughnuts for 40p each, three for £1?' I ask. 'That's it,' they say. 'How did you know?'

At the pits gate, a young family is waiting with barely suppressed excitement. The local newspaper has been running a promotion this evening, in which it offered patrons a goody bag with various souvenirs. Three envelopes have been placed in lucky bags, entitling the winners to a trip to the centre of the infield with Chris Macdonald, the commercial manager of the Eagles, and the promise of autographs from the riders after the meeting. The family is clutching a treasured envelope. The young daughter, perhaps 9 or 10 years old, is also celebrating her birthday. 'There,' says her mother, 'you never dreamed we had this for you, did you?' The child's eyes are full of stars. 'Never dreamed, Mum,' she says. I stand there blinking at the programme, ruefully aware that those of us who do this sort of thing for a living ought occasionally to be reminded of our good fortune.

... the news that the Eagles' rider Joonas Kylmakorpi is 'on fire tonight' conjures a rather unfortunate image

Meanwhile, the inimitable Kevin picks up where he left off. 'Make some noise, Arlington!' he commands. By now, the night is cruelly cold. There is a frosty sheen on the stadium roof, and even the lager drinkers have switched to scalding coffee. Yet the fans respond with a brave cheer and the Eagles finish first and second. Kevin is spectacularly vindicated: 'See!' he yells. 'You make some noise, and the boys perform.' Of course, his touch is not infallible; indeed, the news that the Eagles' rider Joonas Kylmakorpi is 'on fire tonight' conjures a rather unfortunate image. But speedway fans love a trier, and Kevin's enthusiasm has won over his public.

The second section of races sees the Eagles take control. The fans have quite forgotten that there is nothing at stake. Six points ahead at halfway, Eastbourne seal the victory by 49 points to 41. The man who was 'quietly confident' is now dancing with the artless abandon of an uncle at a wedding. The lady in the bobble-hat has just kissed a gentleman who might easily be her husband. But Kevin, a pro to his fingertips, has a public service announcement to deliver: 'Someone's handed in a mobile phone carrying case,' he says. 'If you've lost one, I'll be at the back of the pit lane. If you can describe it, it's yours.' He pauses, pensively. 'You can't just say: "It's a mobile phone carrying case." I've got to have a bit more information than that.' Another pause. 'It might have an insignia on it,' he hints. 'I'm not saying it has, but it might. Anyway, come and see me. If you've lost one.' It is a memorable homage to Alan Partridge.

Chris Macdonald is collecting the victorious Eagles in his pick-up truck. There are two Swedes, a Finn, a Czech, an Australian, a Pole and a Slovenian. Most of the fans stay to acclaim them, and the fact that their heroes have only a nodding acquaintance with Sussex by the Sea seems happily irrelevant. There is more self-conscious waving. The riders do not appear in the least triumphant, merely tired to their bones. And with good reason. Their working schedule is horrendously demanding. Between mid-March and late October, the Eastbourne men ride in the Polish League on Sundays, the Swedish League on Tuesdays and at Arlington Stadium on Thursdays. Add the long-track meetings popular in Poland and Scandinavia, as well as the away matches to be completed in England, and they could be in action six nights in a week.

The rewards can be considerable. Riders are paid by results, around £125 for every point they win. With five rides in a match, and the possibility of five wins delivering 15 points, it is possible to collect £1,875 on a rare 'maximum' night. But costs are oppressive, and the riders assume responsibility for most of their outlay. They need ten bikes in England, ten in Sweden and ten more in Poland, along with mechanics and vans, as well as the ordinary living and travel expenses.

Some maintain apartments in each country; others virtually live in airport lounges.

The problems of eating well and sleeping adequately are obvious, and they are compounded by the demands of competing at the highest level of a dangerous sport. Tomasz Gollob, the 2010 World Champion, is the highest-paid sportsman in Poland, a master of his craft at the age of 39. But few speedway riders can match his longevity, for collarbones break, nerves dissolve, people are enfeebled and exhausted. For most, it is a hectic, hazardous and relatively short career. And those Eagles fans, well versed in their sport, have a strong sense of what the seven riders have endured. Which is why they have stayed to cheer at the Arlington trackside.

The commercial manager drives slowly, milking the applause for his charges. He is naturally eager to promote his sport, yet aware of the danger of overstating his case. 'I tend to describe speedway as Britain's premier summer sport,' says Chris. 'We've got, what, 32 or 33 tracks. That's quite a few people watching. More than county cricket, I'd say. Wouldn't you say? And we do try to involve the fans. Up to 7p.m., they can actually go into the pits, talk to the riders, have pictures taken with them, ask about their preparations. You can't do that sort of thing at Manchester United, can you? People tend to write it off as a sunset sport, but that's not really so. It's very colourful, but it's not choreographed. What you see is what you get. In my opinion, it's excellent value for money.'

Overstatement holds no fears for Kevin. Drumbeating is what he does best. 'Wolves have been put in their place!' he barks. 'Job done! Next stop, Lakeside next Thursday. It's gotta be good, hasn't it? It's gotta be good.'

Back in the pits, the riders jump down from the truck. Three girls, no more than 15 years old and shivering in crop tops and impossibly short skirts, pout prettily at the men in leather. One winks at them. 'Ooooooh!' they squeal, nudging and pushing each other in their delight. A few fans linger to purchase a cheese/egg/salad/burger-burger for the homeward journey, among them my 'quietly confident' friend. The hour is late, the frost is crunching underfoot, and the tips of the trees are glinting silvery in the blackness. The public address pipes up one last time, its voice familiar as an old friend. 'Thanks for choosing us for your speedway entertainment this evening. I'm Kevin Coombes. Good night.'

The Eagles comfortably defeated the Lakeside Hammers in the quarter-final. They then overcame Wolverhampton Wolves once more in the semi. They won the home leg of the final against Poole Pirates by eight points before a crowd of 1,800. But 5,000 fans watched them lose the return at 'The Place of Pace', Poole, by 13 points. The club's official website dolefully reported: 'The Eastbourne "Lifestyle" Eagles Knockout Cup dream is finally over.'

'It's all about you, Frank on the A50'

CHAPTER 6
606 AT THE BBC

On a Sunday evening in September, I am in Studio Four on the second floor of the BBC Television Centre in West London, waiting for Joe Public to speak to Alan Green. And, through him, to the nation.

Green himself is sitting in an empty Stamford Bridge, having covered Chelsea's comfortable victory over Blackpool. A man of combative opinions, freely voiced, Green's Belfast rasp is one of BBC Radio's most distinctive sounds. He enjoys an intelligent understanding of the game, and is a more amenable character than his abrasive public persona would suggest. While he makes no attempt to disguise his own convictions, he handles callers with genuine solicitude, extracting views and ensuring that they all have their say, for better or worse. And his callers seem to appreciate his attentiveness; thanking him for his time, telling themselves that it was worth their while to make the call. This is not always the case with phone-in shows. Indeed, the *Guardian*'s Martin Kelner once offered this solicitous advice to those desperate souls who watch *You're on Sky Sports*: 'If you find yourself at home one night calling up Jason Cundy, you might want to consider Dignitas as a possible alternative.'

The production team behind Green is surprisingly small, reinforcing the suspicion that cheapness is a primary reason why phone-ins are so cherished by network executives. At the rear of the studio, a group of phone operatives field incoming calls, sifting out the loons and passing the plausible candidates through to central control. There sits Dan Garvey, a London Irishman in his late twenties. Unfailingly polite, nimble of wit yet totally merciless, Dan combines the instincts of a fan with the tact of a diplomat. The callers are rated in four categories on his screen: 'Poor, Average, Good, Top Call'. He speaks to the most likely supplicants, teasing out stories and phrases and assessing their potential impact before offering his assessment to the producer, Jo Tongue.

Jo is bright and 30-ish, a Spurs-supporting south-east Londoner who has an impressive track record in both radio and television. She takes the big decisions and runs most of the risks. And those risks are considerable, since there is no time-lapse and no chance to eradicate libel or obscenity. 'We listen to them, and we hope we get a sense of what they might come out with,' she says. 'Callers are quite aware of what they can and can't say.' She pauses, thoughtfully: 'And they do say "alleged" a lot.'

In the background, Dan is checking the credentials of a prospective caller: 'I've spoken to you before, haven't I? Have you been on the show already this season? What?! You think my voice is a double for DJ Spoony? You're joking, aren't you? He's been working on his voice for 30 years. He will be pleased.' Jo listens in to the last 30 seconds of the conversation. She and Dan shake their heads. Ten minutes to go, and there is no obvious opening caller. Yet there is no panic, as Dan auditions two more hopefuls, Frank and Paul. Jo goes with her instincts.

She comes on the line. 'I think we'll start with you, Frank, if you don't mind,' she says. Does he mind? You just know that Frank is thrilled to bits, and says as much.

'Thanks Frank,' says Jo. 'You'll be talking to Alan Green.'

She mutters an aside: 'He's obviously driving. Ask him to pull over.' She clicks a switch: 'Paul, we're coming to you second. Nice to have a couple of Liverpudlians at the top of the show,' she smarms.

'It's all about you, Frank,' oils Dan.

The clock flickers on, and the disembodied voice of Green begins its introduction from Stamford Bridge: 'Chelsea go four points clear at the top after an easy win over Blackpool. A Berbatov hat-trick sinks Liverpool at Old Trafford. Manchester City win at Wigan. What's on your mind tonight? Get in touch. First to the phone is Frank, on the A50. Or at least, that's where I'm told you are, Frank.'

'Ow are yer, Greenie?' chirps Frank. 'All right, mate?' And they're away.

Now when people of a certain age recall how football used to be, they often sound like one of Monty Python's Four Yorkshiremen. That glorious sketch had the quartet exaggerating past poverty and competing in misery by boasting of the days when they lived in a water tank on a rubbish tip, or a brown paper bag in a septic tank. It concluded with the line: 'You try and tell that to the young people today … they won't believe yer!'

… when people of a certain age recall how football used to be, they often sound like Monty Python's Four Yorkshiremen

Similarly with the football fan. Time was when he knew his place – it was almost invariably 'he', since women were actively discouraged – and that place was on an open terrace, with the rain lashing, the wind biting, the crowd swaying on mud-caked steps, and an air of squalor and privation all around. He had opinions, this football fan. He thought the goalkeeper was past it, the centre forward was overweight and the manager was useless. He knew that the catering was a scandal, the toilet facilities a disgrace and the way they increased the entrance fee every August was an outrage. All these views he would pass on to the people who stood on either side, but that was as far as they travelled. For nobody else seemed remotely interested: not the club directors in their imitation oak-panelled boardrooms, not the season ticket-holders in the grandstand with their well-appointed seats and their well-filled flasks. And not even the media, who assumed that the fans, like the poor, would always be with us: silent and uncomplaining. Every so often, writers and broadcasters would deprecate the shameful neglect of the game's most faithful followers. They would then adjourn to the press box, which was sheltered by a roof and was therefore luxurious by comparison.

Fans began to come in from the cold at the start of the Nineties. There was the lifting of the five-year ban on English clubs competing in Europe, following the tragedy of Heysel. There was the publication of the Taylor Report, which was commissioned after the Hillsborough disaster and which pointed the way to all-seater stadiums. And there was the success of the 1990 World Cup, which gave us not only 'Nessun Dorma', Gazza's tears and some infuriatingly resilient Germans, but also the highly unusual sight of an England team reaching the semi-finals and performing with some style. For several years, English football had been commonly regarded as a game played by the uncouth and watched by the uncivilised. Suddenly, it was becoming acceptable, even vogueish.

Having helped to launch the trend, the BBC set about exploiting this new popularity with the creation of 606, a phone-in programme designed to address the whims, fancies and heartfelt concerns of football fans. The presenter was Danny Baker, a silver-tongued, 30-something Millwall supporter. I remember going into Broadcasting House one December evening in 1991, when the show had been running for just a few months, to watch Baker in action.

He was good: quick, bright, at ease with the banter. Since the powers that be were uncertain about the attraction of endless chat, he used to interrupt the dialogue with music, dipping into his briefcase for a batch of CDs. But it was an irritating diversion, because the repartee was so engaging. One caller was asked to name the most inaccessible ground in the League. 'Crystal Palace,' he replied. 'I'll buy that,' said Baker. 'In 1936 the wrong Crystal Palace burned down, in my book.' A dim Scottish chauvinist called in to say that women should only be admitted to football grounds if there happened to be tickets left over. He drew an indignant response from a lady in Luton, who then shredded her feminist credentials by announcing, unprompted, that she'd like to nominate Sheffield Wednesday as 'the best-looking football team in the country'. The most inspired call of the night came from Mike in Reading, who asked: 'Why is it that when you go to matches, you can only ever buy Wagon Wheels? You can't buy them anywhere else. Go into Tesco's and ask for Wagon Wheels, and they'll laugh at you.' Baker's eyes lit up. He knew precisely what Mike was talking about, and his answer was a gem: 'Because, Mike, they are the original stock. They take them into the chairman and say: "Mr Chairman, this is the 16th year we haven't sold these Wagon Wheels." And the chairman says: "Nonsense. Take them back out there till they're sold!" Can you imagine football clubs chucking anything away?'

That was how football used to be, in those distant days before the convulsion of avarice that sent it lurching into the arms of the Premier League, with its sheikhs and oligarchs and wad-waving chancers. Attitudes were hopelessly unreconstructed. The comedian Frank Skinner tells a story of his team, West Bromwich Albion, losing by four goals at The Hawthorns when the public address system blared out a message to a fan whose wife had gone into labour during his absence at the match. She had been taken into hospital and had given birth to a son. The man next to Skinner snorted. 'Poor sod,' he said, with feeling. 'He's been watching us get stuffed out of sight. And when he gets home, he'll have to get his own tea!' As a regular at Millwall's old Den on Cold Blow Lane, Baker recognised the attitudes and relished the daft stories. Yet scarcely a year had passed before he fell out with the BBC and a divorce was arranged, each side citing irreconcilable differences.

When it came to choose Baker's successor, the Corporation was aware of the value of a presenter who was witty, street-smart and steeped in football, a man who might have been plucked from the terraces. Perversely, David Mellor was chosen.

In some respects, Mellor may have seemed the perfect candidate. After years spent in the service of Margaret Thatcher's Conservative Party, he was perfectly at ease with the 'greed is good' ethos of the emerging Premier League. He was, moreover, apparently incapable of embarrassment, as various scandals showed. He claimed to support Chelsea, and frequently mentioned his close friendship with Ken Bates, the popular charmer who then owned the club. I always suspected that he was an opportunist who saw the bandwagon rolling and jumped aboard. I was forever waiting for him to call it 'footy'. And, like so many bandwagon-jumpers, Mellor was never short of bombastic opinions: this player couldn't 'do the business', that manager was 'tactically naive'.

Yet, against all the odds and most of the critical opinion, he endured. At a time when genuine football fans should have been making their case, they found themselves crashing up against this bumptious bundle of self-approval, promising them an hour or more of 'red-hot soccer chat'. I vividly recall his performance in 1997, shortly after the fall of the Tory Government. Citizen Dave had taken a few weeks off to fight the election, in the course of which he had transformed a majority of some 7,500 into a deficit of around 3,000 in the constituency of Putney. It was a memorable election night at the town hall, with Mellor bawling abuse at his opponents and having the abuse returned by such political philosophers as Mr Lenny Beige of the Freedom to Party Party, Mr Michael Yardley of the Anything But Mellor Party, and a screeching grocer named Goldsmith.

So 606 offered him a haven. 'Hello again!' he babbled. 'Just when you thought it was safe to go back to the airwaves – I'm back! ... I hope to be over the moon, but I could be as sick as a parrot.' It was beyond satire, a rural dean attempting to rap, yet Mellor hung around until 2001, untouched by insight, humour or originality. Since then, other presenters have come and gone; none were quite so ill-suited as Mellor, although there have been one or two challengers. And in that time, the fans continued to find their collective voice.

Frequently, that voice has come laden with clichés, most of them directed at managers. Tactical naivety is still a popular charge, as is the demand for greater 'passion'.

It is undoubtedly true to say that several managers have lost their jobs as a direct result of phone-in criticism

Managers are routinely requested to 'step up to the plate', or to 'take us to the next level'. As the blessed Mellor often remarked, they have to be able to 'cut the mustard', since failure to do so would result in their 'losing the dressing room'. Harmless platitudes on the face of it, yet platitudes of a kind that tend to impress the chairmen of football clubs. It is undoubtedly true to say that several managers have lost their jobs as a direct result of phone-in criticism.

So the programmes carry a good deal of clout, and it follows that 606, the first and most popular of all, exerts the greatest influence on football at large. Which is why, on this Sunday evening, I am in Studio Four. Listening to Frank, live from the A50.

Frank has called with a tactical lesson for the Liverpool manager Roy Hodgson: 'When you play one striker up front, you're inviting pressure on you. You can't do it. It's not good enough.'

Green is sympathetic: 'It may take a while for Hodgson to realise that he's not managing Fulham any more,' he says.

Frank is delighted with the qualified agreement: 'Thank you very much, Greenie. He done brilliant at Fulham, but at Liverpool you expect to win every week … He's just too nice of a guy … he's not the guy for the job.'

Green grunts: 'They're not remotely good enough.' Frank repeats himself: 'He's too nice of a guy.'

Hodgson has been manager of Liverpool for just five Premier League matches, but Frank has passed an unforgiving judgement.

Dan is preparing new callers. 'When we come to you, make it nice and lively if you can, Robert,' he urges.

Green is listening to Paul from Huyton: 'I wasn't at the game today. You can't get tickets for Old Trafford, can you? I'm sorry to do this, but…'

'Hold on! What's he up to?' cries Dan, alarmed…

'I'm gonna be a bit enthusiastic,' continues Paul. 'I'm not having all this "mid-table" rubbish, mate … second half we played pretty decent … I've seen a lot of positives … so let's not have all this doom and gloom an' slittin' our throats and all the rest of it, mate.'

'He had me worried for a while then,' admits Dan.

'Let's get a Manchester perspective from Robert in Cheshire,' says Green.

Robert obeys half of Dan's instruction, being nice but less than lively. 'I'm an extremely happy Manchester United supporter … Dimitar Berbatov … absolutely brilliant.'

'What about Rooney today?' inquires Green.

'Quite subdued … Players can't be great all the time … Berbatov stepped up to the plate … quite sublime.'

Jo hopes to fit in 20 callers tonight. With many more like Robert, she could double her target. In fact, *606* regularly attracts between 500 and 600 callers. The highest figure in recent years was something more than 2,000, outraged by England's abysmal World Cup performance against

Algeria. There are no comparable issues tonight, a fact emphasised by Ed in Bradford, a 'first-time caller', who has just returned from the Liverpool match with doubts about Hodgson: 'It was better when we changed to 4-4-2. Why didn't he start like that?'

Brian on the M61 is comically determined to take offence on behalf of Manchester United fans: 'Hi Alan. How're ya doin? You said Blackpool supporters would fill out every ground this season. D'you not think Manchester United supporters would fill out every ground?'

'I just said that Blackpool supporters are wholly committed,' replies Green.

'D'you not think that Manchester United supporters are wholly committed?' persists Brian. He speaks of the players with faux-familiarity. First names abound. He calls Vidic 'Nemanja', and says that they 'possibly could have made Wayne captain, but his mind is still elsewhere. There's still a lot to come from Wayne.' As for Berbatov: 'I've always been behind Dimi.' To the uncommitted, the effect of such devotion is curiously sad.

Neil in Dewsbury takes a different tack. He wanted United's John O'Shea sent off for a professional foul. He asserts that the referee Howard Webb 'bottled it'. He believes it's 'difficult to send off United players at Old Trafford' because of the 'constant drip-drip of intimidation from Sir Alex Ferguson'. And he appears to hold those beliefs as sincerely as the man on the M61. Green, who fell out with Ferguson years ago, affects neutrality.

In the studio, they are anxiously awaiting the call that will lift the show. It will not come from the next in line, a neurotic Evertonian.

'Now, Kevin,' begins Green, 'don't tell me you're panicking, five games into the season?'

'I'm panicking, five games into the season,' replies Kevin.

He explains: 'I love David Moyes. He's been brilliant for our club. We had 63 per cent possession against Villa.' (It is difficult to know who to blame for the fatuous obsession with meaningless statistics, but Sky TV are the leading candidates.) 'I'm concerned about Moyes tactically,' says Kevin. 'We actually have the right players. Moyes just has to find the right formula.' Finally, pessimism wins out, as it invariably does with football fans. 'We play Liverpool in a few weeks,' he says. 'And at the moment, it looks like a bloody relegation battle.'

'Do not despair,' counsels Green. In the background, there is the sound of a barely stifled sob.

'Now, Kevin,' begins Green, 'don't tell me you're panicking, five games into the season?'

Still the studio team searches for inspiration. They had hopes of one caller, but those hopes are fading. 'I'm a bit worried about Andrew,' says Dan to Jo. 'He's listening to his radio.' In fact, Andrew is listening to Peter on the M62: 'Liverpool played poor ... you can't sit back too deep against Man United ... we paid the price ... Liverpool played good for 10 minutes, that's all.' Dan is still worried: 'Andrew's still listening to his radio,' he reports. 'Andrew! Can you hear me? Andrew!' 'Take him out,' says Jo. Andrew is quietly liquidated.

Meanwhile, Green is engaged in a splendidly pointless exchange with Kevin from Manchester.

'Hi Kevin, what's on your mind?' he breezes.

'Not a lot, mate,' says Kevin.

'Unpromising' doesn't come close. Eventually, Kevin is roused to something approaching enthusiasm. 'I've just phoned in to say I'd like to congratulate the Blackpool team for their second-half performance today,' he says. 'Sorry Kevin, can't agree with you at all,' says Green.

'Oh, OK,' says Kevin.

'I think they're a naive team and I think they'll get thumped more often than not,' says Green.

'Well, Alan, that's your opinion. We differ. It's all opinions,' says Kevin.

'Absolutely right,' says Green.

Kevin is mild and reasonable, a throwback to the early *606* standards, when callers tended to be less assertive. Their views were no less firmly held, but they seemed grateful for being considered and overjoyed when actually chosen. Their reaction was that of people who wrote letters to newspapers and were delighted to see their words in print. In this age of email and social media, they are far more used to having their voices heard; yet all too often those voices can sound the same. The ones that stand out are those with originality and passion, laced with a touch of humour. In Studio Four, Dan Garvey suspects he may have found one such caller. He has been put through to the studio, and his name is Geoff.

'So, Geoff, you're a Millwall fan?' begins Dan. 'For your sins, you say? Well, you've been having a great season so far.' He covers the speaker and exchanges conspiratorial mutters with Jo.

'Geoff's a bit of a character. It's your call.'

'What do you think?' she asks.

'I don't know if he'll be mental or quite entertaining,' says Dan.

He turns back to the caller. 'As I was saying to you, Geoff, we don't get a lot of Millwall fans.' Jo nods. Geoff will go on.

Green is currently engaged in mundane chat with Pete in Durham, who wants to have a 'little bit of a whinge about Arsène Wenger, if you don't mind.'

'I don't mind at all,' says Green.

'I didn't think you would, somehow,' responds Pete, archly.

'I've nothing against Arsène, by the way,' adds Green, hurriedly.

'But he's a world champion whinger, isn't he?' teases Pete.

'I couldn't possibly comment,' concludes Green. There is laughter in the studio, where Green's views on Wenger are well known. To Green's credit, unlike some of his journalistic contemporaries, he makes no great effort to ingratiate himself with football managers.

Time for Geoff, on whom hopes are placed. He comes on booming: 'GOOD EVENING, ALAN!'

Green responds in kind: 'GOOD EVENING, GEOFF!'

There is preliminary banter about Millwall's latest defeat. Geoff informs us he has been following them since 1946: 'So that tells you I'm slightly over 21.' He launches into a hoary diatribe about Premier League glory-hunters and the price of players. 'I honestly pray that we don't go up,' he declares.

'What!' gasps Jo.

'Leave off!' grunts Dan.

'Because if we do, it'd be the end of Millwall as a football club,' continues Geoff. 'They won't be able to afford new players. They'd get hammered left, right and centre every week.'

By now, Geoff is into his stride. Green appears to be agreeing with him. They castigate Nani of Manchester United, they mock Glen

Johnson of Liverpool, they pour scorn on modern players in general. 'There are so many footballers, Geoff, you want to get hold of and say: "Will you wise up, son?! Will you rejoin the human race?"' says Green. Geoff is still chuntering as he signs off. Mental or entertaining? The jury is out. But Jo is kind: 'Thanks for the call, Geoff. You were wonderful,' she says. It is the telephonic equivalent of an air-kiss.

Suddenly, more by accident than conscious design, a theme starts to emerge. Jim from Nuneaton draws attention to the growing practice of players blocking off goalkeepers. Jim

> 'There are so many footballers, Geoff, you want to get hold of and say: "Will you wise up, son?! Will you rejoin the human race?"'

has watched this black art exercised at Blackburn Rovers and he seems genuinely concerned. 'Even if it's your team that scores a goal,' he says. 'the real Blackburn supporters, they know it's a form of cheating.' Green indicates agreement. He fell out with the Blackburn manager Sam Allardyce long ago, and a rapprochement is unlikely.

John in London picks up on Allardyce's recent comment that he would find it easy to manage Real Madrid. 'I suppose this was the start of his campaign to be England manager,' he sniffs.

'He's never really stopped campaigning to be England manager,' says Green. 'He's so modest. Such a modest figure … He's got a marvellous track record of success. I'm amazed Real Madrid weren't knocking on his door years ago.'

By now, John is becoming quite angry: 'God help us if he ever gets anywhere near the England job,' he snarls. 'Anyway, last night, Real Madrid went top of their league.'

'How did they do that without him?' says Green. 'I'm sure Mr Mourinho must have been on the phone to ask his advice,' replies John.

Green rounds it up with a heartfelt harrumph: 'The FA have been stupid about certain things in the past,' he says. 'Let's hope that they don't make any stupid decisions about the next England manager.' He pauses, and then: 'Come on Marian in Blackburn, make a case for the defence.' Dan senses that she is agitated, so he whispers a quick warning: 'Nice and lively please, Marian. But we're live, so please, no swearing.' What follows is radio gold.

'Good evening, Alan,' says Marian. 'There is no defence. I cannot make a case. There is no defence for what Allardyce calls football. I am heartbroken as a season ticket holder at Blackburn Rovers. The other week I went to watch Accrington Stanley. It cost me more to watch Accrington Stanley than it did the Rovers, but I tell you what, Alan, I enjoyed the game. Because the ball was on the floor. At Blackburn, Jack [Walker, former owner] would turn in his grave if he were to see what's happening now. Allardyce yesterday was out-thought, he was out-manoeuvred tactically by Hughsie [Mark Hughes, former manager] – my God, how we could do with him back. The man is a joke. Real Madrid, England, for God's sake, anybody – come and take Allardyce off our hands! He embarrasses me. I was in Tesco's this morning and I saw a woman in a Rovers shirt. Hey! Alan! I felt sorry for her because of what we are having to put up with week after week after week. It's not only poor football, it's out-and-out cheating … I watched Blackpool this afternoon. I clapped them off the field. We go there next week and, I tell you what, I'm hoping Ian Holloway [Blackpool manager] can come up with something. And doesn't that sound shocking?'

She articulates her objections to events at Blackburn with passionate precision. Coming from the part of England where the professional game was nurtured and cherished, she feels something akin to shame as she sees her club falling far below the standards she believes it ought to represent. It is not just another empty rant at an unpopular manager. Right or wrong, it is a statement of principle, as impressive as it is unexpected. In a couple of minutes of airtime on national radio, a lady from Blackburn, Lancashire, has told the game a home truth.

In a couple of minutes of airtime on national radio, a lady from Blackburn, Lancashire, has told the game a home truth

Green understands. 'Well, Marian, I can't disagree with anything you said. I really can't,' he says. 'And I'm very glad that you, as a Blackburn fan, and you may have been a fan for many years, you indeed can see what's going on there at the moment.'

You sense that Marian is still trembling from her outburst. 'Well, we have to have some respect,' she says. 'All these other people who ring in to say their team's not doing this or doing that, at least they're playing football. Which is more than what we're playing.'

I am genuinely amazed by the idealism of the callers, the use of words like 'respect', the abhorrence of 'cheating', the uncomplicated love of the game and the insistence that it has far more to offer than a mere result. Of course, some things never change. Chelsea having won by four goals an hour or so earlier, Ben in Woking calls to complain about the referee Mark Clattenberg. 'There's so much money riding on every game. It's a million pounds a point in the Premiership. You cannot afford to get things wrong … I left at 82 minutes … I'm sorry, I pay my £700 a year as a season ticket holder… I saw nothing in the second half, I'm afraid … I was expecting ten! … I'm disappointed.' Ben is the kind of Chelsea fan who might have found common cause with David Mellor.

But others set their sights rather higher. Dave, a Blackpool fan from South Yorkshire, sounds a good sort: 'We play good football … bit naive … We try to play football, unlike Stoke, or Blackburn, with their cheating Diouf and their horrible, horrible tactics, we get the ball on the floor, we pass it around. We've got good footballers. Sure, we might go down. But if we do, we'll go down playing properly. What would you rather watch?'

And Mark, also a Blackpool supporter, is another who is in danger of giving football fans a good name. 'I want to tell you something that happened to me when I was at the play-off final at Wembley back in May,' he says. 'This time-traveller emerged from today, and he tapped me on the shoulder and he said: "I've got some news for you from the future." I said: "Tell me the worst". He said: "You'll lose two of your first five games in the Premier League" … "Who to?" I said. He said: "To Arsenal and Chelsea." What! For goodness sake, what! Three years ago, I was getting excited about an FA Cup win against Norwich … For crying out loud, we were playing Chelsea today! It's amazing!' His voice is shaking. He may well be terminally naive. But I bet he didn't leave Stamford Bridge in the 82nd minute.

The clock is running down. Jo is talking to a couple of callers who are waiting patiently: 'Hello, David. Alan's getting to you in a moment, OK?' … 'Won't be long, Peter.'

Another Peter, from Middlesbrough, is talking. What's more, he is talking sense. 'When is Sir Alex Ferguson going to stop Nani throwing himself about and cheating?' he asks. 'It's disrespectful, it's a disgrace to the game, and it should be stamped out now.'

Green cuts in: 'Are you a United fan, Peter?' He is. 'And you find it as distasteful as people who don't support the club?'

'I do. Because it's unfair. It's like Allardyce and the goalkeepers; it's cheating … no team needs to do it, least of all Manchester United. He's the only one in the team, and it's so blatant. When you watch them, Alan, you're embarrassed. Well, I am.'

Green remarks that it's not only foreigners who dive. Peter agrees. For a United fan, he goes much further. He says that most of the Manchester City players who have come in from abroad are 'quite honest players, I think'. Praise indeed. The closing music sounds. Green winds smoothly down. Jo flicks two switches and issues two apologies. 'Sorry, Peter. We had to get to the next programme. Cheers, mate.' … 'Sorry, David, it's the nature of live radio. Thanks for the call. Have a good evening.'

She thanks the studio staff and sinks back into her chair. She has been working on the programme for a year and she attacks her task with ferocious enthusiasm. She was on the edge of her seat when Marian from Blackburn said her piece, sensing the impact she might make on the radio audience. But does she fear for the phone-in format? Does she worry that the fans might lose interest in waiting in line for the chance to speak, that the supply of callers might simply dry up? She answers with a question: 'Will fans ever get tired of arguing in the pub? That's all it is, really, people arguing over a drink, but without the swearing. Some are difficult, some tend to ramble a bit, but that's what any group is like. And most of them have got interesting things to say. Me, I love football fans. I'd talk to them anyway, for the fun of it. Sometimes, when we get a really good one, I feel like saying: "Never mind talking to Alan, just keep on talking to me".'

You know what she means. The game still suffers its ranters and ravers, just as the pub attracts its bar bores. But these days, there is a crucial difference. When the football fan speaks about matters that are relevant, serious and close to his or her heart, there's an excellent chance that the nation will be listening.

Marian in Blackburn was given her wish. In December 2010, Allardyce was dismissed by the club's new owners. 'I enjoyed a fantastic relationship with the players, my staff and the supporters during my time in charge,' he said.

The day they will never forget

CHAPTER 7

THE RYDER CUP
AT CELTIC MANOR

It's 3.21p.m. on the afternoon of Monday 4 October. An American golfer named Hunter Myles Mahan is standing on the 17th green of the Twenty Ten course at Celtic Manor.

Removing his cap, he extends his hand to denote concession, and the simple gesture provokes an outbreak of frenzied glee. People begin to invade the green; first in their tens, then their hundreds, then many, many more, until the gentle slope is overflowing with humanity.

Everyone is jumping up and down, not in a loutish, carelessly destructive way, but with a mixture of acclaim and relief. Everyone is singing: 'Olé! Olé! Olé! Olé!', the daft little chant that used to serenade Jack Charlton's Irish football team all those years ago. The pleasure is exquisite, the joy almost irrational. Looking back, it is quite impossible to convey the glorious mayhem of the moment. Really, you had to be there in Newport, South Wales, on that wonderful day.

The sun was smiling across the Usk valley and two or three fluffy white clouds shuffled across the flawless blue sky, as if determined to decorate the idyllic scene. It is important to recall the sunshine, since memories of the Ryder Cup at Celtic Manor will involve floods and torrents and dark, baleful clouds. During a notably charmless closing address in Kentucky two years earlier, the European captain Nick Faldo had said: 'See you in Wales, and bring your waterproofs.' In the course of a hapless week, it was possibly the only thing the wretched man got right. But it wasn't the most difficult forecast, since Welsh Octobers tend to be damply predictable. No matter, the people who control the game decided to push back the Ryder Cup so that space could be found for something called the FedEx Cup, a competition that allows sponsors with more money than taste to smother the players in dollar bills from first tee to 18th green. The golf fans of Europe at large, and South Wales in particular, paid the penalty for such vulgar idiocy, and yet the wonder of the occasion eventually emerged through the mist and the rain.

For the Ryder Cup remains the finest event that golf has to offer; a bold assertion, but one which is validated by the response of the galleries. As a rule, the four major tournaments elicit sighs of sympathy and ripples of approving applause, with perhaps a few patriotic cheers when a home player is in contention. By comparison, the Ryder Cup is a kind of protracted bedlam, Us against Them, the Old World taking on the New, with tumultuous roars detonating around the course at every small success, and desolate wails at every drive sliced, every putt squandered. For reasons which are difficult to understand yet impossible to ignore, the event feels viscerally important. Sport, as somebody once observed, is 'a magnificent irrelevance', but ask anybody who has tramped the crowded paths alongside the fairways or joined the huddled masses around the greens, and they will tell you that this one really, truly, desperately matters. And this time, in some curious fashion, it seems to matter more than ever.

This isn't classic anti-Americanism; that would be far too simplistic. In any case, some of the greatest names in American golf – Jack Nicklaus and Tom Watson spring promptly to mind – are equally revered on both sides of the Atlantic. Neither

This isn't classic anti-Americanism; that would be far too simplistic

is there any obvious inferiority complex at work, since before Celtic Manor, Europe had won five of the previous seven matches. Yet everybody remembers just how good it felt to beat America on each of those occasions, how satisfying to trample on decades of effortless superiority. Because they are, in so many small and telling instances, quite different from us. And if we needed proof, then Corey Pavin provided it before a ball had been struck.

Seeking to strike the appropriate tone and gain a competitive edge, the American captain invited Major Dan Rooney, a fighter pilot, to deliver the motivational address. Now Pavin has form in this respect, going back to 1991 when he wore a Desert Storm cap to play Ryder Cup golf at Kiawah Island. He then seemed merely absurd in his inability to distinguish sport from war, but with the introduction of Major Dan, he became genuinely ridiculous. For the major was way beyond satire. When asked to convey the central theme of his speech, he said: 'Flying an F-16 jet looks like an independent act, as it's a single fighter plane. But when we go into combat we become one unit. That was the overarching message I gave: about accountability, working together and having each other's backs.' He announced that leather jackets, the kind worn by fighter pilots, had been presented to the team: 'I handed them over to Corey, Tiger Woods, Phil Mickelson and everybody. It was a very special, very spiritual time we spent together.' And he concluded with the hope that America might 'pull it off on hostile territory'. Woody Allen himself could never have come up with the mad major.

And yet, from everything we know, the American players took him seriously. Instead of laughing him out of the team room, they colluded in his bizarre confusion of bloody conflict and earnest contest. No matter that, long ago and to a man, they rejected the boot camp in favour of the country club, they raised the roof for Major Dan. And those tasteful leather jackets are today adorning the walls of rumpus rooms in some of the most desirable gated communities in Florida and Southern California. Meanwhile, the Europeans were listening to the likes of Seve Ballesteros, Sir Ian Botham and Gareth Edwards. Them and Us.

The notion of Europe as 'Us' is one that took root surprisingly swiftly. It was partly the Ballesteros factor, the remarkable appeal of a man who played the game with style and wit and an impish delight in his own talent. Who wouldn't want a golfer like Seve on their side? And when, in 1979, he opened British and Irish eyes to the possibilities of a broader, grander alliance, he and his friends from continental Europe were instantly embraced. It is one of the happier anomalies of the Ryder Cup that people who regularly bore for Britain on the iniquities of Brussels will readily join the greenside chant of 'Eu-rope! Eu-rope' when there are Americans to be overcome.

If the crowd is partisan, then it is also unfailingly sympathetic to the players. For golf is watched by golfers. The buzz is lively, but the shots are studied in the strictest silence. When a drive is hooked or chip is fluffed, a collective wince ripples round the galleries. They know precisely how the victim feels because they themselves hooked and fluffed and committed all manner of careless errors a day, a week, a month before. Equally, they are well placed to appreciate a player's virtues, because he is standing just a few yards in front of them and he is making the ball do things that are hopelessly beyond the scope of their own ability. All this makes them slow to chide and swift to bless, an attitude rare among those who watch competitive sport.

So they are a tolerant breed, yet the opening day of competition had tested that virtue to the limits. For it rained with such relentless ferocity that even the Welsh were alarmed. Faldo's gauche remark about waterproofs suddenly sounded like prescience. A start was made, and spectators who had each paid at least £100 to watch the day's play came squelching through the gates in the half-light of the soggy dawn, their presence creating that seething air of expectation. Players new to the contest were unprepared for its intensity. Rory McIlroy, the wondrously gifted young Irishman, was required to hit the first drive for Europe. He walked to the tee through the chants and cheers and fervent exhortations of a sodden congregation, and the prevailing passions almost unnerved him. 'I've never experienced anything like that at a golf tournament,' he said later. 'I was just hoping to make contact with it.'

The rain grew heavier, the mud deeper. All the fear and foreboding about South Wales in October was coming to pass. Sure, there were moments of lightly malicious relief; firstly when Captain Pavin drove his buggy into a bog for a few wheel-spinning, mud-churning seconds. Then again when the rumour raced around the course that the American waterproofs were leaking like a Cabinet snitch. What's more, it was true! Waterproof tops could not cope with Welsh rain, while the golf bags were similarly inadequate, with the result that grips became wet and treacherous. The crowds listened to the radio reports of this calamity, they heard how the American team had been forced to turn to the European supplier of wet weather clothing, and somehow it made them feel better when play was suspended after just a couple of hours. Colin Montgomerie, the European captain, remarked: 'Our team room is happier than theirs right now.' It was some small consolation for the communal soaking.

Yet real consolation was hard to come by. Seven hours of play were lost to the weather on that opening day, which seemed a poor return for the £100 outlay. But people were generally uncomplaining. This is, so to speak, par for the course where golf spectators are concerned. The topography of the arena means that sightlines are poor, and a large, mostly unshepherded crowd makes matters far worse. Somebody observed, with rueful accuracy, that watching golf from outside the ropes was like attempting to watch a football match when all you could see was a corner flag. There was a little more play late in the day, but by then Celtic Manor felt as if it had been through a blender. 'It was almost hard to call it a golf course,' said the American Stewart Cink. Meanwhile, the Fourth Estate sat in the press tent and jokily churned out First World War metaphors, and the damply deprived golfing public sank endless pints of cold beer and cursed the fools who had decided that a Welsh autumn could safely be entrusted with the game of high summer.

So how did the Ryder Cup followers react to being soaked and patronised? Why, they came back the next day, in even greater numbers. This time they were better prepared. They wore wellingtons and waterproof capes, and some even brought sou'westers, which gave them the look of stranded trawlermen. There were American matrons in Burberry and Cotswold farmers in Barbour. Over near the clubhouse, a group of lads in Welsh rugby shirts stared at a large screen and supped their ale. A bald gentleman in collar, tie and blazer picked his way past the group, stepping fastidiously through the mud: Sir Michael Peat (Eton and Oxford), private secretary to the Prince of Wales. As he disappeared into the crowd, I heard the forlorn bellow of somebody trying to sing 'Delilah'. I suspect it was not Sir Michael.

And there was much to watch, since extra matches had been crammed in to compensate for the previous day's lack of action. The mud was deeper, with a strong smell of the farmyard, and the wind blew perversely. There was a degree of consternation when the Americans went 6–4 in front after two completed

... somebody shouted:
'How many birdies will
you get today, Tiger?'

sessions. But enjoyment of the occasion and respect for the game and the people who play it never seriously wavered. As Woods walked out to play his foursomes, somebody shouted: 'How many birdies will you get today, Tiger?' The crowd immediately jeered the oafish jibe. They knew that the man had achieved far too much to be the butt of foolish jokes.

Once again, the decision to play in October took its inevitable toll, and the day finished inconclusively, with Europe leading in all six matches on the course. The lights from the corporate cathedrals twinkled across the valley, and Montgomerie spoke of his players: 'They don't need motivation, all they need is passion,' he announced. 'They've got to want to win this, and by God they do!' As the crowds shuffled off to their buses, they quoted the words of the captain. The mood had been set. Tomorrow, they told themselves, would be magnificent.

Here, a confession. It was at this point that I deserted. The shame is with me still. Staying at a hotel in Bristol, I looked out on Sunday morning to see the rain sweeping across the car park. I thought of the mud, the cold, the acute discomfort and the farmyard smell, and I decided to walk away. The man in the next room, a taxi driver who was treating his teenage son to his first major sporting experience, saw me checking out. 'You're not leaving us, are you?' he asked. I started to explain, but he shook his head, slowly and sadly. 'It's the Ryder Cup, and we look like winning it. And you're, like, going home?' For a moment, I thought he was going to give me a white feather. I could hear the reproach in his voice all the way back to London, as I drove down the flooded M4.

I arrived home at lunchtime, soon after play resumed. Magnificent was the least of it. From 6–4 down, Europe won five-and-a-half of the six available points to take a 9½–6½ lead, and the fans never stopped singing. It was one of those days that seem to happen once every three or four Ryder Cups, when a team becomes inspired and the crowd senses that something extraordinary is happening; a thrilling momentum is generated and everything seems possible. The only Europeans to halve their match were the Molinari brothers, Francesco and Edoardo. And even that felt like a triumph, since they were twice required to come back from one down in the last nine holes.

The singles would be played on Monday, for the first time in the event's 83-year history, and Europe would need five of the twelve points available to regain Sam Ryder's trophy. If Sunday was magnificent, then Monday will surely be the day of days.

With untypical decisiveness, I wake long before dawn, climb into the car, and I am crossing the Severn Bridge as Lee Westwood and Steve Stricker walk on to the first tee to launch proceedings. The weather is warm and clear and perfect, as if apologising for the excesses of the past few days. Bright as spring yet ablaze with the beguiling tints of autumn, the valley is wearing her loveliest face. I remember those ancient Hollywood movies, when John Wayne or Gary Cooper would remove the heroine's spectacles, stare into her eyes and gasp: 'Why ma'am, you're beautiful!'

The crowd is smaller, as only those who bought their £130 tickets for Sunday's truncated play have been offered admission today, and many of those could not accept, since they have jobs to do and trains to catch. The corporates too have gone; they have meetings to chair and empires to build. And anyway, there is nobody available to man their marquees and pour their drinks. Yet the enthusiasm is staggering, the fiercest yet. People know, they just know, that something sensational is about to happen. Campaign medals are flaunted by three-day veterans. The phrase 'You should have been here on Friday' is heard repeatedly.

And the mud is still there, deep and shining and treacherous. It tugs off a golf shoe here, traps a senior citizen there. Over at six, next to the water, a small, blonde child slips and falls in the cloying stew. She arises with a large blob of mud on the end of her nose. Her father sloshes across to assist, while her sister turns away, shoulders shaking with laughter. The lady tending the Ryder Cup memorabilia stall watches a portly gentleman slide on the seat of his corduroy trousers. 'Fourteen!' she cries. Then, by way of explanation: 'He's the fourteenth one I've seen go down this morning.' Yet he doesn't seem to mind, not specially. Like the rest of us, he is entranced by the possibilities of the day.

Large screens are posted at various parts of the course to help the public follow events. Crowds stare at these pictures while waiting for the next pairing to arrive. Since the players are out of earshot, the same rules of etiquette do not apply. Here it is permissible to cheer when an American misses a putt or finds the rough or launches a drive into the trees. The cheering is raucous and heartfelt. Television clichés abound: 'There's an alarming amount of red on the board … What a character, that Poulter! … It's not over till it's over.' A New York lady with a Palm Beach tan sees a shot of the American team wives. She is not impressed: 'Those clothes. Outrageous!'

Yet the most impressive feature is the sheer good humour. A few moments before the players appear, the media outriders assemble by the green. Having waited by the 13th for hours, a man in a hooped jersey suddenly finds his view blocked by a couple of gossiping photographers. He mouths an oath. He coughs, loudly. He calls: 'Scuse me, mate.' Finally, he yells: 'Sit down!' And, after a pause, he adds: 'Please.' Impressed by his politeness, the photographers nod and move on. Possibly they are aware that there is no greater media privilege in all of sport than being allowed inside the ropes at a major golf tournament. Given that priceless armband, you can walk just a few, respectful yards behind a player and hear what he is saying, observe what he is doing, practically see what he is thinking. It is an extraordinary insight into his ability to achieve excellence under pressure.

My own experience of watching at close quarters began unhappily, at Royal Lytham in 1979. Green as the grass and uncertain of where to walk, I sought help from a kindly correspondent. He shepherded me around two or three holes, offering endless advice and chuckling indulgently at my more naive questions. As I recall, we were on the par-four 17th when he cautioned me for walking too close to the trio of golfers ahead. 'Never make them aware of your presence,' he said. 'Always hang back, give them space.' As if to demonstrate his point, he halted dramatically and allowed them to walk on and on.

Suddenly, there was a small thud, and my mentor yelped an agonised curse. A golf ball had struck him in the small of the back, and it now lay, reproachfully, at our feet. Away in the distance came the sound of fearsome threats. 'Oh no!' said my friend. 'It's bloody Greg Norman!' A large, ice-blond figure in a Pringle jumper could be seen advancing along the fairway a couple of hundred yards back. 'What do we do now?' I asked. He drew on the experience of a lifetime of golf-watching. 'Scarper,' he counselled. And so we did.

Ever since that traumatic afternoon, I have been a nervous observer on championship courses: fearful of the long drivers behind and anxious to avoid the abuse from the sidelines that an armband tends to attract. But today, trudging the course with the muddy foot-soldiers, everything feels right. Everything except those final singles. As the man said, there is too much American red on the board. The great Westwood is struggling against Stricker. Martin Kaymer, the gifted German, is being taken apart by Dustin Johnson, while Woods is slaughtering poor Francesco Molinari and playing like the player he used to be. There is a droll update at the 13th green, when an elderly man with a light Cork accent and a radio plugged in his ear reports: 'Tiger's just gone birdie, birdie, birdie, eagle. How bad's he?' The thought crosses my mind that, over the next decade, tens of thousands of amateur golfers will play here at Celtic Manor. And we may be quite sure that nobody will score birdie, birdie, birdie, eagle, in the way that Woods has just done.

'Tiger's just gone birdie, birdie, birdie, eagle. How bad's he?'

But Woods cannot salvage things for America, can he? Nobody could do that, could they? Surely it couldn't go wrong now? Not at this stage, not when the watchers have suffered as much as the players. And not at such a venue. For all the flooding of the past few days, all the brooding mist and the ceaseless drizzle, all the stumbling and the splashing, the place has grown on us. True, the River Usk is the colour of mud, and instead of flowing it seems to slurp. And the clearest views of the play are reserved for those who stand more than 6½ feet tall, with sharp elbows and thick skin. No matter. In some mysterious fashion, the whole thing has come together. The stewards are infinitely courteous – 'Stay on this side of the rope please, gentlemen. That'd be great, thank you' – the shared adversity has brought about a curious bonding, and the sunshine has worked its wonders. In the great state of Georgia, they would have dyed the river green or blue or whichever colour best suited television's taste. Here in South Wales, they leave it to nature's whim, and they are right to do so. Heresy it may be, but already Celtic Manor feels more comfortable, more natural, more civilised than Augusta National, that raddled dame with her store-bought traditions and her preposterous airs. No, it couldn't go wrong, not on a day like this.

Suddenly, I sense a great deal of agitated trampling. Some are moving back down the course, eager to encourage the European efforts. Others hang on at 17, even 18, gambling that they will be on hand when victory is delivered. For most, the outcome is a matter of genuine emotional importance. Others are rather more nonchalant. Two 40-ish men climb the slope to a vantage point and, in the accents of their Home Counties tribe, speak in arch terms of the awe in which they hold the players. Says the first: 'I've been wasting my time in all those bunkers and that water. You see, what you do, you hit every fairway, make every chip, plonk it on every green.' 'And single putt,' replies his friend. 'Ah yes, single putt,' comes the reply. 'I don't know why I never thought of it before.' And, chuckling affably, they trudge off in search of glory.

At first, glory is hard to come by. Westwood, the Englishman who embodies the spirit and soul of the team, falls to Stricker. The crowd emits a vast roar of consolation, but they are starting to worry. Woods is quite unplayable, forget Woods. Likewise Johnson. But Ian Poulter is retaliating vigorously for Europe, and meanwhile, two of the pivotal battles are going all the way. Rory McIlroy and Cink are all square at 18. The crowd loves McIlroy, partly because he is brave and bold and Irish, partly because he plays with the joy of one who still believes he is outrageously fortunate to be doing this for a living, but also because they sense that he will be around for the next 15 years or so, winning everything and giving immense pleasure. McIlroy ad Cink have similar shots to the green. Cink, older and shrewder, lays up. Rory, as they knew he would, takes it on. 'Brave lad!' comes the call while his ball is in the air. It soars into the blue, then dies in a greenside bunker. Forgiveness is instant and unconditional. Cink's short iron takes flight. 'Get in the wa-ter,' squeals a Welsh voice. It is a rare lapse of form. 'Shhhhhhhh!' comes hissing from a hundred throats. 'Nasty, that,' remarks the man next to me. The ball comes to rest 8 or 10 feet from the pin. There is generous applause. They like Cink. They detect class and decency in his manner.

But still they love Rory, and they will love him still more if he can get away with this. He climbs down into the bunker and addresses the ball. Around me, I count four people who are living out the cliché by biting their nails. A swing, an explosion of sand … and the ball catches the lip and drops back into the bunker. Rory's face crumples, his caddy grimaces. 'He didn't give it enough,' concludes my neighbour, superfluously. He repeats the stroke, and sees it float to 6 feet. Cink misses his putt for the match and a few thousand people bite their tongues and uncross their fingers. Rory, who is now looking about half of his 21 years, settles over the crucial putt, and sinks it to halve both the hole and the match. There is a cascading roar of relief and acclaim, as the two men hug in mutual respect. Rory hurls his ball into the crowd, where a man in a yellow T-shirt drops it. I refuse to see this as an omen.

The audience is still bubbling at this piece of theatre when the figures of Luke Donald and Jim Furyk are glimpsed in the distance. Furyk is another favourite of the crowd, with his idiosyncratic swing and his unforced modesty. Donald is patently pleasant and pleasingly capable, but there have been doubts about his nerve. Today, he has been putting like a magician and arrives at 18 a hole to the good. Nerves are jangling; nobody seems quite convinced. And then as the players prepared to play their chips to the pin, something outrageous happens.

A fat man, wearing only a thong, appears on the fringe of the green: capering, striking poses. He is probably drunk and palpably stupid. There is a befuddled grin on his face and a jokey little slogan scrawled across his chest. Donald shakes his head, Furyk shrugs, and at the side of the green, Corey Pavin looks as if he could split him in half with a pitching wedge. This time, I am at one with Pavin. As is a Welsh voice behind me. 'Prat,' it says. And then, after reflection, 'Fat prat.'

Two security men race forward to seize the prat and lead him away. A few minutes later, a member of the Gwent Constabulary walks past. 'Where you bin, then?' a voice inquires. 'We could have done with you just now.' The officer glares as the gallery giggles.

In the event, Donald is unmoved by the crass intrusion. He plays a nerveless approach, rolls his putt to the lip, and the hole is conceded, along with the match. There is much cheering, and one poor fellow rolls messily down the muddy bank. Everybody points and laughs, and somebody whips out a phone and takes a picture. But the Cup is yet to be won, and you can touch the tension.

I am starting to worry about Montgomerie. A default shot of the on-course coverage is of the European captain scurrying around the course on his buggy, his mobile features registering every nuance of triumph and disaster far more dramatically than anything the scoreboard can manage. A gentleman from Dundee, who tells me he once met Montgomerie's father and thought him a most agreeable chap, shares my concern. 'It's getting to him,' he says. 'Look at him. He looks like someone on the edge. If we don't win this, well, I don't know. He could do anything.' It is an alarming prognosis, yet I find myself nodding agreement. Deep down, I suspect that British golf galleries have harboured these fears about Montgomerie for the past decade or so. Wonderful player, technically superb, strikes the ball as purely as anyone we have seen. And yet, how to put it? There are days when you wouldn't leave him too close to sharp instruments. If you took his pulse at this moment, it would sound like a demented drum solo. He is clearly an excellent captain, but he does not inspire quiet, understated confidence.

Mercifully, a degree of relief arrives in the form of Miguel Angel Jimenez, who combines the torso of a darts player with the touch of a pickpocket. Throughout the day, his drives have been landing 50 yards or more behind those of his opponent, Bubba Watson. The deficit leaves him totally unmoved. He trusts in his flair and touch and imagination, and those timeless qualities do not let him down. People are actually dancing as they turn from the screen near the 18th green to watch Jimenez slide in his winning putt for his 4 & 3 victory. 'Olé! Olé! Olé! Olé' breaks out all round the course. And the

Spaniard smiles a rascally smile, shakes the hand of everyone in sight and raises an imperial arm, a gesture which says: 'You too could play golf like this. If only you had the talent.' Then he fumbles for his cigar, lighting it flamboyantly, bestowing a blessing on the watching world. The chanting drifts across the valley, and the opposition seem vaguely perplexed. I suspect that of all the golfers in the whole of the USA, perhaps only John Daly could begin to understand Jimenez. After all, it was Daly who once said: 'I never go to the gym. They don't let you smoke in there.'

By now, we know that we are destined for a dramatic finale. The nature of the contest demands nothing less. The scoreboards are reading like casualty lists. People are standing in the mud and staring at the evidence of the numbers. Ross Fisher has been beaten, as have Peter Hanson and Padraig Harrington. Woods has dealt brutally with Francesco Molinari. His brother Edoardo has halved with Rickie Fowler, who sounds like an *EastEnders* extra, looks like a member of an Eighties boy band, but is said by those who know to be the finest golfing prospect on the planet. Since Fowler finished with four birdies, including a 20-foot putt on the last hole, to secure equality, the half felt like abject defeat.

Jimenez ... raises an imperial arm, a gesture which says: 'You too could play golf like this. If only you had the talent'

Depression is hovering over Celtic Manor. As we hurry down to the 16th, the music has died, the dream is fading, and that Scotsman's assessment of Montgomerie keeps running through my mind. The crowd is buzzing with 'what ifs'; putts that slid past, drives that found water or rough. Only European 'what ifs' are cited, opposition frailties being quite forgotten. A trio of American males begin a chant of 'U-S-A! U-S-A!' It is quite inoffensive, yet we know that had they attempted something similar at Swansea City or Cardiff then consequences might have ensued. Here, the home fans affect a sniffy indifference. One man turns to glare, but his wife tugs his arm. 'Ignore them,' she advises. 'They just want to be noticed.'

The man of this desperate moment is Graeme McDowell, or 'G-Mac' as everyone has started to call him, partly because it is short and neat, and partly because it implies chummy acquaintance. As the winner of the US Open four months earlier, he understands pressure, but this, we sense, is pressure of a different nature. He has to win this tussle with Mahan, since a half would share the match and see America retain the trophy. Once he led by three holes, now he is only one up, and the momentum is with Mahan.

Thousands upon thousands of us wade through the shimmering brown Windsor foothills to take our slippery stance on the slope beneath the Kidwelly Pavilion. Poulter, his own match won, passes us on his buggy, ostentatiously thumping the European badge on his chest. There are shouts of 'Go Poults!' He does not appear embarrassed by the attention. The bank is full, and we all stretch and strain to improve our view, always with an eye to our neighbour's comfort. We feel we are in this together. 'The man from Portrush', as the commentators are calling him, is oblivious to our plight and to the noises we are anxiously suppressing. He is considering a 15-foot birdie putt with a mild left-to-right break. Success will leave him two up with two to play. Failure will probably see the men in white coats collect Montgomerie. On runs the ball, and on and on, and the screams follow every inch of its course, concluding in a sustained screech of delight as it vanishes below ground. 'Never doubted it. Not once did I doubt it,' the man in front tells his chum. Later, with the smugness of hindsight, we shall all peddle the same message about the final acts of this drama. But we shall be lying.

And so to 17. Another slope over another green, beneath the Conwy Club and the Caerphilly Pavilion. Both are closed for business, this being an unscheduled Monday. Impossible that it could be more packed than the last, but it surely is. I spot an opening some 30 feet above the base of the bank, the entire green stretching before me. Amazingly, it is still there when I slither up. On my left is a lady in a London Irish rugby shirt. On my right, a plump Italian, emoting into his mobile phone, informing his brother in Milan of the progress of events. Above me are countless thousands of neurotics clinging to each other for safety and reassurance. Briefly, I wonder what might happen if just one person slips and starts a chain reaction. But the thought is swiftly banished, as G-Mac prepares to drive the 211 yards from tee to pin. 'Come on son, you're a legend!' booms a voice from the north of

Ireland. He isn't helping. 'It's going to be all right. It'll be fine. I know it,' insists the London Irish lady, with a prayer in her throat. In flies McDowell's approach. It clings to the fringe of the green, and everyone offers up their thanks. Mahan to play, and the tension is unendurable. This is the part that we civilians can never understand. In these circumstances, with his colleagues ringing the green like a hanging jury and crowds clinging to the slippery slopes and cameras clicking and television staring and the whole world watching and waiting and wondering, we should find it impossible to lift the club.

Amazingly, we discover that poor Mahan is prey to the same pressures. He seems to swing half-heartedly and the clubhead burrows into the ground inches behind the ball, causing it to make a short, apologetic hop. It is a bewildering error from a superb player, and we don't know whether to cheer or to cough. Everybody watching has made such a mistake a hundred times before. But only Hunter Mahan has done it with the Ryder Cup at stake. McDowell putts, and leaves it short. Mahan plays again, this time he has to hole the putt or accept the consequences. The crowd is hushed. The ball does not fall. The game is up. Mahan removes his cap. People are coming on to the green. They know it's all over. The scoreboard is streaming the message: 'EUROPE 14½-USA 13½ – EUROPE WIN THE RYDER CUP.'

There is an explosion of delight, shot through with shrieks of ecstasy. A strange thought occurs, unbidden. Why didn't Mahan let McDowell knock in his putt, so the event could have ended in triumph rather than failure? Would that have made the event more joyful? Because the joy is of a special nature; an extraordinary collaboration of the watchers and the watched. It is one of those rare and precious sporting occasions when the audience deserves almost as much credit as the actors in the drama.

The head of Montgomerie, a touch greyer since Thursday, can be seen at the heart of the melee. Flags are appearing, the flags of Europe. Francesco Molinari is being heaved onto anonymous shoulders, while the crowd chants: 'Two Molinaris, there's only two Molinaris'. Francesco is conducting, arms aloft, two fingers raised on each hand. You never saw a man enjoy himself quite so gleefully. Still more people surge forward, as the tune changes to 'Olé! Olé! Olé! Olé!' It is an 'I was there' moment. I find I am singing along with the rest, hands clapping above my head, a reaction normally reserved for Ireland landing a Grand Slam or Charlton Athletic avoiding relegation. But this was wonderful beyond words; the better for being so close, so thrilling.

It is one of those rare and precious sporting occasions when the audience deserves almost as much credit as the actors in the drama

While the greenkeeper walks off into the woods, carrying a pearl-handled revolver, the cavorting assembly stumbles back down the 18th; jostling, cheering, singing 'We've got our trophy back'. The American fans are attempting to appear philosophical; the Europeans are trying not to gloat. Both are failing. The forecourt is scanned for vaguely familiar figures. Somebody spots that ginger-haired chap from the radio. 'One Chris Evans…', the chant breaks out. Evans buries his face in his hands and scuttles ostentatiously around the corner, in the manner of one who really, really hates being recognised. Down on the 18th, a group of uniformed men, 30 or 40 strong, are gathering. They might be official, but could easily be a male voice choir. At a signal, they surge forward, race across the green and leap into the greenside bunker, causing an avalanche of damp sand. And there they lie, giggling foolishly, stunned by their own daftness.

Moments later, familiar faces appear on the clubhouse balcony. And still more flags are sprouting: St George of England, the Red Hand of Ulster, the German for Kaymer, the Italian for the wonderful Molinaris. Padraig is draped in the Irish tricolour, spraying champagne with a silly grin, as if he had just invented the trick. There are calls for Montgomerie, who is inside, searching for his sanity. Every player is serenaded when he appears.

Items of golfing gear are flung from the balcony: shoes, caps, sweaters; all of them grabbed and prized. Jimenez wraps himself in the flag of Spain, puffs his Havana and beams his benediction. A friend tells television interviewers that nobody drinks or smokes quite like Jimenez, and you wouldn't doubt him. The Molinaris seem dazed, thrilled, their smiles as wide as the valley. And in the middle of it all stand the two Ulstermen: Rory having champagne poured over his curly mop, and beaming his delight at the sheer devilment of it all; and McDowell, the bold G-Mac himself, mouthing sounds which go beyond words. Later, he will tell a press conference that, compared with this pressure, winning the US Open was like 'playing the back nine at Portrush with my dad.' But for the moment, he is standing there with his friend and countryman, their arms around each other's shoulders, grinning and drinking and savouring the magic. God willing, the two of them will stand at the centre of many a stage over the next few years. But this is the day they will never forget. And neither shall we.

'Send her vic-torrr-ri-ous!'

CHAPTER 8
RUGBY AT TWICKENHAM

Three hours to kick-off, and an argument is breaking out on the station concourse. Two men, each in his late thirties, each wearing white replica shirts with a red rose on the breast. One man is purposeful, the other thirsty.

'Time for a swift one in the buffet, then?'

'No, we said we'd see them in the Cabbage Patch.'

'But one won't hurt, will it? Just the one?'

'No, our train goes in 9 minutes.'

'So we have got time for one, then!'

Waterloo has staged the same daft little quarrel down the decades. Do we drink cold lager now, at 11.30 on this drab November morning, or do we abstain for half an hour until we reach the pub? Friendships have foundered on the answer.

With poor grace, Thirsty yields to his purposeful chum. Still squabbling, they spill on to the Twickenham train. There they stand alongside men, and a few women, who have arrived at a similar decision. Four miles down the line, at Clapham Junction, more people press into the crowded carriage. Some of them wear the black shirts and scarves of New Zealand. There is token barracking, much of it involving sheep, all accepted quite amiably. The train noses through some of the more desirable suburbs of south-west London, admits a few breezy red roses at Richmond – 'Room for a little one? … Move right down inside!' – then sidles along to Twickenham. Throughout the entire journey, nobody has mentioned the match.

The two men next to me have been discussing the internal politics of their company's human resources department. The New Zealanders have been ruminating on the cost of their London lodgings – 'In Wellington you could get a suite for that money' – and a father and son over by the door have been talking about Chelsea's start to the Premier League season. Now you could scarcely imagine a more intriguing contest than the one we are about to witness. The All Blacks team reads like a threatening letter, with names like Joe Rokocoko, Ma'a Nonu, Richie McCaw and the finest rugby player in the world, Dan Carter. England are taking promising shape, led by Lewis Moody and featuring unproven players of exciting potential in Courtney Lawes, Chris Ashton and Ben Foden. Yet not one of those names has been spoken in the carriage. It is as if we are all off on a communal blind date.

If it were a club match, it would be quite different. The fans would be aware of the players, the tactics, the strengths and the weaknesses. And that knowledge would spring from familiarity. Having pledged themselves to a team, they would have watched that team perhaps twice a month throughout the season. But Twickenham is different, especially in the autumn. Whereas the Six Nations develops a rhythm, a narrative, the autumn matches challenge the watchers to fit names to faces. And, given that a good many of those watchers are there for the occasion rather than the contest, those names can be slow to register.

Twickenham will accommodate 82,000 people, most of them telling themselves how fortunate they are to be there

No matter, the occasion alone is a powerful attraction. Twickenham will accommodate 82,000 people, most of them telling themselves how fortunate they are to be there. Their sense of good fortune is enhanced by the ticket touts barking their wares on the 15-minute shuffle to the stadium. 'Who wants tickets? Buy or sell': I count 27 of these manipulators of supply and demand, many blocking the pavement, all curiously ignored by the Metropolitan Police. Two or three ticket-holders stop to inquire about price; they have no intention of selling, they just want to be reassured that they are holding something of real value. In any case, they feel they have a right to those tickets, since most have acquired them through schools or England's 1,900 rugby clubs, or via the ballot organised by the England Rugby Supporters Club.

A small crowd has gathered on the South Stand piazza to observe Twickenham's most recent attraction, a 27-foot bronze sculpture depicting a line-out. It was unveiled in June, it weighs 5 tons and it cost £455,250, a point of some contention among the hierarchy of the Rugby Football Union. However, John Owen, the immediate past president of the RFU, was in no doubt of its merit. 'This is not art for art's sake, but art for rugby's sake,' he declared, a touch obscurely. He added: 'We've dedicated it to the core values of our sport.' The sculptor, Gerald Laing, chose to depict a line-out as it was a 'particularly dramatic part of the most dramatic of games'. He compared the potential catcher to the Knight of the Round Table, Sir Percival, in his quest for the Holy Grail. This is not a comparison I hear from the crowd in the piazza, many of whom are idly wondering if the jumper will actually catch the ball. The so-called 'core values' are engraved in the granite base of the statue: 'Teamwork, Respect, Enjoyment, Discipline and Sportsmanship.' Those who have paused to study the innovation should know that these are the 'principles that lie at the heart of the game in England'. They are the results of an exhaustive study by a seven-strong Core Values Task Group, set up by the RFU in 2007. They should not be mistaken for a statement of the bleeding obvious.

Some of the arrivals have paid £5 for a 'ref-link'. Now this is something that defines modern rugby union far more succinctly than any of those so-called 'core values'. The ref-link is a radio earpiece that enables us to eavesdrop on the referee's exchanges with the players. He will inform them of the decision he has made and his reason for making it and, given this ammunition, we shall either nod knowledgably or disagree vigorously. For a paltry fiver, the ref-link makes sages of us all. I struggle to think of another major sport that is conducted in such a fog of incomprehension. The laws of rugby union are a smorgasbord of edict and suggestion, nuance and interpretation. They change with each passing season, sometimes it seems with every passing week.

What is acceptable to a southern hemisphere referee is abhorrent to a northern official, and players must proceed on the basis of trial and error until they discover where the lines are drawn, which rules must be observed and which can safely be disregarded. The one unifying factor is that nobody, but nobody, can agree on the offside law. It is rugby's Schleswig-Holstein question, that diplomatic imbroglio of which Lord Palmerston remarked: 'It is so complicated that only three men in Europe have ever understood it. One was Prince Albert, who is dead. The second was a German professor, who is mad. I am the third, and I have forgotten all about it.' If those who play the game are eternally surprised by the sound of a whistle, then those who merely sit and watch can have no understanding whatever of why the play was halted. In the kingdom of the blind, the man with the ref-link is king.

Thus equipped, we troop into what the publicity brochure calls: 'The largest dedicated Rugby Union venue in the world.' The reception is affable, although we are informed that entry will be denied to anyone carrying cans, bottles, glasses 'and fireworks'. I find myself wondering who says: 'It's the All Blacks today. Mustn't forget the roman candles and the catherine wheel.' In the programme, a thick and glossy investment at £5, new RFU President Richard Appleby bids us: 'a very warm welcome to Twickenham Stadium for the first of four 2010 Investec internationals'. Most civil. At the corner of the North Stand, a pleasant young man with a canister on his back and a beer pump in his hand approaches hopefully. 'Pint, sir?' he asks. I decline with thanks. 'Only £4.10p,' he says. Again, I decline. 'Oh, go on,' he urges, wrongly detecting a weakening of resolve. 'Ne'mind. Worth a try,' he says. One hopes that the England team will be even half as motivated this afternoon.

All around the ground there are subliminal pressures to partake. In the Rugby Store by the West Stand, they are playing the 'Drinking Song' from *The Student Prince*: 'Ein, zwei, drei, vier, lift your stein and drink your beer'. And then, as if this seemed excessively Teutonic, a blast of rose-tinted reverie: 'There'll always be an England, while there's a country lane; wherever there's a cottage small, beside a field of grain.' Suddenly even Sigmund Romberg sounds positively palatable.

Merchandising opportunities abound. This is an affluent, captive, stridently patriotic audience, many of them slightly the better for drink.

For a salesman, it amounts to a handwritten, personally delivered invitation. Replica rugby balls sell for £19.99, match-day scarves for £7.99, England shirts for £49.99. A man emerges from a shop, stuffing his new shirt into a bag. 'I'm going to the Welsh game next year,' he explains. 'Got to have an England shirt.' Across the forecourt, another man is shouting into a mobile phone in a broad Yorkshire accent. 'I got it, Richard. XXL. That right?' I imagine Richard at home in Leeds or Bradford, booming his thanks while reaching for another pasty.

So the big spenders spend, the drinkers drain their plastic mugs and the peckish linger at the fish 'n' chips stall or the Great Australian Pie Company. And as I watch the passing parade, I realise how difficult it is to generalise about rugby followers. Long, long ago, Twickenham stood alongside Cowes and Royal Ascot as the embodiment of privilege, and something even darker. In the Thirties, George Orwell – or possibly Philip Toynbee, accounts differ – could assert: 'A bomb under the West Stand at Twickenham on international day would end fascism in England for a generation.' As little as 20 years ago, it was possible to paint a picture of Twickenham Man in the expectation that the portrait would carry some resonance. He wore the uniform of his tribe: waxed jacket by Burberry, tweed hat by Dunn's, shirt by Viyella, complexion by John Courage. He found his physical exercise in his evening stroll to the pub, where he ordered 'my usual poison', served in his favourite jug. For intellectual exertion, he turned to the *Daily Telegraph* crossword. His own rugby career was a distant memory of tussles with Home Counties adversaries: Esher Thirds, Sidcup Seconds, Old Gravesendians Extra A. Not so much the playing, but the japes and the jokes, the singing and the drinking, the bawdy cast of Saturday night characters, from Barnacle Bill to Eskimo Nell to O'Reilly's remarkable daughter. The caricature is gone, vanished with the tribe. Sure, the odd vestige of antiquity lingers. There are countless, respectful poppies in this mournful November, and hats of familiar tweed. But ties, even club ties, are no longer de rigueur, elbows are no longer clad in leather patches, and Barnacle Bill is home from the sea.

Twickenham Man was most at home in the old stadium, with its angular, dark green stands, virtually free of advertisements. It was a place where you could hear the line-out calls, savour the thud of colliding packs, inhale the sharp tang of embrocation. 'Slap it on, lads,' the skipper would call. 'If we can't be fit, at least we'll smell fit.' I first visited almost half a century ago, when Brother Senan took our school First XV to watch Ireland knock

'Slap it on, lads,' the skipper would call. 'If we can't be fit, at least we'll smell fit'

seven bells out of their erstwhile lords and masters. At least, that was our hope and our intention. In the event, a fly-half named Richard Sharp played the Irish on his own, and trounced them with something to spare. It was a princely performance, culminating in a sumptuous outside break; back straight, fair hair streaming and legs stretching in smooth acceleration before dapping the ball down beneath Ireland's posts. 'They always find one, don't they?' lamented the reverend Brother. 'Always one like him.'

England would be thankful to find one like Sharp today, in this relatively new stadium, before this demanding audience. The seat prices have only increased the demands upon them. Even after taking all manner of financial factors into account, we paid just a handful of small change to watch Sharp work his wonders. Today's top price is £85, and for that kind of outlay, modern Twickenham Man expects an inspiring performance as well as a satisfactory result. For too long, England have given him neither.

And if expectations are high in the £85 seats, try to imagine how the customers paying more than ten times that amount might be approaching this international. A couple of hours ago, some 400 temporary members of the 'Captain's Club' arrived at the Carling Room, which is situated, according to the publicity blurb, in 'the most exclusive area in the Twickenham stands'. There they sipped coffee and munched pastries before moving on to a champagne reception, at which they were introduced to the man from whom the room takes its name. Will Carling first captained England at the age of 22, the youngest ever to achieve the honour. In the course of an utterly distinguished international career, he won 72 caps and led his country on 59 occasions, including three Grand Slams and a World Cup final. In 2001, he formed the corporate hospitality company which is hosting today's event.

A number of former internationals are scheduled to assist Carling with his meet-and-greet duties, including the All Blacks Andrew Mehrtens, Justin Marshall, Jerry Collins, Tana Umaga and Zinzan Brooke, as well as England's Matt Dawson, Kyran Bracken, Richard Hill, Josh Lewsey and Dean Richards, who is currently serving a ban from rugby following his central role in the Harlequins 'fake blood' scandal. In return for their fee, they will exchange harmless confidences, pass on a few jokes, offer informed forecasts of the likely outcome of today's match, and generally furnish the corporates with sufficient anecdotes to enthral the golf club bar for weeks to come.

The guests are now working their way through a four-course luncheon 'served with fine wines'. They will then collect their Official Match Programme before picking up their Premier Official Match Ticket, which will enable them to sit in some style with their chums. The cost of all this – including the 'Full Complimentary Bar, the souvenir mini leather rugby ball "personalised with your corporate logo", the souvenir baseball cap, the post-match tea, the sweepstake for a signed shirt and the personal reflections of some of today's England and New Zealand players', works out at £875 plus VAT per person.

If Carling's operation is at the top end of the hospitality market, then there are others who run him close. The Keith Prowse organisation, along with Twickenham Experience, offers a package that promises a 'Who's Who of international rugby' in the Green Room, where Lawrence Dallaglio, another former England captain, will 'ensure an entertaining day is had by all'. Other hosts will include Will Greenwood, an England World Cup-winner, and Austin Healey, who will apparently provide 'good healthy banter'. There will be question-and-answer sessions and most of the features offered by the Captain's Club. There is no mention of a baseball cap or a mini rugby ball, which may help explain the cost of £795 plus VAT.

Other hospitality options include the East Stand restaurants, Obolensky's and Wakefield's, which overlook the pitch and are named after titans of the English game. They will cost £699 plus VAT today, and will feature all the usual ingredients. The cheapest package is Rugby House, with a slightly scaled-down range of benefits and a guest speaker before the match, but 'only in suites/restaurants with more than 100 people'. These particular clients may therefore miss out on a certain amount of 'good healthy banter', but since the day has cost them only £599 plus VAT, what do they expect?

Now some of us are faintly hostile to the concept of corporate hospitality. We feel that sport is demeaned by being used as a business tool, we believe that seats should be occupied by those who want to see rather than be seen, and we are uneasy about exposing our captains of industry to the post-luncheon platitudes of ancient heroes. (The most objectionable tend to come from the Sixties and Seventies, tedious troglodytes who drool over the days when heads were hacked and bodies were trampled and nobody ever complained. Quite the reverse: when the game was over, they'd all go off, and get roaring drunk and trash a hotel. You made friends for life that way. Especially in Seventies South Africa.) But no matter. Times and circumstances change. The building and maintenance of a modern stadium is, in part, made possible by the contribution of the corporates. This is the way that a steadily increasing number of people choose to watch their sport. Some 3,000 clients/fans are being lavishly wined, dined and healthily bantered for this game against the All Blacks, and their presence is essential to the balancing of Twickenham's books. It is not a question of taste, merely a matter of economics.

The last of the port is sliding down corporate throats when pitchside fireworks announce the arrival of the teams. These garish pyrotechnics always seem terribly un-Twickenham. They are the kind of eruptions designed to accompany hapless British heavyweights on their walk to the ring. Recent experience teaches that on windless days, the smoke thus generated can blot out the action for the first 10 or 15 minutes. Mercifully, this is not such a day, and we watch a lady named Camilla Kerslake belt out the respective anthems. For a good many people, the singing of the national anthem is one of the principal reasons for attending an England rugby match. At Twickenham, faces flush, jaws clench, and they bellow the bewildering lines as if they really, truly mean them:

'Send her vic-torrr-ri-ous; Ha-ppy and glorrr-ri-ous!'

This is not an exhortation; it is an instruction. And God had better do something about it, if He knows what's good for Him. As the crowd finish serenading his grandmother, the stadium screen picks out Prince Harry. Now there's a Twickenham type. Put him on an identity parade in the North Car Park, and I'm not sure you would pick him out. And Twickenham defers to him quite slavishly. Three years ago, as England toiled unimpressively against Italy, English rugby's Elite Director, Rob Andrew, spent the whole of the second half chatting with Harry. It was an extraordinary spectacle. One of the most important men in the English game was pretending that he had nothing better to do with his Six Nations afternoon than explain the finer points of rugby to this occasional visitor. So Andrew pressed on with his tutorial, while Harry wore the look of a man killing time until the Boujis nightclub opened for business. And nobody seemed to think it unseemly.

The anthem done and the deity duly instructed, the All Blacks assemble for the haka. Over the past few years, the Maori dance has ruffled a few feathers in rugby circles. Why, it is asked, are they given a free ride for a performance which psyches them up, gives them an edge, enhances their fearsome image? Nobody has explicitly suggested that the haka is the primary reason why New Zealand have won 26 of their 33 matches against England, but the suspicion hangs in the air. As the men in black embark on a ritual which their team has observed for more than a century, the England players respond with intelligent discretion, standing shoulder to shoulder along their 10-metre line and screwing their features into resolute frowns. The Twickenham crowd is less impressive: first jeering, then bellowing 'Swing Low, Sweet Chariot'. This is the default reaction of English rugby: when you are unsure of how to respond to a given situation, bellow 'Sweet Chariot' and all will be well. When the noise has subsided and the dance is done, the stadium speakers burst into 'Land Of Hope And Glory', as if to say 'There! See if we care!' Nobody knows who dreamed up that little wheeze, but the suspects include a Torquay hotelier named Fawlty.

Then it begins, a game that a proportion of the crowd can scarcely recognise. Since turning 'open' in 1995, rugby union has changed more significantly than any major sport. Its players are bigger, faster and

… when you are unsure of how to respond to a given situation, bellow 'Sweet Chariot' and all will be well

infinitely stronger. The statistics are conclusive. Toby Flood stands 6 feet 3 inches tall and weighs 14 stone 9 pounds. Twenty years ago, he might have been a candidate for England's second row. Today, he will play at no. 10. The front row comparison is still more revealing. For the 1991 World Cup final, the combined weight of the English front three – Jason Leonard, Brian Moore and Jeff Probyn – was 48 stone. Today's trio of Dan Cole, Steve Thompson and Andrew Sheridan have a combined weight of 56 stone. Their percentage of body fat is considerably less, their powers of endurance significantly greater. This is a direct consequence of professionalism, that evil which rugby union held at bay for so long. Another consequence, equally vivid, is the change in attitude about how the game should be played. Way back in the dark ages, people used to turn up to watch the ball repeatedly kicked into touch. It was a multi-purpose ploy, in that it gained yards of territory, gave the pack a welcome breather, and demonstrated that William Webb Ellis had been wasting his time when he picked up the ball and ran.

In 1963, Wales possessed a talented line-out jumper in Brian Price. They also possessed, in their captain Clive Rowlands, a scrum-half who was unashamedly pragmatic. Playing Scotland at Murrayfield, on a wet day which discouraged handling, Rowlands simply pumped the ball into touch each time he received it. As a result, there were no fewer than 111 line-outs in the course of 80 minutes, or one line-out every 43 seconds. Wales won 6–0 and the ball spent far more time in the crowd than on the pitch. They should have returned the admission fees after that travesty; instead, they changed the laws, and not a moment too soon. By contrast, the modern game is played with ball in hand. Possession is treasured, passing is sharp, athleticism is taken for granted, and adventure is considered desirable rather than reckless. It is a game which Twickenham Man scarcely recognises.

Yet some things never change, and one of these is the aura of the All Blacks. England's coach Martin Johnson has encountered New Zealand a time or ten, and he understands how that aura can affect opposition minds as well as bodies. In the last moments before his team took the field, he warned his new players not to be overwhelmed or intimidated by the men wearing the silver fern. His warning is unheeded. Although they lost to Australia just a week earlier, the All Blacks are carrying themselves with the air of men for whom defeat is not a serious option. Like Brazil at the round-ball game, they exude the assurance which derives from prodigious ability and glittering tradition. They are thrillingly aware of their pedigree. They take the right decisions at precisely the right time, and inside 23 minutes they have scored two converted tries. They are threatening to do something truly damaging. The fans seem to share the uncertainties of their team. They are

... the All Blacks are carrying themselves with the air of men for whom defeat is not a serious option

people who customarily treat the rest of the Six Nations as prospective cannon fodder, yet today they are quiet, almost meek in the face of the onslaught.

It is half-time, and England are 14 points down. Johnson has marched to the dressing room with a face like thunder. New Zealand have been given far too much respect. As a player, he had a nose for these things. He gave nobody more respect than they deserved, and usually a great deal less. As the game unfolds, he senses that the All Blacks may be flattering to deceive, that they are more vulnerable than they appear. And that England, his England, have been a sight too deferential. He has harsh things to say.

As it happens, I have some small experience of a Johnson mood. A few days before the 2003 World Cup final in Sydney, I interviewed the then England captain at his seashore hotel in Manly. We were in a relatively small room, and at 6 feet 7 inches and 18½ stone, Johnson was occupying most of it. He had spent a difficult morning when a host of small problems had presented themselves. His mood was vaguely tetchy. I was asking about his routine in those last hours before the biggest match of his life. How would he order his thoughts, what would he actually, physically do to keep from worrying and wondering? He thought for a moment.

'Well,' he said, 'I suppose I'll read for a while.'

'Yes,' I said, 'but can you read...?'

His face darkened: 'COURSE I CAN BLOODY WELL READ,' he roared. 'WHO D'YOU THINK I AM?'

Pathetically, I tried to appease him. 'I didn't mean can you read. I know you can. But at a time like that, with all that tension, all those things on your mind, so much depending on you…'

He watched me squirm, then he burst out laughing. 'Just keeping you on your toes,' he said.

At this moment, Johnson is keeping England's rugby players on their toes. I wish them well.

The corporates have shuffled off to their various suites, their Full Complimentary Bars, and the chummy wisdom of retired warriors. The un-privileged have joined the long queues for pressure-pumped lager and a Great Australian Pie. And a good many have remained in their seats, to study the programme. It is a rewarding exercise. There is a diverting Q&A with the prop, Dan Cole:

'Q: Have you ever been mistaken for anyone else?

'A: Occasionally, people get me mixed up with a Calvin Klein underwear supermodel. But what can you do?'

There is a cheery, confidence-building stat which informs us that 'New Zealand's current run of eight successes since 2003 is the best winning sequence of the series'. Above all, there is a truly telling line from John Steele, the new chief executive of the RFU. Requesting that sportsmanship be shown to the kickers of both teams, as well as to other supporters, he adds: 'We would please ask you to resist Mexican waves.' Clearly, the RFU has made an inspired choice in Mr Steele. For the Mexican wave is a vacuous pantomime for the swiftly bored and easily distracted. Those of us who have endured this slack-jawed intrusion in stadiums across the world have long awaited some expression of official disapproval, and Steele's polite request may well offer an even better solution than that which advocates a team of rooftop snipers, with authority to take out the first clown who leaps to his feet with his mouth wide open and his arms flung high.

The teams have returned, and we see that Johnson's words have been digested. England are more positive, less subservient, and the fans are falling in behind them. Chances are created, a try is scored, and although Carter is kicking goals with disconcerting ease, 'Sweet Chariot' is being sung like a hymn of hope. The gap is narrowing, and Johnson is pacing and bawling and thumping his huge fist into his enormous palm.

With 9 minutes remaining, the All Black flanker Jerome Kaino is sent to the sin-bin, and the crowd are trying to scream England home. But New Zealand fall back on their pride and their cunning. Pinned to the ropes, they roll with the punches; stealing a play here, pulling a trick there, exploiting to the full the byzantine obscurities of that offside law. They have learned how to win, and home they come by 10 points, puffing and panting and knowing, deep down, that they have ridden their luck. Naturally, they behave as if everything had proceeded precisely to plan. Their coach, Graham Henry, is shamelessly patronising. He says England were 'quite competent', that they 'played quite well in patches' and that they will 'probably get better'. It is undoubtedly calculated, yet curiously clumsy. As he speaks, he seems to be looking for an English head to pat. As well he didn't choose Martin Johnson's.

On the pitch, in front of the East Stand, they have erected a podium on which the winners will receive a trophy. Few have stayed around for the ceremony. The corporates have retreated once more to their retreats, for one last session of booze and banter, followed by the ritual exchange of business cards. The rank and file have moved on, in great numbers, to the Scrum and the Drop Kick bars for 90 minutes of karaoke. There is a queue of willing singers for a string of familiar songs: 'Sweet Caroline', 'New York, New York', 'Rocking All Over the World'. I find myself wondering if anyone will have the nerve to attempt 'My Way'. I move closer to the door: 'My friends, I'll say it clear, I'll state my case, of which I'm certain.' I needn't have wondered.

The bars serve drink for a further hour, and shortly before 7p.m., a crowd, several thousand strong, is swaying and staggering down Rugby Road, en route to the station. Some are loud, some are shrill, but so far as I can see, nobody is loutish or threatening. On Whitton Road a teenage lad – tall, beanpole slim, vaguely drunk – kicks a traffic cone across the street.

'Go and get it, son,' says a constable, emerging from the shadows.

The lad complies instantly, sheepishly. 'Sorry, officer,' he mumbles.

'S'awright, son,' says the policeman. 'Safe home, now.'

On Chudleigh Road, a fiddler sits on a stool and plays a stream of jigs and reels. He is very good, too good for a cold night on Chudleigh Road. Two middle-aged men, with drink taken, begin to dance; backs straight, arms held stiffly at the sides as they spin and jig and whoop to the lively lilt of 'The Irish Washerwoman'. They start to fade, and the fiddler subtly curtails the melody. They nod their thanks, pass over some coins and go on their way. Everyone applauds.

The match ended more than 3 hours ago, but the queue for the station is long and sluggish. People bump together, nobody complains. One man sinks into a hedge, still clutching his drink. He lets out a small sigh. 'Good night,' he mutters, and closes his eyes. His friends retrieve him, brushing the twigs from his coat, chuckling at his helplessness. Three broad-bottomed ladies in All Black scarves shuffle along with the rest. They are supping from pint mugs and smiling superior smiles. They simply reek of smugness. 'You were bloody lucky today,' says a mildly resentful red rose. 'Aren't we always?' replies one of the women, raising her mug in a mocking toast. Nobody is offended. It is the first time I have heard the game mentioned.

'You were bloody lucky today,' says a mildly resentful red rose. 'Aren't we always?' replies one of the women

We tumble down to the platform. As ever, the station staff are polite, tactful and wondrously good-humoured, treating the unsober masses like honoured guests.

'Please stand behind the yellow line,' warns a guard.

'Why?' splutters a man in his mid-twenties, prematurely bald, with the neck of a hooker and a can of beer in each hand.

'Because you might fall in front of the train,' replies the guard. 'And we don't want that, do we?'

The hooker considers the reply, nods a couple of times, then concedes: 'Yeah. All right. Fair point.'

We struggle on to the Waterloo train. There is a brief sprint for seats, then people stand up to let the women sit down. There is an overpowering smell of stale beer and worse, and all around me people are delivering befuddled monologues. One man, grey-haired and slurred of speech, racks his brain for evidence of previous sporting experience. Finally, he blurts out: 'West Ham United!' He tells a story of how, during the Seventies, his merchant bank gave him £200 to buy a pair of season tickets at Upton Park.

His face lights up: 'I used to go there every home game. With a client. Usually a Jap. And I'd sit there and shout: "Come on, West Ham United!" And I'd get him to shout as well: "West Ham United!" They're still my team. I look for their result every week. Every week.'

One of his strap-hanging neighbours, feigning interest, asks: 'How did they get on today?'

'Who?' he says.

'West Ham.'

He seems perplexed by the question. 'Don't ask me,' he says. 'I haven't got a clue.'

A quartet of New Zealanders push their way in at Richmond. They meet the three pint-drinking ladies, whom they appear to know. They speak of Auckland, and the social scene thereof. They establish mutual friends, shared contacts. Nobody shows the remotest surprise at this chance encounter, London being such a small town, and they agree to go to a party in Clapham. They all leave together at Clapham Junction, in search of an off-licence.

By now, the jam has eased. Looking along the carriage I can see a group of England fans, seven or eight strong. One of them, a small man in his mid-forties, is shouting into his phone, unaware that the rest of the train is listening. He is telling his wife what a wonderful day he's had, with wonderful friends, watching a wonderful rugby match. Yes, he has had a couple of drinks. Yes, he did promise to be home by seven, but it isn't easy to get away. He knows she will understand. He summons the dregs of his courage: 'So what I was wondering,' he says, 'I was just wondering if you could pick me up at the station, about half past nine?' There is a long pause as he listens to the response. Once or twice, he tries and fails to interrupt. Finally, he nods his head. 'I see,' he says. 'That's fine. So, er, d'you think you could give me that taxi number?' The roar of derision fairly shakes the compartment. One of his wonderful friends starts a chorus of 'Why Was He Born So Beautiful?', a hoary old song, yet strangely appropriate.

He curses. He smiles a bashful smile. The singing continues: 'He's no bloody use to anyone, he's no bloody use at all!' He throws back his shoulders in a show of defiance we know he will live to regret. 'Sod it,' he says. 'Let's go and have one in the White Hart.'

CHAPTER 9
A NIGHT AT CRAYFORD DOGS

The evening rain is bouncing off the tarmac, drenching the lads in their hooded tops as they sprint across the car park. Shall I follow their dash, or sit in the warm car, listening to a particularly compelling episode of *The Archers*? 'Dum, dee, dum, dee, dum, dee, dum. Dum, dee, dum, dee, dah, dah!'

Fifteen minutes later, Ambridge is mourning the tragic death of Nigel Pargetter, the laird of Lower Loxley, who has plunged from the roof of his ancestral home. On the brighter side, the rain has eased sufficiently to allow me a comfortable stroll to Crayford dog track.

There is a faint din of distant barking, a trundle of laden cars from the adjoining Sainsbury's superstore and, inside the greyhound stadium, the low buzz of anxious conversation. For a fanciful moment, I suspect they have been told of poor Nigel's demise. But no, up there in the Heathview Restaurant they are staring hopefully at their racecards, searching for the winner of the 7.30. The women are smart, the men casual, and all wear an air of frowning indecision. The public address system pipes up at intervals: '5 minutes 'betting time … 2 minutes' betting time,' it is the kind of voice which clears theatre bars. At the bottom of the card there is a form guide; this one is 'a slow starter', that one has 'a tendency to finish second', this has 'yet to trouble the judge', that is damned as 'not a threat lately'. Knowing less about the sport than anyone in the restaurant, and possibly less than anyone in the entire stadium, I conclude from the pessimistic tone that none of the six animals is in with a chance.

But bets are laid, fingers are crossed and, as one, the entire assembly turns away from the panoramic window above the track and seeks out the relatively small screen at the rear. There is a flurry of action, a surge of pace, a few stifled roars of encouragement. Then, 25.01 seconds and 380 metres later, it is done. A dead heat between the bitch who was damned as 'a slow starter' and the hitherto habitual runner-up. Third is the lady who never bothers the judge. I check the programme's form selection. It has chosen the first three. For those who have paid £1.50 for the programme, it seems a remarkable bargain. As the field crosses the finishing line, a woman diner claps her hands, just once. It is not the despairing gesture of the inveterate gambler, more the mild frustration of somebody who has just come close to winning an office raffle. Her husband pats her back and pours her a consoling glass of rosé. She starts a conversation with her friend across the table, the race already a fading memory. The evening has far to go.

The greyhound racing industry is aware of its rackety reputation. 'Going to the dogs' remains a pejorative phrase, while for many the sport still evokes Arthur Daley, fat cigars, loud suits, betting coups and animals stuffed with more illegal substances than a Seventies rocker. The image is vigorously resented. As one industry figure privately remarks: 'Given what we now know, greyhound racing might well be a lot straighter than Test cricket. But the perception is different, so we have to try hard.' At Crayford, where south-east London nudges into north-west Kent, they could scarcely try harder.

The greyhound racing industry is aware of its rackety reputation

On this wet and windswept Friday evening, the restaurant trade is pleasingly brisk. The Heathview accommodates 250, but tonight they are seating around 160, with waitresses attending and people placing bets on hand-held terminals. The usual price for a three-course meal is £27.50, but they have endless promotions at Crayford, and throughout January they are offering a 'Winter Warmer' for £19.95. Since this includes the £6 admission fee, the patrons are effectively getting a choice of five starters, six main courses and dessert for £13.95. Clearly, the meals are heavily subsidised by gambling revenues, but no matter; there are racecourses in Britain where £13.95 would scarcely cover the cost of a sandwich.

People come to the restaurant for special occasions. At one end, a shimmering column of blue balloons hovers above a 25th birthday party. At the other, five tables of laughing, chattering young people mark the 18th birthday of Kellie Carroll. Above them all, at a bar table close by the Tote window, the track's most faithful fans stare down incuriously at the scene. Crayford is open for 'matinee races' on Tuesday, Thursday and Saturday afternoons, when entry is free, as well as on Friday and Saturday evenings. Jean and Alan attend almost every session: 'Although sometimes we give it a miss on Saturday nights,' says Jean, with a hint of apology. They have been married for 60 years, and a few months earlier they celebrated their diamond anniversary with a party at the track. 'We took three tables,' says Jean. 'Lovely night, it was. And we had a nice card from the Queen. "Elizabeth R", she signed herself. Nice. We've already booked for our 65th. Another three tables. They treat us lovely here. Where else would we go?'

The various tables are studying form for the second race. If anything, it is less promising than the first. 'Engine tending to misfire early ... Last victory was facile, but so long ago ... Could gain advantage, can he keep it? ... Three wooden spoons, form as poor as rivals.' The tone is curtly dismissive. If dogs could sue, then writs would be flying. It is explained to me that this is graded racing, with races ranked from one to eight. The prospects are assessed by the track's racing manager, who works from the form book with the aim of producing a level playing field. Thus, the outstanding dogs are rated at one, the ones who are 'not quite so good', are rated eight. The second race is for the grade eighters, greyhound racing's equivalent of cricketing tailenders. The restaurant follows the same routine: bets are placed, hands are waved, muffled cheers are uttered, condolences are exchanged and drink is poured. It is won, with remarkable ease, by the dog who not only gained the advantage, but held it. Second is the misfiring engine. The form guide selects not only the first, but also the runner-up. Such service to punters is way beyond the call of duty.

A thought strikes me: nobody, but nobody, seems remotely interested in the actual race, other than its implications for future contests. People are concerned about the result and its financial consequences, but they appear to regard these beasts as little more than bouncing balls in a roulette wheel: a quick spin, a few brief moments of indecision, and a sudden finality. Not so much a spectacle, simply a vehicle for deciding a wager. Virtually every other sport sets some store by its aesthetic appeal. Horse racing revels in the beauty and movement of its contestants, and endows the horses with all manner of noble qualities. From the little I have seen tonight, greyhound racing views them merely as a means to a lucrative end.

I move downstairs, past the posters of speeding dogs carrying the caption 'We can't keep our traps shut', past the security men, affably anticipating another peaceful evening. Then outside, through the small, damp section of smokers, all addicted and some vaguely resentful of the temporary exile which their addiction imposes. To a long-reformed smoker such resentment feels irrational, yet strangely spirited. I remember meeting one cantankerous ancient outside a pub in Dublin. It was a winter evening, brutally cold with sleet in the wind. He was coughing his way through a packet of Marlboro Lights and complaining bitterly about the injustice of his exclusion. The night air, he protested, was terribly bad for his chest.

Crayford's sandy track is heavy and cloying. Ideally, I am informed, it should have the texture of a tide-washed beach, but the rain has done its worst and the surface is discouraging. The third race is run over hurdles. It is a discipline that attracts some of the finest human athletes. In all of sport, few things are more graceful than the sight of the great high hurdlers – a 'Skeets' Nehemiah, a Colin Jackson – flowing across the barriers at a sprinter's speed. But at least they acknowledged the existence of those barriers. The dogs make no such concession, clearing them in full stride and finishing in a time only fractionally slower than a comparable flat race. Viewed from the trackside, it offers a fleeting excitement. These are undeniably handsome animals, tall and slender, with deep chests, arched necks, small ears and darkly expressive eyes. The fastest dogs in the world, their acceleration generates speeds of around 40mph, the 60-lb bodies brushing and bumping as they fight for ground at the corners. Yet it lasts for just that handful of seconds, and when it is done everyone moves on. There is a 12-race programme to be completed, and the next race is 16 minutes away, with a lot of betting to be crammed into the interval. There is no time, nor any apparent desire, for reflection. And that is a pity, since any sporting event ought to leave us with memories more durable than a blurred photo-finish or a torn Tote ticket.

The fastest dogs in the world, their acceleration generates speeds of around 40mph

I try this thesis on one of the smokers. He is not impressed. After some thought, he mentions sprinting, and that Jamaican fellow everyone makes such a fuss about. That's all over before you can look up, but nobody worries about that, do they? Why pick on the poor old dogs? It is a reasonable argument, but it ignores the human element. When Usain Bolt walks to his blocks in an Olympic 100 metres final, he is grappling with all manner of emotions: fear, trepidation, hope, pride, all competing for the upper hand. We understand this because we know something of his personality. Over a period of years, he has articulated his ambitions and discussed his anxieties. The fact that his race will last for just a blink longer than 9½ seconds is irrelevant, because we know precisely what is at stake for him, as an athlete and as a man. Animals are different. They are motivated not by dreams of glory but by the prospect of their next meal. Not one of the dogs or bitches here tonight will go home, push aside that meal and reproach itself for a sluggish start, an ill-timed finish, a general failure to try that bit harder. And even if they did feel that way, they couldn't let us know.

This is not the kind of argument that Ian Bland appreciates. When it comes to greyhound racing, Ian is something of a zealot. He loves it, he lives for it, and he has felt that way almost forever. 'I was on holiday in Broadstairs with my parents, and I went walkabout,' he says. 'I was gone for ages. They sent for the police. And they found me in a bookmaker's shop. There I was, 9 years old, on my own, listening to the dogs.' When he was 11, he came to the old Crayford Stadium, the one they knocked down to build the superstore. After that, he was smitten. 'I'm a Crayford man through and through,' he says. 'Always will be.'

That is the kind of enthusiasm more often encountered at Anfield or Villa Park, but he makes no apology. He spent most of his working life in banking, yet you sense he was only marking time before destiny called and Crayford played its hand. First he became marketing officer, then they added the job of restaurant manager 'for my sins'. He loves the punters, relishes the atmosphere, and adores the dogs. Several years ago, he and his wife approached a leading trainer and offered to work with his dogs. 'We didn't want payment, we just wanted to understand how the sport functions,' he says. 'Fantastic experience.'

Everybody seems to know him. They pass his table and call him by his first name. Some compliment him on the food, and his face lights up. There are 28 registered tracks in Great Britain, and a year earlier, Crayford was the top track in the country for growth, in terms of both attendance and turnover. 'We pamper customers, you see,' says Ian. 'Drinks, meals, bets. This is part of the leisure industry, isn't it? We're all competing for what they call "the leisure pound". The days of the cloth caps are long gone. We try and cater for everybody. All sorts, all ages. D'you know, in this restaurant, we've got three high chairs for young babies. Everyone's welcome. People just want a good night out. That's not a bad thing, is it?'

Consciously or otherwise, he tends to underplay the contribution of gambling, which lies at the heart of the whole event. After all, the course is owned by Ladbrokes, and greyhound racing accounts for a significant proportion of the company's profits. It is surely important to keep the punters punting? Ian gives a little shrug. 'People here are not what I call gamblers,' he says. 'Serious gamblers tend to do their business at home, online. The vast majority of betting's done online these days. We mostly get people who do it for a bit of interest. Some of them are students of form, but not a lot. Some like the name of a dog. Some back the number, and stick to it religiously. Others just look out of the window and pick what they fancy. The form book's irrelevant to them.' As a man who knows his way around the form book, he shudders at the heresy.

In fairness, there is little obvious evidence of huge bets being struck. At the evening meetings, stakes tend to be £1, with forecasts and trios in 50p units. In the afternoon, when admission is free and pensioners are the principal punters and races are staged for the benefit of betting shops, the betting may be done in 10p units. Untutored in these matters, I query the figure. It is correct; a 10p bet on a 3–1 winner would win 40p, including the return of the stake. There is something innocently endearing in that statistic; 10p for a piece of harmless diversion, 10p to take part.

And yet the perils are there and they are recognised on the opening page of the racecard, which features a prominent advertisement for the gambling charity GamCare. It offers help with problem gambling and carries these warnings: 'Placing a bet is buying fun, not investing money/ Spending outside your means can create problems for yourselves and others/Only play with money you can afford to lose/Set limits on how much you will spend, and keep to those limits.' Solid stuff, every word. But whether it has more effect than 'Smoking kills' is open to question.

The races flash past in 25-second bursts. Downstairs, in the fast-food snack bar, the customers are more inclined to shout home their investments. Again, they look away from the windows, as if they too distrust the evidence of their eyes. Instead, they turn to the screens, growling at first, then roaring louder still and louder in a great climactic bellow until the favoured animal crosses the line. They then return abruptly to their meal: sausage and chips and perhaps a lager at £3.50 a pint. The children, of whom there are many, tend to ignore the entire proceedings, preferring to swill cola, crunch crisps and work the controls of electronic games.

The bookmakers are out there ... awaiting customers ... Lonely creatures, you could almost feel sorry for them

Outside, the rain is easing, but the wind is blustering. The bookmakers are out there, at the end of the stand, shivering beneath umbrellas. Their pitches are lit by thin bulbs, and they are awaiting customers (minimum stake £5). Lonely creatures, you could almost feel sorry for them.

In the Heathview Bar, the screens are beaming birthday congratulations to Kellie Carroll: 'Love from all your family'. They have sponsored a race in her honour, and she will preside over the presentation. Ian Bland is mustering his forces. A party of three lads and three girls watch the Kellie Carroll 18th Birthday Stakes from the restaurant. 'Hare's on the move!' chirps the commentator, the traps spring open, and a jet-black bitch called Ardera Saphira comes swishing through the drizzle to defeat the field. The 5–2 co-favourite, she was the selection of the racecard's form guide, and she repaid that confidence. The greyhounds are going through their brief, ritual scuffle over the imitation hare. It is an implausible contraption, worked by an unseen hand high in the eaves of the grandstand; a hand entrusted with one of the more unlikely tasks in the world of sport.

The dog paraders, the spear-carriers of the meeting, emerge from the darkness of the infield to attach leads to their charges. Straight-backed and solicitous, they march them away. Meanwhile, the presentation party descends to the lower level, walking past the fast-food counter, past the bar where the drinkers have gathered in numbers, and out into the night, led by the pretty, dark-haired teenager who is celebrating her coming of age. I fall in line at the rear of the ranks.

'Did you back the winner?' I ask one lad.

'No chance,' he says.

'Did the birthday girl?' I inquire.

He shakes his head.

'Did anyone?' I persist. 'Not that I've heard,' he grins, totally unconcerned. People step back as we reach the door. 'They're the sponsors,' comes a whisper. I notice that Ian has something over his arm, a piece of red velvet with gold braid hanging from the seams. A jacket for a dog.

Bare boards form a gangplank over the sodden track and on to the infield. We squelch across the muddy sand. At either end of the presentation platform stand silver greyhound statues, indolently sprawled. And in the centre, on a raised green dais, still panting from her efforts in covering 540 metres in 34.66 seconds, is Ardera Saphira. She is wearing a red velvet jacket, with a message running along the length of her body in gold capitals: 'HAPPY BIRTHDAY FROM LADBROKES'. Kellie and friends gather round. Ian fishes in his pocket and pulls out a camera. 'Move closer everyone! Closer! Ready?' There is a click. 'That'll do nicely,' he chuckles.

The party moves back inside and Ian watches them leave. 'Nice crowd,' he says. 'But then, most of them are. We're very lucky here.

We get a lot of stag and hen parties, but there's never any trouble. Just high spirits.' A chance memory makes him smile. 'There was one girl, a good while ago. She turned up for her hen night dressed in whoopee cushions. Can you believe that? Not a small girl, either. Anyway when she got out there in the middle, all her friends sort of jumped on her. And as each one landed, the cushions made "that" noise. You know what I mean? Well, I had my work cut out trying to get them all off and away. There was another race coming up. Difficult night, that was. But, as I say, most of them aren't a bit of trouble.'

By now, the memories are flowing. 'We're very big on birthdays at Crayford,' he says. 'The oldest was a gentleman of 103. We made a great fuss of him. Then there was Reg. He came here for his 102nd birthday. A hundred and two. Dear old Reg.' A small shake of the head. 'He went home and died next morning. Very sad. And just recently, we've had a big run of 80-year-olds holding birthday parties.' And you just know that he treated every one of them with the care and attention he lavished on young Kellie's clan.

He is searching his pocket for another jacket. 'We try to do them for all occasions … "Happy Birthday" of course. Or, when we're holding a race for a deceased patron, "In Loving Memory". Quite often, they've asked for their ashes to be scattered on the track. Not a problem. Or there's "Congratulations", "Happy Retirement", we try to cover all angles.' He finds what he is looking for, a piece of green velvet with that familiar gold braid. It is inscribed: 'Congratulations on 100 races', and it will be awarded to In Rainbows, a bitch running in the next race, who has competed in more than a century of races at Crayford. 'We award around 50 a year, a jacket and a glass trophy,' he says. 'The owners treasure them. They say they'd rather have that than the prize money.'

The owners play an important role in greyhound racing. They take an almost defensive pride in their pastime; the syndicate that owns one of the runners in the third race this evening is brilliantly entitled Only Fools Have Horses. Their investments are not huge, but they play their part in keeping the sport going, and they do so for minimal reward. The total prize money for tonight's 12 races is £3,185. The largest winning prize is £148. It repays an interest, but it is scarcely a path to instant wealth. Yet while they accept that the sport is not especially lucrative, they want to be sure that it is straight. The issue of drugs looms large, indeed, tonight's racecard touches on the perils of prohibited substances. A dog has been positively tested for the steroid Laurabolin, and one of the Crayford trainers has appeared before a disciplinary committee. The track has ten contracted trainers who provide the dogs. It is a considerable operation, since there are between 650 and 700 dogs on the racing strength at any one time. The committee heard that a previous owner of the greyhound had accepted responsibility for administering the drug in Ireland, it was also told of the trainer's previous good record. But it cautioned her and imposed a £250 fine, since it was 'mindful of the need to impose a sanction that acted as a deterrent'. Such vigilance may appear high-minded, but it is also heavy with self-interest. If there is even the sniff of suspicion that dogs may be nobbled, then the gamblers will grow wary and the Kellies of this world will take their birthday celebrations somewhere else.

Crayford's general manager, a former City figure named Barry Stanton, allows me a short tour of the kennels where, for obvious reasons, security is at its strongest. The place is throbbing with soul music. I assume this is for the delight of the handlers. Not so. 'It dampens down the noise of the hare going round outside,' says Mr Stanton. 'They go mad when they hear the hare. They're trained to react to the sound. The music calms them.' Again, I am struck by the sleekness of the creatures, their streamlined bodies bred for speed. Everything about them is known. There are tattoos inside the ears, blood and urine samples are taken, there is a microchip in the neck, which is checked against a computer screen before entering the arena, and they are carefully weighed before racing. There is a narrow band to indicate the optimum weight. If they weigh too much, they may have been over-eating; too little and they may be sick. This means, according to Mr Stanton, that 'ringers' – dogs competing under false identities – are things of the past. In a small room at the rear of the kennels, a young vet sits in a small room, watching the races on a closed-circuit screen. She counts them all out, and she counts them all back. The meeting could not take place in her absence.

The racing life of the greyhound is short, from 15 months to around five years. At one stage, large numbers were routinely put down at the end of their usefulness. The numbers destroyed are still sufficiently large to concern animal welfare organisations, but today there are various charities and 'adoption groups', along with the tracks themselves, making efforts to find them homes as domestic pets in the five years or so which remain to them.

We walk back to the grandstand, Barry Stanton assessing the numbers. 'We've got around six or seven hundred in the place tonight; tomorrow we'll have more than a thousand. Saturdays, we always do. We're so close to London, they have so many options, and these are tough economic times. So we're doing pretty well. The restaurant apart, they spend around £6–£7 per head at the bar and £1 at the snack bar. At the Tote, they spend around £30 per head. We take 26 per cent of that. The whole spend is around £40 per head. If they don't enjoy the experience, they won't come back.' He pauses, then dangles the hook to catch the gambler: 'And of course, they could go home with more money than they came with. That's a selling point, isn't it?'

As he says, competition is fierce. Greyhound racing has been functioning in Britain for more than 80 years, and in the immediate post-war years it shared in the dramatic expansion of all sports. In 1946, it attracted an extraordinary 34 million spectators to its tracks, only marginally behind the numbers who watched the matches of the old Football League.

But the numbers of tracks dwindled down the years, as stadium owners became increasingly aware of the value of their inner-city sites. Venerable punters can recite the names like a litany: New Cross, whose infield Millwall footballers once used as a training ground; Harringay, which accommodated crowds of 50,000 in its heyday; Catford, regarded by the cognoscenti as the most atmospheric venue of all; Walthamstow, the 'Stow', where Winston Churchill addressed 20,000 people in 1945, just two days before the nation rejected him at the polls.

Attendances have shrunk to around ten per cent of the mid-Forties figure; yet it remains one of the leading spectator sports in the land. And people have their unswerving loyalties and firm habits. The tracks closest to Crayford are at Sittingbourne, Wimbledon and Romford (which in 1937 conducted a short-lived experiment with cheetah racing. It drew a large crowd, but was ultimately abandoned when the beasts revealed no great appetite for competition). But these are not regarded as rivals, since Sittingbourne is Kentish, Wimbledon is an eternity of suburbs away, while Romford is in Essex, and a visit would involve crossing the Thames. You may as well ask punters to cross the Danube.

Attendances have shrunk ... yet it remains one of the leading spectator sports in the land

But Crayford works hard to retain that loyalty. With 260 meetings a year, it is the busiest track in the kingdom. Up in the restaurant, they are pushing aside the debris of the chicken casserole, belly of pork and cod Florentine, and racecards are being fiercely studied, as if concentration alone might tease out the next winner. Over by the window, a small drama is being played out. A husband is making earnest attempts to engage his wife in conversation, while she ostentatiously ignores his efforts. Time and again he tries and is rebuffed, while the rest of the table feign ignorance of the stand-off. By contrast, Kellie's crowd are in the best of spirits, without a whoopee cushion in sight.

Ian Bland surveys his kingdom. 'All well, I think,' he says, with some satisfaction. 'You know, we have all sorts of dos up here. We do functions for solicitors, banks, Masonic lodges, rotary clubs, PTAs. You name them. They book a party for a night out, and they expect to enjoy themselves. A very diverse bunch of customers. The Mayor of Bexley's coming next month. Big charity do. Be a very good night, that.' But not as good as Boxing Day, apparently, when the stadium sells out its capacity of 1,200 customers, and they start queuing outside the front entrance at 9.a.m. 'Twelve months to go, and we've already sold out the restaurant for next Boxing Day's brunch,' reports Ian, boasting slightly. 'And we're now accepting bookings for 2012. What d'you think of that?' I am impressed by the amount of forward planning that goes into a Crayford Christmas.

'Hare's on the move!' the commentator barks out his catchphrase once more, and the audience turns once more to the television. Ian looks down on the brightly lit track, as the dogs streak along the straight, past the advertisement for Dartford FC 'Support your local club', past the hoarding for Holsten Lager, past the board for Clarks

Farm Greyhound Rescue. I mention my visit to the kennels and my surprise at learning that the music was aimed at the dogs. He gives me the indulgent laugh that experts reserve for the woefully uninformed. 'Very funny creatures, greyhounds,' he says. 'I've got one at home. Bought it for the wife from this track. They're very lazy, you know. Very gentle, good with people, but lazy. All my one does is eat and sleep. Seriously. I'm hard pushed to get her to go for a walk. Even when they're in training, they conserve their energy. But when they finish racing, they just lie on the couch. That's my one; she's a couch potato. Anyway, I sometimes watch the dogs on television when I'm at home. And she watches too. Just opens one eye, not that interested, even when the hare gets going. But recently, I put on a DVD of a race at Crayford. Didn't give it a thought. So the camera takes in the track, the hare starts running and … whooosh! She's off that couch like a bullet, screaming across the room. I could hear the clunk as her nose hit the glass of our telly. And there she stayed, pressing her nose flat against the screen. It was the sound of the Crayford hare, you see. She's been well trained.'

He smiles at his tale, but again you catch a whiff of his genuine respect for sporting animals. You find it to an equal degree in horse racing, but there at least the credit is shared with the jockey. Bland argues that greyhound racing is, in a sense, more pure because of what he calls 'the minimum level of human involvement'. He shows me an article he once wrote for a racing magazine. It is a thoughtful piece, in which he says: 'It is, I fear, a regrettable fact that any sport in which humans take part will also incorporate human traits, some of which are not entirely desirable. Let's just call it human nature. None of that here though, just six dogs doing their best to catch that orange bag that they think is a hare. I never implied that they were as intelligent as humans, just that they may be more sincere in their reasons for wanting to win.'

A man in his early twenties walks away from the Tote window, counting a small wad of banknotes. Ian nods at him. As an employee of Ladbrokes, he is not allowed to bet. Indeed, he is not even allowed into a Ladbrokes betting shop. But he is allowed to tip dogs, and he writes a tipping column in the *Kent Messenger* under the nom de plume 'The Informer'. He tipped a 6–1 winner in last week's column. 'My Christmas present to the readers,' he called it.

They are preparing for the 12th and final race. The paraders escort the dogs along the darkened path, up and down, then back to the traps. 'Five minutes' betting time … two minutes' betting time…' Every ritual is observed. Up go the trap lids, two frantic circuits, and a dog named Inishowen Bill scampers in at 5–1. The racecard had said that he was 'finding the grade tough'. Not that tough, apparently. Ian blesses the scene with a beam. 'A good night,' he declares. 'Everyone seemed to enjoy themselves. I'll go home and relax. Nice cup of tea and some paracetamol.' He may love his job, but he is not immune from its stresses.

Around the restaurant tables, they are pouring the last of the wine, draining the dregs of the lager. Nobody is remotely the worse for drink. Downstairs in the snack bar, two families – mothers, fathers, aunts, uncles, aunts, six or eight children – are having their picture taken. The photographer is taking an age to set it up: 'Everyone smile. Come on, smile! Can't see you at the back! You've stopped smiling.' As the camera flashes, I notice the small boy in the middle of the front row; the one with eyes tightly closed, and tongue stuck out in derision.

A bookie hurries past, collar turned against the returning rain, anxious to be home. Outside, above the back straight, a train slides slowly past on what we knew as the Dartford Loop Line. Raindrops are bouncing off its roof. A security man holds open the front door, bidding us all a courteous good night, trusting we'll soon be back.

The dark car park is almost empty, save for a few late night superstore shoppers. As I walk to the car, I see the lads in the hooded tops across the way, laughing, jostling, sharing a carton of chips. Ambridge may be mourning the loss of Nigel Pargetter but, all things considered, Crayford seems to be holding up pretty well.

'Aw look, mate, this isn't for me'

CHAPTER 10
THE ADELAIDE TEST MATCH

The whiff of breakfast bacon comes wafting from the hotels on North Terrace and mingles with the scent of sun cream from the crowds gathering on King William Road.

The start of play is still 2 hours away, so I take the beautiful route, slipping down through the side streets to the green banks of the Torrens River, where fountains play and floppy-hatted children feed the pelicans and black swans. The heat is rising, and the spires of St Peter's Cathedral are etched darkly against a sky of blinding blue. Crossing the bridge, I meet an Australian journalist, and we stroll through the parkland to the gates of the most beguiling Test ground on earth. 'What a wonderful town this is,' I say. He seems surprised. 'A lot of Poms like Adelaide,' he says. 'Buggered if I know why.'

Australians treat Adelaide as if it were the school swot, the one who for whom sport and laughter run a distant second to an early night with a good book. 'Sniffy' is the word my colleague favours. When we reach the members' entrance on this, the first morning of the second Ashes Test match, a young man wearing a blue, long-sleeved vest, is being chastised by a steward: 'I'm gonna let this go, just for today,' says the official. 'But if you even think about wearing a shirt without a collar tomorrow, don't get out of bed. All right?' The young man nods, but my friend shrugs. 'See what I mean?' he says. But I recall the pavilion dress code at Lord's: 'Ties and tailored coats and acceptable trousers with appropriate shoes.' Turn up in a long-sleeved vest in St John's Wood, and they'd place you under house arrest. No, Adelaide isn't sniffy.

'A lot of Poms like Adelaide,' he says. 'Buggered if I know why'

Yet it is stunning, an authentic cricket ground which has yet to be reduced to the status of a stadium. With its Edwardian scoreboard, its crowded, grassy hill and its elegant, idiosyncratic stands, it is an arena in which great deeds are done. Four years earlier, England had declared on 551 for six in their first innings (S.K. Warne 53-9-167-1). In their second innings, hopelessly mesmerised, they managed 129 all out (S.K. Warne 32-12-49-4), and Australia won by six wickets. Six Englishmen, including the top five batsmen, remain from that team, yet this time they are vibrantly confident. The first Test in Brisbane has been drawn, but England compiled a monumental 517 for one in their second innings to secure an important edge. This match threatens to be the one that shapes the series. There is the prospect of genuine drama, some of which will reverberate around the members' lawn.

The South Australia Cricket Association has around 20,000 members, each of whom was held on a waiting list for up to five years before paying an entrance fee of A$299 (£203). The new Western Stand, however, built at a cost of some £80 million, has seats for only 14,000 of these members. A large number of the excluded are therefore left to their own devices on the lawn behind the stand, following the match on large screens and enjoying the refreshments provided. Not that they mind. They seem a relatively decorous bunch as they sip morning coffee, acknowledge old friends and watch their children imitate the gods: a Ponting here, a McGrath there and, over by the wall, a tubby lad who does a passable Warne. It is good to see the children allowed space to play. The Harris Garden, behind the Lord's pavilion, is somewhat less spacious, and certainly less indulgent towards youth.

Dotted among the crowd are men whose faces do not fit snugly into a city, even a city as green as Adelaide. Big men, with skin leathered by the sun, they have come from the sheep and cattle country of the north to visit the 'social Test'. Their various stations are vast, far beyond my comprehension. The largest mentioned is a cattle station, Anna Creek, which apparently occupies some 6 million acres. I ask the conventional British question: 'Would that, by any chance, be bigger than Wales?' My informant, seeking a European dimension, replies: 'Bigger'n Belgium.' Then, with more confidence: 'Bigger'n Israel.' The size of Israel being a matter of some dispute, I change the subject. But these are people whose workplaces are so immense that a light aircraft and several landing strips are required to administer them. And here are gathered those farmers and drovers, perched on dining chairs on the western lawn of the Adelaide Oval, toying with coffee cups and awaiting the start of a cricket match.

It is an eventful opening. Having chosen to bat, Australia lose Simon Katich, run out without facing, off the fourth delivery of the first over. The captain, Ricky Ponting, is held at slip next ball with his team on nought for two. Michael Clarke departs in Anderson's next over to leave Australia three wickets down with only two runs on that Edwardian scoreboard. It is their worst start to a Test innings in 60 years, and on the lawn they are already seeking stronger sustenance.

Inside the Oval, the screens are full of ecstatic Englishmen, capering across the hill. It is a temptation the lazy director never resists: at the fall of an Australian wicket, cut to the Barmy Army. And they answer the cliché in kind, cheering and chanting, pointing and posing, gleefully waving at their own images. 'Look at us, look at us!' they seem to be saying. 'Are we wacky, or what?' Whenever I watch them in full cry, I recall David Brent's dance in *The Office*; gauche, artless, cringingly unaware of his own absurdity. In fairness, this trip is costing them dearly, since the Australian dollar has been on a steroid diet. At the time of the last Ashes series in 2006–07, £500 would have bought around A$1,250. It now buys around A$750. This means that a pint of beer costs the equivalent of about £5, it also means that the number of English fans able to make the trip has shrunk to around half of the 37,000 who travelled last time. Most of them have paid about £3,500 to attend the Brisbane and Adelaide Tests, which sum does not include the extraordinarily high cost of eating and drinking. So the Barmies do not take kindly to gratuitous abuse from those who are being paid to be here. But we shan't let that stop us.

Of all the fans whose doings are detailed in these pages, I find the Barmy Army the most difficult to love or understand. It is partly the choreographed nature of their celebrations; the songs led by the tedious trumpeter and that loon of a Jimmy Saville lookalike, or the sad little dances directed by three or four appointed leaders, who stand with their backs to the cricket and conduct operations. They have travelled 10,000 miles in order to ignore the Test match. It is partly the songs themselves; the po-faced 'Jerusalem', the lumpenly pathetic 'God Save YOUR Gracious Queen', or the tritely offensive eruptions, three or four times daily, of 'You All Live In A Convict Colony'; always followed by a spontaneous chuckle, as if they had just fired off a Wildean shaft.

Of all the fans whose doings are detailed in these pages, I find the Barmy Army the most difficult to love or understand

Wade through their website and you will discover that they actually possess a set of rules, a Boy Scout's charter which includes: 'Have Fun – good, clean and entertaining fun … Show Respect – for all players, officials, fans and grounds' rules and regulations … Give Consideration – to people's views, beliefs and cultures.' Now consider some of their songs:

> *Ponting is the captain*
> *Of the Aussie cricket team*
> *But once the match is over*
> *He is a gay drag queen…*

> *Ponting's special friend*
> *Is a man called Glenn McGrath*
> *You'll see them holding hands*
> *At the Sydney Mardi Gras.*

And if that suggests that Cole Porter lived in vain, then try:

> *Here we come, walkin' down your beach,*
> *Get admiring looks from*
> *All the sheilas we meet.*

Hey, hey we're the Barmies,
And people say we're vulgar and loud.
But we're too busy singing
To put anybody down.

You're just trying to be nasty,
We've come to watch our team play.
You're bad losers and convicts,
And you've got nothing to say.

Who churns out this formless doggerel? Who knows? I see a lonely man, possibly with acne issues, who spends too much time with his computer, typing earnestly beneath a sign which reads: 'You don't have to be mad to work here, but it helps.' Then I look across at the Hill, and I see him a hundred times over.

And yet, they take themselves seriously. They have convinced themselves that they are appreciated by England's cricketers and secretly envied by the Australian public: 'Get admiring looks from all the sheilas we meet.' During the Brisbane Test, members of the media received the following email: 'Barmy Army members will be available for lunch and post-play discussion/interviews throughout the final day at the Gabba. Available will be Paul Burnham, founder of the Barmy Army and Bill the Trumpet, plus selected Barmy Army members. Please find us during lunch and after play at The Chalk Bar, Stanley Street, Woolloongabba.' Their artless self-promotion is pompous beyond parody, yet it illustrates my principal objection: these people are here to be seen. Their presence has little to do with support for a team and everything to do with being noticed, behaving with such buffoonery that the television cameras cannot ignore them, and then waving at themselves.

The Australians retaliated in 1997 with the Fanatics, a faintly self-conscious attempt to replicate the Barmies. To their credit, their heart isn't really in it. Occasionally they surprise themselves with a daring jape, as in the Ashes series of 2009 when they set off a fire drill at the Leeds hotel where the England team was staying, forcing the players to stand on the pavement while the building was searched. Their leader, one Warren Livingston, said: 'At first I thought we're just doing our bit for Australia. But I can't condone this sort of thing.' True, they still go through the motions with their rhetoric: 'Summer in Australia is all about going to the beach, holidays and best of all: a cold beer at the cricket with your mates. Every four years we enjoy one of those special summers when the soap dodgers return down under for the Ashes.' But they don't mean it, for they are insufficiently crass. 'We are hoping like-minded Aussies will be interested in providing some vocal and colourful support for the Baggy Green,' they bluster. A good effort, but it won't do. It simply lacks that essential, barmy edge of puerile offensiveness.

In fact, most Australians are keeping a low profile after the calamities of the first three overs. Mike Hussey and Shane Watson are carrying the team prudently through to lunch, and this modest advance is marked by a degree of discomfort out there on the lawn, where they have yet to come to terms with the notion that England may just have cobbled together a cricket team capable of humiliating Australia's finest. After England's 'whitewash' tour of 2006–07, I recall listening to this magnanimous appraisal by one of the countless former Australian Test cricketers who now pursue media careers: 'To be perfectly honest, I thought we were a bit flattered by five-nothing,' he said. 'I thought 4–1 would have been about right.' This was the way of things, the natural order, through the Nineties and deep into the new decade under captains like Mark Taylor, Steve Waugh and Ponting. And yet this morning, in Adelaide, there are indications that the plates are shifting, and the times are a-changing.

In truth, this fin-de-siècle feeling has yet to penetrate the tone and content of the messages that are broadcast at each break at the Oval's captive audience. Every boundary is greeted by the award of one of Shane Warne's favourite chicken burgers on the large screens. Every outstanding shot is immortalised by a two-burger award. The burgers have been in short supply this morning. Some ads are heavy with unintentional irony. In Brisbane, a stern warning was emblazoned across the front of a stand: 'Don't be a galah. Set a limit and stick to it. Gamble responsibly.' The next advertisement but one was for Betfair. When a record is broken or a notable statistic established in this series, the screens record the moment as 'a Johnny Walker Milestone'. This also doubles as a public service message: 'People are reminded that anyone caught throwing items in this venue will be evicted. Remember, if you throw, you go.'

But weirdest of all is the nudge-nudge, 'Carry On' tone of much of the advertising. One little saga features a handsome handyman sealing cracks in a wall with professional expertise. Repeatedly, he is interrupted by the lady of the house offering tea, cakes and winsome smiles. After the latest interruption, he turns to the camera and asks, rhetorically: 'Would you leave me alone in the house with your wife?' Then follows the punchline, designed to sell the brand of sealer: 'Do it yerself – before someone does it for you.' Yet even this seems almost sophisticated when set alongside the advertisement that opens with Australia's vice-captain Michael Clarke walking into a dressing room and starting to unstrap his pads while the voiceover gibbers: 'Karen from Canberra told us: "I just love Michael Clarke. Could you get him to show me his dongle, please?"' There is a theatrical intake of breath: 'Karen, steady yourself!' Clarke pulls his 'Oooh, missus!' face, then he delves into his pocket and produces – a piece of plastic. 'Mag-nificent!' drools the voiceover. 'Get your limited edition Clarkey USB modem and three-gig starter credit for A$49.' Do they really know their audience? I hope not.

As it happens, the various toe-curling sales pitches are bypassing large numbers of that audience. The corporate troughers have set to work promptly, and there is a drone of pleasantries and a tinkle of cutlery from the Gil Langley Dining Room in the Bradman Stand, where A$550 per head has purchased lunch, 'a premium selection of wine, beer and soft drinks', an MC, a guest speaker, air conditioning and, intriguingly, 'one match-day programme per two guests'.

Out on the lawn, where the fare is less formal, the commercial messages are floating past unheeded on the warm summer air. Unlike the English bowlers, the out-of-towners have been slow to find their line and length, but now they are off and running to the attractions of the giant marquee. Some join the long queue for the beer stall, others wait their turn at the Johnny Walker stand, some purchase pies and pizzas and a few, a brave few, patronise the wine bar, where they hold at arm's length plastic glasses of sauvignon blanc, hurrying across the grass with a fiercely masculine frown which says: 'Aw look, mate, this isn't for me. It's for her.'

Despite the travails of their team, this has the feeling of a very happy, very Australian gathering. There are lots of women, many more than for a comparable occasion in England. They sit mainly in feminine groups of eight or ten, exchanging compliments, remembering schooldays, swapping proud tales of their children. An elderly lady, seated beneath a striped umbrella and fanning herself with a menu, winces discreetly at the loudness of the laughter and the shortness of the skirts. Clearly, she has never attended Royal Ascot on Ladies' Day. The men sprawl in masculine bunches, drinking beer, telling familiar jokes and casually boasting: 'Wonderful cruise. You name it, we went there: Venice, Nay-pools, Mar-saay. Bloody everywhere.' From time to time, their thoughts turn to the team they have come to support. There is serious conversation about illusory strengths and manifold weaknesses, and the conclusions are not flattering. 'Useless baastards!' seems a popular summation. One man, catching my accent, tells me in hushed tones that he expects and even hopes for an English victory. 'We're just not that good any more,' he says. 'Anyway, it's your turn.' He is touchingly generous, and he may well be right.

The temperature is now nudging 34°C, causing the members to cluster beneath capacious umbrellas. Bitter experience has taught Australians a proper respect for ultraviolet perils. This respect is not widely shared by their visitors inside the ground. Up there on the hill, the white, northern skin of the Barmy Army is already acquiring a worrying blush as shirts come off and strong drink slides down. The comparison with conditions back home could not be more vivid. Two days earlier, I met Richie Benaud, strolling through town with his wife Daphne. The day was dazzling: fresh and bright with the promise of bone-warming heat. I said that things were sadly different in Britain, where heavy snow had closed schools, airports and motorways, trains had stopped running and towns had virtually closed down. Richie sympathised.

Despite the travails of their team, this has the feeling of a very happy, very Australian gathering

'Terrible,' he said. 'And I hear 16 race meetings were abandoned.' He walked away, shaking his head.

But 12,000 miles to the south, there is diversion at hand in the outfield, with relay races involving teams of young athletes. These affairs have become rather more sophisticated with the passing of the years. They used to involve men of various ages and athletic talent giving a young woman the advantage of a start and attempting to catch her before she reached the finishing tape. In those days, it was called: 'Chase the Sheila'. The decision to dispense with the title was apparently condemned in certain unreconstructed quarters as 'political correctness gone mad'.

The expansion of the ground has attracted an attendance of 38,000, the biggest first-day gate since the Bodyline tour of 1932–33. Around 8,000 of these are believed to be English, an extraordinary turnout in the depths of a recession. And England's cricketers are rewarding that fidelity. Watson falls soon after lunch, and while Hussey proves frustratingly adhesive, Jimmy Anderson is bowling with splendidly controlled hostility to which the Australians have no response. You find yourself feeling particularly thrilled for Anderson, who will be returning to England at the close of this Test to be present at the birth of his daughter. Some have publicly criticised this eminently civilised gesture, including the ray of sunshine that is Bob Willis. 'I don't agree with the Mothercare buggy-rolling thinking that modern man has,' chuntered Willis. 'He should be on the cricket tour, that's his job.' Anderson has declined to react to this Neanderthal slur. He is, as I say, a civilised man.

So the wickets are tumbling at a comforting clatter, and on the lawn reactions are mixed. Most of the women seem oblivious to the happenings on the various screens, just as most of their counterparts at Ascot never quite get around to watching a race. The children continue with their private cricket matches, happily uncontaminated by the example set by Australia's batsmen. And many of the men are cursing in disgust. They have not travelled two or three hundred miles to see the blokes in the green baggies play like, well, like Englishmen.

Australian patriotism is staunch and fierce, although lightened by a certain, saving self-mockery. I recall the Sydney Olympics of

2000, when a brewer of lager ran a brilliant television advertisement for his product. It featured a raucous Aussie listing the virtues of his country, his patriotic fervour growing with each bellowing boast. 'I fight wars but I don't start 'em! ... I ride in the front seat of the taxi! ... And I believe that the world is round – with Australia on top!' It was at those same Games that I saw a matronly lady directing visitors to the station at Olympic Park. 'G'day,' she said as they arrived. Then she turned up her nose. 'I don't really go for that "G'day" crap,' she confided. 'Cultural clee-shay, I reckon. But the visitors seem to like it.' In both examples, there was an irreverence that said that they didn't wish to be taken too seriously, but neither were they intending to be undervalued. And today, cricketers they once venerated are inviting the derision of the oldest enemy. Australians expect a great deal more.

Australian patriotism is staunch and fierce, although lightened by a certain, saving self-mockery

Australia are dismissed for 245, their lowest first-innings total at Adelaide in 17 years. Various talking heads emerge to offer various explanations, but in the end all agree that they just weren't good enough, that they had fallen far below the standards they used to set, that the rest of the match could only involve pain and humiliation. The western lawn had arrived at a similar conclusion some hours before. A week or so earlier, at the start of the Brisbane Test, an Australian sage was asked his opinion on the outcome of the series. 'Tight as a duck's, mate,' was his considered response. At the time, it seemed an accurate assessment; today it appears impossibly generous to Ponting's dysfunctional team. Small wonder that the members are sinking their drinks at a disconcerting rate as the shadows lengthen across the lawn, and a sense of futility seeps through this most social of Test matches.

This evening, I eat at a small, kerbside restaurant in north Adelaide. While I am waiting for coffee, three middle-aged men in Barmy Army T-shirts come marching along the road. They pause dramatically, point accusingly at the diners and chant: 'You All Live In A Convict Colony, Convict Colony, Convict Colony'. They repeat it, loudly, and then they pause. I wait for their spontaneous chuckle. It arrives on cue.

*

Ed Delaney wakes at seven o'clock on the morning of the second day. He showers, watches the BBC World Service and reads the newspaper over breakfast. He drops into Woolworths to buy lunch, which he will eat at the ground. Then he joins the throng on King William Road, walking together to the Oval.

Ed is 65 years old, he lives in Ashby de la Zouch, and all his life he has loved cricket with a quiet passion. A self-effacing man, he merges easily into the crowd, with his trim, grey beard, his thin-rimmed spectacles and his sensible shorts. He describes himself as 'semi-retired', and he owns a modular manufacturing company in the Midlands.

This is his seventh visit to Australia, and while he concedes that it's a 'very expensive country', he insists that 'from a fan's point of view, it's the place to come'. His wife came with him on the last Australian tour, but this time she has opted for a holiday in Barbados with a friend. 'Last time, we went to the Perth, Melbourne and Sydney Tests,' he says. 'We went with the Barmy Army. To be honest, it's not something I'd want to repeat. Perth was great fun. We got a bit involved with the singing, and for a while it was a bit of a laugh. Then it became very monotonous, very difficult to take. We extricated ourselves at the MCG. My wife and I found other seats. Nothing personal, but we couldn't take any more.'

This time, he has come with the travel company Gullivers, to watch the Brisbane and Adelaide Tests with a group of 37 England supporters. He is among six of his group to opt for business-class travel, and the cost is considerable. 'I'm paying £11,000 for the trip. Well, £11,040 to be exact.' Yet, clearly, he doesn't regret a penny. 'It's a wonderful way to do it,' he says. 'Everyone's really friendly; everybody's always helping each other. They tend to be around 55 to 65, in couples, most of them. And there's three single ladies, real cricket aficionados. We did go to the vineyards of the Barossa Valley, but apart from that, it's just been the cricket. You get into a routine here: cricket, food, sleep. Cricket, food, sleep. Perfect. I found the Gabba a bit cold and impersonal, but Adelaide's wonderful. During the match, I never leave my seat. I sit up there in the Chappells Stand and watch every ball. Then I'm back to the hotel, a couple of beers in the bar, and out to eat with a nice couple from Luton. It all goes so quickly. I'm never bored. Honestly, I'm amazed at how short the days are. And the Aussie fans are great. The banter's always good and friendly. The Barmy Army? They're OK, if they're on the other side of the ground.'

A more contented man you never saw, and he feels he has good reason: 'For one thing, there's the camaraderie. And for another, there's the cricket. We've played marvellously well so far. I'm really pleased for Alastair Cook. He needed that double-hundred in Brisbane. And all our group loves Pietersen, because of the way he tries to play. If he comes off, England'll be all right, I reckon.' While the price he paid is beyond the capacity of ordinary pockets, Ed Delaney represents a relatively silent majority of England supporters. They have been called the Alternative Army. They sit and study, applaud and appreciate. They find their pleasure in the game, and they never forget that they are here to watch rather than to be watched.

And today is a day beyond their dreams. It is the day when England take the match by the throat, with a wonderfully satisfying ruthlessness.

On go England, and on and on. Not so much a productive innings, more a protracted reprisal for the sufferings of the years

There is a small, obligatory panic when the captain is bowled for just a single, but the newly prolific Cook forms an alliance with the pragmatic Jonathan Trott, and on they sail through the sweltering day, painstakingly exploiting the advantage which their bowlers had established. The attendance is some 5,000 down on yesterday, although the lawn seems more crowded than ever. I ask the barman in the beer tent to explain this phenomenon. 'It's 'cos you can't see the cricket from here,' he replies, as if this truth were self-evident. On go England, and on and on. Not so much a productive innings, more a protracted reprisal for the sufferings of the years. After Brisbane, Cook appears incapable of error. You can almost hear the exhortation of his mentor Graeme Gooch: 'Be greedy, son! Be greedy!' Cook remains splendidly unsated.

The partnership has yielded 173 runs when Trott departs and a barrage of Aussie boos marks the entrance of Pietersen, who wears the smirk of a pantomime villain. He seems to enjoy the role. If he had a moustache he would certainly twirl it. But as he takes guard and surveys the field, he recognises the possibilities. The Australians are bounding to their positions and barking messages of mutual encouragement. But they are singularly unconvincing, for they know that Pietersen is the very last batsman they would wish to see when it's this hot, and the score is 176 for one.

There are times – too many, perhaps – when self-indulgence wins the upper hand and Pietersen perishes prematurely. But this is not such a time. Instead, he is a paragon of responsibility: first playing himself in, then employing a sublime conspiracy of hand and eye to punish and bully the fading bowlers. The Barmy Army runs through its limited repertoire, their Alternative counterparts simply purr with pleasure, and the Adelaide Oval is unanimously aware that this Test match, and possibly this Test series, is being decided by the onslaught.

Irked by the reversal of traditional roles, the Australians are starting to lose interest. As I leave the ground this evening, I encounter two radio men at the media entrance. They are discussing tomorrow's phone-in topic. Usually, they opt for something vaguely triumphal: 'Just how bad can the Poms get?' or 'Should we make them play our second team?' This time, one of them is making a case for deodorant: 'Simple question: "Roll-on or spray? You decide".'

'It's a winner, mate. We'll get the biggest response of the whole bloody summer.' The times, as I say, are a-changing.

Nine thirty on another flawless morning, and the lobby of the Stamford Plaza hotel is buzzing with English anticipation. The lift is disgorging a stream of Identikit guests, wearing shorts and carrying bags filled with lunch packs, cameras, binoculars and, in one case, an old-fashioned scorebook in which every ball will be neatly and faithfully recorded. One lady of middle years is wearing a T-shirt which bears the motto: 'Dear God: Thanks for Chocolate, Champagne and Cricket'. A gentleman of similar vintage wears a rather older shirt that details the venues of England's Ashes tour of 2002–03. He nods to the hotel porter as he passes the desk.

'Where are we off to today then, sir?' asks the porter, archly.

The guest plays the game: 'I thought we'd try a couple of galleries, then maybe look in at the concert hall,' he replies.

The porter smiles: 'Enjoy the cricket, sir,' he says.

'I will,' says the guest. 'I will.'

His confidence is not misplaced. A commendable number of spectators, more than 32,000, have turned up on this Sunday morning. Some have come with the intention of giving their team one more chance, others are here to enjoy the social scene. For his part, Pietersen is here to play the innings that has escaped him for too long. Starting on 85, he is moving from milestone to milestone with commanding inevitability. On the lawn, reality is swiftly recognised, and the screens are little more than wallpaper as drink flows and conversation bubbles and Australian bowlers falter and fade, and England's cricketers enjoy the kind of day that many had feared would never come again.

Pietersen is hitting the ball pretty much where he chooses. His hundred comes quite quickly, and by lunch he has passed 150. With three wickets down, England's lead is now beyond 200. There is a beer tasting in the media tent, with examples of South Australia's finest nectar presented for approval. Yesterday, they were offering oysters. 'Just like our own dear Headingley,' remarks a broadsheet scribbler, after checking that Geoffrey Boycott is not within earshot. For Australia, the news keeps getting worse through the afternoon, as England pass 500 and Pietersen reaches his double-century. But the rain arrives at tea, and is greeted like an old friend.

Moments later, another old friend makes his entrance on the large screens. He is wearing a diamante-studded, body-hugging white suit and he is gyrating across the Cathedral End while miming the deathless lyrics of 'Suspicious Minds':

We're caught in a trap.
I can't walk out,
Because I love you too much bay-bee!

Within moments, the ground is transformed into a mass karaoke as the Oval crowd, along with the semi-detached drinkers on the lawn, sing along with The King.

We can't go on together,
With suspicious minds.
And we can't build our dreams,
On suspicious minds.

It is splendidly surreal, Elvis hip-grinding his way through the intricacies of an Ashes Test. It is also vaguely ironic: here is a man who can bring off a passable impersonation of Presley, yet closer examination reveals his deficiencies. Likewise Australia's cricketers; they may strike the right poses and make the right noises, but they will never be mistaken for the real thing. For they are essentially a tribute act in baggy green caps.

Elvis leaves the building, but the music continues. A familiar introduction comes lilting through the speakers: 'Doo dee doo dooo…' and the crowd is 'Singin' In The Rain'. In the middle of the dancing Barmies on the hill, a young man flourishes a placard which announces 'I Hate Poms'. Perhaps nobody notices, certainly nobody cares. It is only when the Oval DJ excavates 'Raindrops Keep Falling On My Head' that I decide that enough is enough.

Although play has been abandoned for the day, the members are drinking more earnestly than ever. The women are speaking more loudly; the men are more assertive. Nobody behaves too outrageously, but I see two lads, who clearly have not met for some time, fling affectionate high-fives at each other. They miss, both stumble, and one topples into a puddle, where he finishes his drink before finding his feet. In the shadow of the stand, a large gentleman dressed as Merv Hughes is running in to bowl at a dustbin. The crowd, clapping and shouting, urges him on. His balance betrays him in the delivery stride, and the ball sails 5 feet wide, while Merv slides on his front for 10 muddy yards. There is much applause. 'I've seen him do this before,' says an appreciative young woman. 'He's very good, isn't he?'

Ed Delaney is back at his hotel across the Torrens. He confesses that he has spent much of the day quietly gloating at the ongoing carnage. Soon, he and his fellow guests will gather in a private room to listen to the thoughts of Michael Atherton, Jonathan Agnew and David Lloyd, aka 'Bumble'. 'Everyone sort of mingles for drinks, then they answer the questions we've already submitted,' he says. 'They're excellent, very approachable. You wouldn't get that with football, would you?'

Three hours later, a small party of visitors is finishing a splendid Italian meal in the city. The restaurant owner appears at the table, and hesitantly approaches one of the guests. 'I hope you don't mind,' he begins, 'but me and my friends, we think we know who you are. You're a famous cricketer, aren't you?' There is a long, non-committal pause, but he presses on: 'You're Garry Sobers, aren't you?' Another pause. 'Well, we're both left-handers,' replies David Gower.

England are in remorseless mood next morning, batting on belligerently until deciding that 620 for five is probably sufficient. They have Australia at 238 for four when bad light curtails play. English celebrations are slightly constrained by the promise of a violent storm next day, which may arrive in time to save Ponting's team. They need not worry. The last six wickets fall in just 86 minutes, and victory is England's by an innings and 71 runs. Unused to such treatment at English hands, the Australians react with something like panic. Straws are clutched. The coach, Tim Neilsen, publicly muses on the possible return of Shane Warne. The man may have been a towering genius, but it is a sign of Australia's desperation that the nation could even think of turning to a 41-year-old who these days does little but text and talk and tout chicken-burgers. Warne ends the speculation by flying off to England for an assignation with an actress, but the damage has been done.

Unused to such treatment at English hands, the Australians react with something like panic

The rain arrives as promised, a mighty deluge exploding in squalls, the more satisfying since it is too late to affect the outcome. But the out-of-towners have long since departed the social Test. They are now back in Coober Pedy and William Creek, Buckleboo and Bookaloo, telling their tales of high living and late nights, of feeble surrender by the impostors in green baggies, and of Englishmen who have finally worked out how to play the greatest game.

For their part, the English are leaving in triumph; singing their songs down King William Road and striding back along North Terrace for a convivial afternoon before taking on the restaurants of Rundle Street. There will be bends and bumps in the road, and one will present itself in Perth. But a new and exciting course has been set and it was set in Adelaide, a place which the Poms regard as a wonderful town. And I think I know why.

Into the fire with Rocky of the oche

CHAPTER 11
DARTS AT THE PALACE

Teatime at the Palace, and the guests are drifting through the Great Hall. They assemble beneath the rose window to exchange gentle banter and genial reflections on the events of the day. An eclectic gathering, their number includes seven nuns in mini-skirts and stilettos, half a dozen friars, a couple of policewomen, a Blues Brothers tribute band, a leprechaun and a forest sprite, who is searching for the Gents. 'Fancy dress,' explains the attendant at the entrance to the Hall. Then, more helpfully: 'It's Christmas.' And Christmas, as the man on Sky Sports so pithily explained, means just one thing: the Ladbrokes.com World Darts Championship.

> *Christmas ... means just one thing: the Ladbrokes.com World Darts Championship*

Alexandra Palace is a Victorian pile perched upon a hill in North London. Its notable features are the Willis Organ, installed in 1875 when it was considered the finest concert organ in Europe, and the radio tower, which in 1936 began to transmit the world's first public television service and tonight is enveloped in the December murk. In truth, these attractions alone would not have tempted almost 3,000 people to pack the place every evening for two weeks in the deep midwinter. No, what brings them in night after rollicking night are the efforts of 72 contenders, whose skills are extraordinary and whose hearts are as big as their waistbands.

Around 35 years have passed since I last set foot in the Palace. They were heady days. I was on the sports desk at the *News of the World*, whose sports editor regarded darts as a sobering counter-weight to the glamorous, head-turning attractions of football, cricket and track and field. In vain did I protest that there was nothing sober about darts. I was detailed to cover the regional finals of the *News of the World* Championship, Britain's only national darts tournament. This involved an extended trek around town halls, corn exchanges and civic centres to watch the champions of various pubs and working-men's clubs take their shot at the big time. I remember being introduced to the darts master of ceremonies, a dapper man in a dinner jacket, who used to stand at centre stage, barking out the scores.

'Hello,' he said. 'My name's Les Treble.'

'Treble?' I said. 'That's very, sort of … suitable.'

'How d'you mean?' he said.

When the evening was over and the local mayor had presented the trophy, along with a voucher for a week at a Pontins holiday camp of the winner's choice, I would dictate ten paragraphs of essentially unchanging prose: 'Charlie Farnsbarns is the new Eastern/Western/Midlands/Northern Area champion of the *News of the World* Darts Championship. He took his title before a packed crowd at the Muggleswick Recreation Centre, when he defeated...' Unprompted, I can still recite the turgid copy, including the last line which carried the promotional reminder that the said Charlie would take his tilt at the title in the Grand Final at 'London's Alexandra Palace on...' The date would usually clash with the FA Cup semi-finals, and I would plead for the chance to cover real sport rather than an inflated pub game. The sports editor would smile a cruel smile and remind me where my duties lay.

It was at this time, the early Seventies, that television first began to show an interest in covering darts. Naturally, they chose the *News of the World* tournament, since it was the only show in town. One of the grand finalists in those early years was a stout, practically toothless character, who spent his waking hours in a country pub, would only compete with four or five pints inside him and always played in a blue cardigan with an enormous hole in the elbow. He would hurry through his matches in a flurry of bull's eyes and doubles before declaring: 'Now I can have a proper drink.' The newspaper executives, a notably fastidious bunch, instructed their junior reporter to have a word with the maverick's 'connections'. Pathetically, I obeyed. On the night before the final, I sought out his local publican. 'If it's not too much trouble, would you mind saying something to him about saving the boozing until after the final?' I mumbled. He gave me a dubious grunt. 'And another thing,' I persisted. 'I really hate to mention this, but could you possibly ask him to wear something other than that blue cardigan?'

Next day, I saw my bold contender at the pre-finals lunch in a function room. He was wearing a green cardigan and sinking a pint of lager. He looked up and spotted me. 'S'alright,' he said, flashing his gums and winking. 'I'm only having this one.' And he tugged knowingly at his jumper, as if it were our secret. Then he raised his mug in an expansive toast, which was when I spotted the enormous hole in the elbow. He won, of course. Absolutely strolled it. 'Thunk! Thunk! Thunk!' went his darts. 'Game shot, sir!' piped Les Treble. They gave the new champion a Pontinental holiday, as well as a gleaming Skoda. I'm not sure he ever took the holiday. And, given his drinking habits, I hope and pray that he never tried to drive the Skoda.

Anyway, after that little lot, I resolved never to return. Indeed, when a large chunk of Alexandra Palace was burned down in 1980, I remember feeling less regretful than I should have been. But slowly, inexorably, and around 35 years later, that which the wordsmith on Sky calls 'the magic of Ally Pally' has enticed me back. I sense it has changed. For one thing there is the smoking, which is conspicuous by its absence. Smoking used to be almost compulsory at the Palace, great curtains of yellow smog rising from the audience and floating towards the distant rafters. I believe the event was part-sponsored by Embassy, whose gorgeous, pouting young ladies would risk all manner of indignity by moving among the throng and passing round packets of cigarettes. Every match, every shot, was played out to a chorus of chesty, throaty coughing and carried its own health warning. No longer. Smoking is mercifully forbidden, the fog has lifted, and you can actually see the players from the back of the hall, as well as the two large television screens, which depict the flight of the darts and the details of the score. From time to time, the telly people will show the winning dart bury itself in the double in super slow motion. It is an absurdly irrelevant affectation, yet it never fails to spark a cheer.

People sit and watch those screens, since the board itself is clearly far too small. Effectively, they have travelled from all over the country to see what could be seen in their own homes. But they do not complain because, as they will tell you, being here is all that matters. Plus the fact that their outlay is relatively modest: for this afternoon's matches, they paid £20 per head for the tiered seats at the side of the hall, and £30 for a place at the central tables. This evening's programme, which will last from seven to some time around eleven o'clock, will cost £25 and £35 respectively. There are also corporate tables in a roped-off area, in which food is served to feckless dilettantes paying £100 a head. In the old days, most of the audience was left to stand and peer at an enlarged duplication of a darts board, on which the destination of each dart was symbolised by a single, twinkling bulb. The switches were assiduously flicked by Les Treble's brother. A conscientious cove, he never made a mistake worth mentioning.

... they have travelled from all over the country to see what could be seen in their own homes

Yet, however momentous the advances in facilities; the basic attraction of darts is unchanged. There is a conviction lurking somewhere in the corner of every mind that says: 'It could have been me.' Apart from the fantasies of starry-eyed children, this does not happen in other, more authentic sports. The fans accept that they could not take a punch from a heavyweight champion, or ride a Grand National winner. But darts is not so much a sport, more a knack. And so they watch the homely, tubby, largely unremarkable characters who come shuffling on to the stage at the Palace, and they tell themselves that, with sufficient practice, firmer discipline and a good deal of determination, they too could have mastered the knack, they could have been a contender. And even now it may not be too late. Accordingly, they empathise strongly with the men on that stage. Because they are not watching gods, but ordinary mortals, fallible souls like themselves. Apart from that cursed work ethic, and that knack.

Those who run the entertainment have long been aware of the virtues of appearing ordinary, and so they seek to cast the players as warm, jolly, unthreatening individuals by the liberal use of nicknames. Some are puzzling, some funny, some clumpingly obvious and some too daft for words. Thus, among the players in this championship, we have Kevin 'The Artist' Painter, Mark 'Special Brew' Walsh, Denis 'The Heat' Ovens, Steve 'The Bronzed Adonis' Beaton and, from Watford, the shameless Alex 'Ace of Herts' Roy. I should also mention Wes Newton, who was once known as 'Av It!' and is now, a mite less aggressively, called 'The Warrior'. In fairness, none of these can hold a candle to the sport of boxing, where an original nickname is almost as important as a decent left hook. I give you just three: James 'Lights Out' Toney, Michael 'Second To' Nunn and, a personal favourite, O'Neil 'Give 'em Hell' Bell. Who could fail to support a fighter calling himself 'Give 'em Hell'?

I am pondering these matters when the hall braces itself for a confrontation between Andy 'The Pie Man' Smith and Mervyn 'The King' King. Mervyn, it transpires, is not the Governor of the Bank of England, but a large man with a fierce frown. He is 44 years old and the sixth best darts player in the whole, wide world. Yet if Mervyn is large, then The Pie Man is from a different species. Andy is just huge. Raymond Chandler's description of Moose Malloy springs to mind: 'A big man, but not more than 6 feet 5 inches tall, and not wider than a beer truck.' The height may be an exaggeration, but in a collision with Andy, you wouldn't necessarily favour the truck. He has a shiny skull, the stare of an amiable panda, and he wears his nickname across the back of his tunic. It is a 'forgiving' garment, with every stitch up to the job. His wife, a slender lady, is watching from the front row of the guest seats. She too has 'The Pie Man' etched loyally across the back of her T-shirt. The odds are against Andy, who is rated at 250–1 to win the title, Mervyn being a 40–1 shot.

Mervyn bears an advertisement for a speedy loans company among the four patches on his chest. It strikes a strangely depressing note. The crowd noise is high, but when a small section starts to sing the song from the football dugout, 'Mervyn, Mervyn, give us a wave', the King responds promptly. Both men are staggeringly good at what they do.

Whether it is a skill worth acquiring is an open question, but the levels of nerve and touch are astonishing. Each match this evening will be played over the best of seven sets. Each set will be decided over the best of five legs. And each leg will be won by the first player to 501.

Although Andy's skull is now glowing pinkly beneath the lights, his darts appear to be obeying him. Whenever he scores the maximum of 180, he turns away from the board and dedicates the feat to his wife. She leaps up, fists clenched, her voice swelling the growing din. A frantic atmosphere is crucially important to the success of a broadcast, so there is brazen collusion between sponsors, cameras and public. Long before play begins, placards bearing the Ladbrokes logo are strewn around the tables. On the front is the figure 180, in the manner of cards bearing the numbers 6 or 4 in one-day cricket. On the back is space for brief, pointed messages to be written. The cameraman roves the hall, checking the messages, setting up shots. 'Steak and kidney pie, please!' shouts one slogan, pointedly. 'Hello Plymouth!' pipes another. 'Rat!' snarls one alarming scrawl. The players press on, blow for blow, their mathematical agility as dazzling as their accuracy. 'Andy, you require 121,' bawls the MC. Smith responds with 60, 25, double-18 before I can even begin to work out the sum.

The pressure eventually tells on the pair of them and they start to make nervous errors, like a golfer facing a 4-foot putt. But The Pie Man comes through 4–3, flinging an arrow into double-8, shaking his fist, blowing a couple of kisses, mopping his brow and making his exit, stage left. 'King won't be crowned at the Palace,' pronounces the man from Sky. Andy, still mopping, says superfluously: 'I'm sweating.' He shakes his head. 'It was hot up there. People don't realise,' he says. He recalls the delayed start to his match, the problems involved in waiting offstage for the previous match to finish. 'Difficult,' he says. 'You don't know how much you've had to drink. Have you had enough? Have you had too much? I mean you've got to pace yourself. Do you go to the toilet now? No? When do you go?' Too many decisions. Too much information. The panda stare appears perplexed. Then he remembers that he really did win. In his broadest Brummie, he drawls: ''Appy days, eh? 'Appy days.' Truly, he is an engaging man.

As the contest ends, the fans leap to their feet. They all sing a daft song which involves much pointing and ends in a collective 'Oi! Oi! Oi!' I ask an official for the name of the tune. 'Chase The Sun.' Planet Funk,' he answers, without hesitation. 'I've never heard it,' I say. 'You don't want to, mate,' he replies.

There is an interval between sessions, and the customers use the break to explore the delights of the Great Hall. There is a betting stand, heavily patronised, as Ladbrokes indulge in a spot of niche marketing. There is a drinks stall, with the drinks paid for with tokens. These are sold at a cost of £1.80 per token. A pint of Boddingtons bitter costs two tokens, the same price as a pint of Gaymers cider or a large white wine. A four-pint pitcher of lager is on sale for eight tokens. There is a brisk demand for the pitcher, which most of the patrons seem to regard as a cocktail. There is also a stall for pies and roasts. I purchase a pie, which is a great mistake. The meat inside is darkly mysterious and the gravy, as Alan Partridge remarked of his apple turnover, is hotter than the sun. It is served, along with an infusion of mushy peas, in what appears to be the lid of a cardboard box. 'You'll need this,' says the man behind the counter, handing me a wooden fork. As I deposit the entire, noxious concoction in the waste bin, I spot the debris of several similar feasts, glowing sickly, like nuclear waste. The British are, by and large, an accepting, uncomplaining race. It is a weakness which mass caterers have been ruthlessly swift to exploit.

Across the hall, a revealing little scene is unfolding. Beneath a sign which reads 'Meet the Legends', fans are invited to have their photograph taken with Eric 'The Crafty Cockney' Bristow and Keith 'The Kid' Deller. Bristow won the title five times in the Eighties and generated a vast amount of publicity, some of it favourable. Deller was the youngest-ever world champion when he won at the age of 24 in 1983. They stand, somewhat awkwardly, in a small enclosure, assessing likely customers. But for darts fans, history is what happened last week. I am told that most of them have brought a great deal of money for drink and a few coins for food. They are not clamouring to pay £20 for a 12 x 8-inch framed picture. Eventually, a middle-aged lady in spectacles comes hesitantly forward. Bristow and Deller seize her and smile for the camera. She pays her money and receives her picture, which they sign with a flourish. They wish her well, then they continue to scan the crowd: furtively, hopefully.

A burst of music from inside the hall sends the strollers hurrying off. 'Barney!' they cry, as the crashing chords of 'Eye Of The Tiger' rattle the building. 'Barney' is Raymond van Barneveld, from The Hague in the Netherlands. And they are playing his song. The champion in 2007, now ranked third in the world, Barneveld is another whose paunch suggests a weakness for second helpings. A pre-written card is held up, beseechingly, to the camera: 'I'm Barmy about Barney'. The crowd begins a chant of 'Barney Army!' Scarcely cutting-edge, but the enthusiasm is irreproachable. His opponent, Kevin McDine, is described in the programme as a 'Geordie-born ace'. He is 25, immensely tall, chubby of face, and he smiles a lot: too much and too easily, I should judge, for one who hopes to overcome Barney and his Army.

Barney wins a leg, and the Geordie-born ace seems not so much annoyed as vaguely miffed. This is not a good sign. Barney wins another leg. 'He's a clinical assassin,' says the man next to me. I nod, knowledgably. Another losing leg goes by, and Kevin gives a cheery wink to a friend in the crowd. A very bad sign. There is the occasional maximum, signified by a Gregorian chant of 'One hun-dred and eigh-ty' from the MC. In the end, the Dutchman saunters home 4–1.

Not content with being the finest darts player to come out of The Hague, our Barney is also a splendidly shameless ham

Kevin heaves a theatrical shrug, which says: 'Never mind. I didn't have much of a chance anyway, did I?' and tramps nonchalantly from the scene, pausing to bless his fans with a breezy wave. Barney waits for Kevin to depart before offering himself to his screaming public; a process which involves standing at the front of the stage, flinging his arms dramatically wide, thrusting out that formidable paunch and gazing mutely at the gods for several seconds as the ecstasy washes over him. Not content with being the finest darts player to come out of The Hague, our Barney is also a splendidly shameless ham.

Barry Hearn, who is chairman of the Professional Darts Corporation as well as being a sporting entrepreneur and occasional social commentator, surveys the packed house with satisfaction. 'People are living in rotten times. Hard times. Everything's difficult,' he says. 'So they say bollocks, let's forget it all and have a right good night out. Tonight, they'll drink between six and seven pints per head. And they'll see some real characters. Like Andy Smith. He famously went into a restaurant and, when they gave him the menu, he said "Yes". Ate the lot. He's a character. See, most people don't much like Premier League footballers. They think they earn too much, and they don't deserve their money. Now these blokes, these darts players, they might earn a few hundred thousand a year, the ones at the top. Fair enough. People don't mind that. So they come along, have a good laugh, cheer on their man, then get up and sing a little song every 15 minutes or so. And they love it. And I'll tell you something else: it's straight. We've never had a complaint to the Gambling Commission about darts, even though it's probably the easiest game in the world to bend. These blokes can throw a dart a millimetre out, and you and I would never know. But it doesn't happen.' I don't doubt that he's right although, given that nobody would ever know if the odd dart were to go deliberately astray, I do wonder how he can be quite so sure.

Still, Ladbrokes, proud sponsors that they are, will be relieved to know that their hard-won profits are safe from darting blackguards. The prize money alone is costing them £1 million, yet for Stephen Vowles, the impressively titled Director of Customer Experience Ladbrokes E-Gaming, the investment is worth every penny. As he writes in the tournament programme: 'Christmas wouldn't be Christmas without a trip to Alexandra Palace, although I will be making my debut here having only joined Ladbrokes in early December.' That's Stephen for you: he's never been before, but if he missed out, then his Christmas just wouldn't be the same.

All his prospective punters, all these people wearing red Stetsons with the Ladbrokes logo, are enjoying themselves enormously. They are generating a busy hum of expectation. The Palace feels like a boxing hall before a world title fight as the emotional temperature rises notch by notch, drink by drink. With the merest nod to showbiz convention, Mark Hylton and Mark Webster take the stage. They are the final bout of the supporting bill, the people who must keep the audience adequately distracted until the main event of the evening. Hylton, from

Rugeley in Staffordshire, is rated a 500–1 chance to win the title. He is an Eng. Lit. graduate who boasts the slightly disconcerting nickname of 'Mile High'. This, I discover, may be traced to his previous job as an airline cabin manager. Webster, a young Welshman of serious mien, with a conventional hairstyle and half-rimmed spectacles, is thought to be something of a prospect. He has a touch of the insurance office about him and his nickname is a faintly uninspired 'Webby', but you sense that his very lack of charisma may ultimately prove quite charismatic. The prosaic tone of the contest is reflected in the content of the thrusting placards. No blinding shafts or yelping insults, but the worthy 'Happy Anniversary, Mum and Dad' and the wonderfully surreal 'My Dad's Got a Fish Pond!'

All evening, something odd has been developing among the audience, a rumbling irascibility that needs only identifiable adversaries to give it shape and context. One of the rules of entry insists: 'No football colours will be allowed in the venue', experience having shown that strong lager and conflicting loyalties can produce distressing results. But most of the watchers are football fans, for whom no event may be considered legitimate without an exchange of musical insults. Early in the 'Mile High' v 'Webby' encounter, the battle lines are drawn: this will be a collision between the tiered seats (£25) and the central seats with tables (£35). And so there is concerted pointing and the odd, incoherent threat. There are mildly obscene gestures and scabrous jibes. There are all the trappings of tribal antagonism without a tribe in sight. An anthropologist could organise field trips. It is quite bizarre.

From time to time, they are pacified by an eruption of the old Johnny Cash song 'Ring Of Fire'. The entire arena leaps up as one, arms pumping and heads bobbing:

I went down, down, down
And the flames went higher.

Long ago, in Atlantic City, I was given tickets for a Cash concert. The good ol' boy was clearly suffering from a mixture of strong drink and exotic substances. He missed a few notes, forgot a few lines and once he dropped the microphone, cursing violently as he went in fumbling search. The highlight of his performance arrived when he invited one barracker in the third row to step outside and settle their differences. Since that memorable evening, I have never regarded the late Mr Cash as a natural conciliator, yet here they are, tiers and tables, bellowing together:

It burns, burns, burns,
The ring of fire, the ring of fire!

Yet it is less than a genuine truce, more a ceasefire. For they are becoming excited by the imminence of the main event.

Television has started to send out offstage shots of Phil 'The Power' Taylor, the world champion and the most celebrated player the game has ever known. If this were a big fight, Phil would be shadow boxing frantically, throwing a stream of hooks and jabs with bandages on his hands and a snarl on his lips. But it isn't a big fight, and anyway, Phil is 50 years old, so he gives the camera a polite little nod and twiddles his fingers and looks as if he is torn between the Ovaltine and the cocoa.

Every camera shot detonates a roar around the arena, for Taylor is their shining star. A week or two ago, he came second to the jockey A.P. McCoy in the nationwide vote for the BBC Sports Personality of the Year. Some of us found it curious to see a darts player finishing ahead of the world champion heptathlete Jessica Ennis or the world's no. 1 golfer Lee Westwood, but that was how the viewers voted, and darts celebrated its finest hour. For his part, Taylor appeared suitably pleased, although far from overwhelmed; having won the world title 15 times, recognition is not something he lacks. In fairness, those who know him suggest that he is well aware of the value of publicity. This very morning, he played his part in planting a harmless little fable in several newspapers, indicating that he was furious with a Sky pundit for suggesting that he had fallen beneath his own exalted standards. He threatened to have strong words with the faithless hack who doubted his talent. Yet, for all the nonsense, he retains the air of a modest man, battling daunting odds: a 'Rocky of the oche', as one besotted journal fetchingly described him. And Taylor inspires fierce, some might say blind, loyalty. The young man in the row behind me is explaining to his girlfriend Phil 'The Power's' place in the pantheon. 'He is the greatest sportsman England's ever had,' he says. A telling pause. 'No question.'

Thus elevated high above the likes of Bannister, Redgrave, Botham, Finney, Moore, Coe, Thompson and Grace, Taylor prepares for his ring-walk. This ritual was invented

Phil the Power's … the greatest sportsman England's ever had,' he says. A telling pause. 'No question'

long ago by a fight promoter anxious to please his television paymasters by drumming up a little bogus hysteria. At its best, it was Mike Tyson: bare-chested, black-booted, a towel at the neck and a stare of disturbing menace. At its worst, it was the various light-flashing, firework-crashing, toe-curling extravaganzas that accompanied a string of hapless pugilists to their fate. The modest promenade of a grandfather from Stoke-on-Trent ranks somewhere between the two extremes.

Sky have cranked up the atmosphere a little with a moody sequence of Taylor in action, along with a stream of understated slogans: 'Darting Genius … Exponent of Excellence … Precision Personified', and the like. And because the fans view everything through the prism of football, everyone sings 'Walking in a Taylor Wonderland', to the tune which used to serenade Kevin Keegan at Newcastle. Taylor starts to move down the central aisle, and although he has made many of these entrances, he seems almost taken aback by the noise. A tall blonde sashays along a yard or two ahead of him, wearing the self-conscious smile of a ring-card girl. Phil 'The Power' looks around, nodding his thanks, smiling a polite little smile, and finally climbing the steps to the stage, where destiny awaits.

This evening, destiny has made the trip from Lowestoft. Peter Wright looks like the kind of heavyweight that Don King used to cast in the role of opponent. He is 40 years old, and somebody has advised him that the best way to get himself noticed is to have his hair spiked with grease and dyed a vivid shade of green. It is a great mistake, although not as great a mistake as the red and green braided extensions which are dangling from his fluorescent crown. We cannot know who bears responsibility for them, but since he wears on his chest a patch which reads: 'Hairways Hair Salon', we have our suspicions. His nickname is

'Snake Bite', a title he wears in glittering capitals across his shoulders. With all these exotic hostages to fortune, and a blankly bewildered expression on his face, the signs suggest that Wright may have a problem with Phil 'The Power'.

That impression is strengthened when Taylor wins the first set 3–0. Concentrating intensely, like an opening bat awaiting a fast bowler, he ignores his opponent completely as he goes about his business. I try to analyse his technique, but to me it looks just like all the others. The second set has the same, abrupt outcome. And by the time Taylor wins the first two legs of the next set, most of the crowd have lost interest. Apart from periodic, communal bursts of 'Ring Of Fire', the tiers and the seats are going at it like the Montagues and the Capulets. 'You're not singing any more!' accuse the £35 plutocrats. 'Bor-ing, bor-ing tables!' reply the defiant £25 paupers. It is the purest farce. Take away the language and the venom, and we could be in the nursery. I force myself to look at the man that Lowestoft knows as Snake Bite. Having gone to so much trouble with his ridiculous hair and his risible nickname, he has now lost the first eight legs. Might he be feeling just the slightest bit foolish?

Clearly not. Taylor has been exchanging pleasantries with a cameraman, but his attention is retrieved as Wright wins the ninth leg. Then the tenth. And soon after that, the set. Phil gives a little wince, stuffs his darts in his top pocket and strides off stage for a drink of whatever it is that these finely tuned athletes consume during intervals. The crowd din is tremendous, yet it has nothing whatever to do with the match. Instead, the weird altercation between tiers and tables rages on. 'Tables, tables give us a wave' taunt the tiers, while their chosen opponents clamber up on their own tables and retaliate with ripely abusive chants of their own. Occasionally, the factions step out of character. When they consider a chant particularly witty, they will stand and applaud. Their applause is returned. For a few bright, shining moments, mutual admiration reigns. I sneak a look at the house rules: 'Drunkenness will not be tolerated … If you shout out, whistle or boo whilst players are throwing, you may be ejected without warning.' They are printed in exceedingly small type at the foot of the inside back page of a 52-page programme. As such, they are quite easy to overlook.

The match lumbers on through the prevailing chaos. To my inexpert eye, it hinges on one interchange in the fourth set. Wright needs double-9 for the third leg. He sets himself, walks away, then walks nervously back. Had he been a golfer, you would have backed him to miss the putt. As it is, he misses his double. Taylor hurries to the oche and promptly buries his own double for the leg. Precision personified, indeed. The crisis is over and, by four sets to one, he reaches the quarter-finals of the championship for the 18th successive year. The news slowly penetrates the bedlam of the arena. Taylor appears to be taking a bow, which suggests that a conclusion has been achieved. But most seem not to notice, because by now the tiers are standing on chairs and the tables on tables, and everyone is chanting and cheering and pointing and shouting, as if United were playing City, with the title at stake. The champ slips away, almost unnoticed. Later, he acknowledges the distraction. 'It was difficult to concentrate,' says Taylor. 'When I went six-nothing up, the crowd started to amuse themselves. They seemed to lose interest. Funny that.'

Barry Hearn had spoken about people who come with the firm intention of enjoying themselves. As they make their way out into the freezing fog to search for cars and buses – many wearing Father Christmas hats, a few walking with a stumble in their step – they appear to have achieved their ambition. The bus drivers have been sitting for hours in their darkened cabs: some dozing, some gossiping, a few leaning out of the window to puff at illicit cigarettes. They are bored beyond words, but they try not to show it. So they switch on tight smiles as their passengers come weaving through the mist, preceded by the sound of their song:

It burns, burns, burns,
The ring of fire...

It's a long, long way to Wigan or Wolverhampton. Many a mile, many a chorus.

I remain more convinced than ever that what we have seen this evening is not really sport, not as most of us understand that term. Rather, it is a game show, an entertainment requiring no special physical attributes yet demanding a strong nerve, steady hand and the ability to ignore the wail of hostile choristers. And does that matter? Probably not. For as Hearn also said, we live in hard times, difficult times. If it takes somebody like 'The Power' or 'The Pie Man', or even dear old 'Snake Bite' from Lowestoft to give them 'a right good night out', then so be it. For such is 'the magic of Ally Pally'. As that chap from Labrokes will tell you, Christmas just wouldn't be Christmas without it.

Events took one or two unexpected turns after that day at the Palace. Taylor was beaten in his quarter-final by Mark 'Webby' Webster, who was himself defeated by Adrian 'Jackpot' Lewis in the semi-final. This match was attended by Prince Harry, who has yet to acquire a memorable nickname. The Prince was made most welcome at the Palace. When he hugged the portly 'Jackpot' in celebration, he received a kiss on the cheek. Lewis went on to win the world title by beating Gary Anderson, 'The Flying Scotsman'. He said he was 'over the moon … living in dreamland'. It was put to him that the title, along with the £200,000 prize, might be 'life-changing'. He nodded reflectively, then his face lit up: '£200,000!' he said. 'I can pay me tax bill now. I only owe £108,000.' 'Appy days.

'He'll blow them away. Trust me.'

CHAPTER 12
SNOOKER AT WEMBLEY

Despite the sombre bleakness of the January afternoon, the man in the Wembley car park is in ebullient mood. 'Where we off to today, then?' he asks. 'The Arena,' I say, 'for the snooker.' He nods his head, politely unimpressed. He gazes across his broad acres, at the hundreds of untenanted spaces. '*Strictly*'s on the week after next,' he says. 'We'll be packed out for that.'

He seems quite cheered by the prospect; on two midwinter evenings, a total of 25,000 people will converge upon the London Borough of Brent to watch a bunch of D-list celebs and Ann Widdecombe perform an indifferent tango. And what has ignited public interest in the arcane world of ballroom dancing? Why, the enduring power of television. The combination of peak-time exposure and regular engagement with the participants has created an entertainment phenomenon that sells tickets the length and breadth of these islands. Just as it did with snooker.

If television had not recognised the possibilities of the game, then snooker would still be confined to the back rooms of pubs or to small, raffish clubs on humble high streets. Until the late Sixties, the public was largely indifferent to its charms, to the extent that no world championship was held between 1958 and 1963. The cameras, or more precisely the colour cameras, changed everything. From the mid-Seventies, hours, days and weeks of coverage became increasingly common. It was easy, cheap and relatively undemanding. And by virtue of this relentless exposure, it produced its own cast of characters, each of whom acquired his own defining image. Thus, Steve Davis was 'robotic', Jimmy White was at first the 'crowd-pleaser', then later: 'The best player never to…' The young Stephen Hendry was 'dour' yet undeniably successful, while Alex 'Hurricane' Higgins was given the trite label of 'flawed genius', and he wore it like a badge of honour.

People knew them as they knew the cast of a soap opera. Loyalties were pledged, antipathies were nurtured, and all manner of meaning was read into the smallest gesture, the most fleeting facial expression. The game itself appeared little more than a vehicle for parading the personalities of those who played it. To those of us who were largely immune to its charms, it seemed to involve a high degree of ball skill, a rudimentary grasp of geometry and the smallest smattering of strategy. Of course, it was a good deal more subtle than an uncomplicated pub game like darts but, like darts, it demanded no physical effort or commitment. We wondered what might happen to the phenomenon when the familiar cast of the Eighties and Nineties started to yield to the next generation.

Well, the flower of that generation, a field 16-strong, has assembled for the Ladbrokes Masters. It offers prize money of £500,000, with £150,000 to the winner. Only the world championship is more lucrative. At the box office, a tall man with a pointed beard is pondering an investment. The cost of the afternoon match between the former world champion Mark Williams and Ding Junhui is £10. The evening match between John Higgins and Graeme Dott is priced at £15. An all-day ticket costs £20. But news has reached us that Ding is leading by four frames to one, and needs just two more frames for the match. Should the bearded one settle for just an evening ticket, or should he pay an extra fiver on the off-chance of witnessing a decent finish? He continues to debate the point with himself until the lady behind the glass coughs politely. Whereupon he hands over a £20 note, as we always knew he would.

Inside, the Arena floor has been divided into sections by sliding walls and curtains. The place can accommodate 12,750 people, but snooker can be watched by only a fraction of that total. It must have been somewhere close to this spot that, almost a quarter of a century ago, I sat at ringside to watch Frank Bruno fight a 17-stone South African. In the opening round, I looked down to scribble a note when a large, lifeless head came smashing down on my writing pad. Bruno had knocked his man clean through the ropes. I recall the din of the crowd, and the bark of the referee's superfluous count. Most of all I recall a small, heart-rending voice, cutting through the clamour. It came from beneath the ring, and it pleaded: 'Will someone get that big bastard off me?' It was the voice of a *Daily Express* photographer, who had been struck by a falling heavyweight.

No din today. No clamour, no noise at all, save the click of the balls and the low hum of the air conditioning. It had never occurred to me that the silence would be so profound. Why, nobody even coughs. This is London in early January, midway through a particularly miserable winter, and it appears that nobody has so much as a sore throat! The National Theatre would kill for an audience half as healthy. In truth, the NT might like a slightly larger audience than this afternoon's congregation. Attempting to count the customers, I get to 427 before a group moves seats and spoils my calculations. But they are concentrating hard, helped by the informative commentary they receive from radio earpieces which they bought on the way in for £6.

No din today. No clamour, no noise at all, save the click of the balls and the low hum of the air conditioning

Ding Junhui, seeded nine, was born near Shanghai and resides in Sheffield during the snooker season. A small, serious man in his early thirties, he was once presented with 276 pies as part of his prize for winning the 2009 UK Championship. I can think of one or two darts players who might have tucked right in, with some brown sauce and a few jars. Ding passed them on to a local charity. He has perhaps 12 or 15 of his compatriots dotted around the banked seats, each of them conveying support by an encouraging smile or a sympathetic frown. He seems quite unaware of their presence as he circles the table in his black shirt with its mandatory Ladbrokes logo, concentrating fiercely, chalking his cue with meticulous care, a surgeon contemplating his first incision. From time to time, a brief patter of applause will acclaim a particularly deft pot. Totally ignored. Those who know about the game suggest that Ding's temperament is a trifle suspect, that his finishing is less than ruthless and that from time to time he buckles beneath the pressure. And yet, he seems to exist in a world of his own, and his skills are remarkable. Every so often, Ding does something amazing, and people clap and look at each other, as if to say: 'Fair dos. The boy can play.'

Mark Williams, by contrast, seems to be seeking distraction as Ding accumulates points and frames. He spends a great deal of time in his black leather armchair, occasionally looking up despairingly to the crowd, to somebody I take to be his manager. Williams is in his mid-thirties, comes from Cwm in South Wales and appears thoroughly out of sorts. It is difficult to think of another game which requires one player to sit in full public view, looking on as his opponent racks up point after point. Clearly, he is yearning for Ding to miss. But etiquette forbids him to reveal a trace of emotion. So he sits and stoically stares into the middle distance, his cue leaning against his leg. Occasionally, he wipes his hands on his towel or toys with his sponsored water. But mostly, he just sits. Helpless, and full of foreboding.

Seeded five, he is plainly an outstanding player; twice champion of the world and twice winner of the Masters. A year earlier, he beat Ding in the final of the exotically named Sanyuan Foods China Open in Beijing. Apparently, he is known in China as 'the man who won the Sanyuan'. The victory is rarely celebrated in Cwm. And yet, for all his success, even his best friends might not call him 'charismatic'. I delve into his background to seek a hint of devilment. He is partly colour-blind, which may be of no great matter to, say, a rugby prop forward but is a significant affliction to a snooker player. Somewhere on his body, he bears a tattoo depicting the Welsh dragon eating the English flag. And he has been nicknamed 'The Welsh Potting Machine', which makes him sound like a garden implement. All very well, but it doesn't come close to urinating in the sponsors' plant pot or head-butting the referee, the sort of pranks which the 'Hurricane' got up to when he was being more 'flawed' than 'genius'. It is difficult to squeeze a headline from a potting machine.

Yet most of the crowd are supporting Williams, largely because it is much easier to get to Wembley from South Wales than from Shanghai.

'G'orn, Mark!' they call, three different voices earnestly entreating as he goes 5–1 down. It is difficult to spot the callers, the hall being dark and the voices modulated, for fear of upsetting fellow members of the audience. Mark reacts with a forlorn twitch of the shoulders. I recall a quite different reaction from the terminally graceless Jimmy Connors who, when being beaten out of sight at a long-ago Wimbledon, bawled at the sympathetic crowd: 'I'm trying, for Chrissakes!'

Mark pads miserably offstage for the brief break as music crashes out: 'Back to life, back to reality'. Ding sets off with purposeful stride, like a man who could use 10 minutes' practice. Strobe lighting sweeps the arena, dramatic as a school disco. Lots of people begin to cough, having stifled the irritation throughout the past frame. Small knots of spectators assemble to discuss events and hazard forecasts. They speak in strangely hushed tones, as if someone, somewhere might be disturbed by full volume. A light comes on in a raised studio at the far end of the arena. I spot the robotic Steve Davis talking to the Irishman Ken Doherty, another former world champion. Belatedly, I realise that both men are live on television. Now if this were a darts event, the fans would be waving placards, bellowing witty ditties and making all manner of saucy signs in an attempt to find a place in the picture. Here, they maintain their dignity as they discuss Williams' chances of finding a way back into the match.

The players return, offering themselves to the scrutiny of two cameras drifting some 10 feet beyond the table and trained on the action. You suspect those cameras are not going to miss much action. After all, this is not ice hockey, rather it is a game with all the pace and energy of a state funeral. The referee encourages that leisurely illusion. Jan Verhaas is tall and Dutch, with steel-grey hair and the white gloves of his calling. He wears a dinner jacket emblazoned with the logo of the people who supply the green baize for the table. And he drifts discreetly around that table, murmuring the scores in a soft incantation. For some, he resembles a functionary at Sotheby's, purveying priceless porcelain in pristine gloves. For others, he has the bearing of one of nature's head-waiters: 'Chef says the turbot's awfully good

… this is not ice hockey, rather it is a game with all the pace and energy of a state funeral

today, sir.' But those of us who have read the programme are aware that this paragon is not entirely infallible. He confesses that his most embarrassing moment was 'oversleeping twice in the same day when he was supposed to be refereeing Premier League matches in Cleethorpes'.

The return of the players signifies a change in Williams' fortunes. The 'Potting Machine' starts to live up to his name. Balls of many colours start to disappear. He gets the score back to 4–5, and 'G'orn Mark' becomes the muted cry of the hour. The watchers are entranced, studying the happenings on the table, then checking them with the big screens strung around the arena. They seem to be concentrating more intensely than ever; the old couple, chin wedged in palms in the top row, the Liverpool shirt halfway up, the West Ham shirt five rows back and the stout young man in the Alice Cooper T-shirt, plumb in the centre of the front row. Ding sits, arms folded, still as a statue as his lead evaporates. It doesn't last. Williams misses, to a suppressed 'Ooooooh!' Ding takes a last swig at his water, rises from his own black leather chair, and strides to the table. Click-click-click, pot-pot-pot! A final pink slips from view. With a morose little frown and the shadow of a wince, Mark signals his concession and accepts his first-round defeat. To his credit, he signs two or three autographs before disappearing. Ding scrawls a few and poses for a picture with a beaming Chinese girl. There is applause. It is all very civilised.

Leaving the arena, I pass through several empty corridors. Some have pictures of Wembley's more celebrated acts: Madonna, Jagger, Status Quo. None, so far as I can see, of the 'Hurricane' or Steve Davis. Turning a corner, I see a player stretching across a practice table. He is wearing a tracksuit. I never imagined that they might ever wear anything other than a waistcoat.

I pause at the merchandise stall in the foyer. They are offering snooker cues for £115, a ball marker for £7, cue tips for £3, white cotton gloves for £10, T-shirts bearing the logos 'Nugget', 'Jester', 'Wizard', 'Rocket', 'Whirlwind', and 'Give Me A Break'. They also offer, intriguingly, a yo-yo that carries the World Snooker logo. I feel I am missing the point. Across the foyer, a small stall has been set up and a queue is starting to form. After 5 minutes or so, with the queue now

28-people strong, out walks the victorious Ding Junhui. He greets them all with an affable grin: shaking their hands, signing their programmes, posing for their pictures. It is an impressive little scene, which reflects well on both the player and his game.

With 2 hours to kill before the evening session, I take a walk around the complex, crossing the bridge which leads into Wembley Stadium. As always, I feel a quite illogical sense of ownership. Around a decade earlier, I served on the council of Sport England, the body which distributes National Lottery funds throughout the sporting nation. Our most controversial project was the new Wembley Stadium, when we attempted to steer a prudent course between the public interest and the outrageous demands of professional football. After anguished deliberation, we agreed to subsidise Wembley to the tune of £120 million. The entire scheme was finely balanced until the last few days of negotiation, which involved a number of talented civil servants and lawyers, and one of my council colleagues, a celebrated entrepreneur named David Ross. He had worked unsparingly throughout the final stages, driving bargains and concluding contracts. And when the deal was done, two signatures were needed on the final document: David's, of course, and another council member. I was the only one available, since I lived just half an hour away.

'Sign there, there and there,' said the lawyer.

I hesitated. 'If it all went wrong, I wouldn't be liable for anything, will I?' I asked.

'Like what?' asked the lawyer.

'Well, like £120 million,' I replied.

'Some chance,' said the sleep-deprived Ross.

'Just sign the bloody thing.'

And so I did.

Returning from the stadium, past the swirling fountains that always seem such a good idea in summer, I search out the Arena restaurant. The choice is wide, the staff attentive, the food good and the prices reasonable. As one who has learned to expect the worst from a British sporting venue, this is a surprisingly pleasant experience. The process is simple; you present yourself at the reception desk and, after being shown to a table, you are given a menu with dishes such as gammon with eggs, mushroom risotto, roast pork, all for less than £10. You then return to the desk to inform the supervisor of your choice, and go back to the table to await its arrival. I overhear the conversation on the next table, at which five people are seated. A young woman, late teens to early twenties, is concerned about the progress of her university course. Her tutors have been offering conflicting advice, and she is uncertain about her next move. Her mother, clearly an academic, offers a view, then her father weighs in, followed by her boyfriend and her brother. The pros and cons are carefully debated, then, when the subject is exhausted, they start to discuss Mark Williams' dismissal at the hands of Ding Junhui: 'Nobody saw that one coming, did they?' 'Remarkable!' Across the way, a teenage boy sits with his father and brother. He is taking a call on his mobile: 'You saw us on telly, then? ... Really? ... You're not kidding? ... So what were we doing?'

I walk back down the restaurant to order coffee. The desk is empty. Across the way, at the Ladbrokes stand, five people are perched on stools, staring at a bank of screens. They appear to be watching dogs at Wolverhampton and horses at a track in Philadelphia. Having studied the form, they place their bets with irrational confidence. As I am observing this surreal diversion, I feel a tug at my elbow: 'May I order a coffee, please? Large, white. And where would you like me to sit?'

I turn to find a lady of advanced years, with a pleasant smile, a bag over her arm and a snooker programme in her hand. I explain that I am not the restaurant manager. 'You looked as if you might be,' she said. 'You're wearing a tie.' As we wait to be served, she tells me she is a snooker fan, and that she will be 80 years old in three days' time. I ask her name.

'Pat Collins,' she replies.

'Mine too,' I say.

'Extraordinary,' she says, and smiles politely.

So we take our coffees, Mrs Patricia Collins and I, and we find ourselves a table. She has travelled in on the Metropolitan Line from Croxley Green in Hertfordshire. She restricts her outings these days, but she always finds time to visit the Masters. 'It's snooker, you see. I find it quite hypnotic. I discovered it when they brought in colour television. Like most people, I imagine. And I found that you sort of sided with certain players. Mother was quite obsessive about it. If anybody beat her Steve Davis, she'd just go mad! Really, she'd be dreadfully cross. I like Hendry myself, though I never dared say so. Not in front of Mother.' I offer her the dessert menu. She declines, politely. 'Not for me, thank you. I brought my own food from home. Nice sandwiches, a bit of fruit. That way, I know what I'm getting. Is that terribly old-fashioned?

'It's snooker, you see. I find it quite hypnotic. I discovered it when they brought in colour television…'

'I've been coming to this event for 15 years. I suppose I could easily watch the whole thing on the television, but I like to collect the programmes. That's one of the reasons why I come. I always send off for a World Championship programme. Never been, of course. Sheffield. Much too far. They used to hold the Masters at the old Conference Centre near here. It was all subsidised by the tobacco companies then. And it was so cheap! I used to come on two or three days a week then. Embassy would ring me up and tell me the times of play and who was playing. It made everything quite easy. The current people don't seem to bother. My husband didn't want to come to snooker himself. Never cared for it. So I'd settle him down with meals and things, and he'd watch his favourite programmes, and he was fine. And off I'd go, off to the station. It wasn't always easy. I mean, people used to be allowed to smoke in the Conference Centre when I first went there. Embassy, d'you see? It was revolting! But I persevered because I was fascinated.'

I ask if she attends any other sports. 'Not really, no,' she says. 'I certainly don't like darts. All that beer-guzzling! That doesn't appeal at all. No, snooker's the one that caught my eye. And even that's not really a sport, is it? Not what you'd call a sport. You don't get out of breath doing it. Football, tennis, badminton, things like that. Now they're sports. I don't see snooker players as a sporty sort of people, do you? But I enjoy it. I'll wait around to see some of this evening's match. Higgins and Dott, is that right? I'll probably stay until halfway. It's not really very comfortable to sit here much longer than that. I'll watch the finish at home, on television. I've got my programme now. That's the main thing.' She sets off for the Arena, to enjoy her annual treat. I doubt there will be anybody older than Mrs Collins out there today. And I'm quite sure there'll be nobody nicer.

I follow her a few minutes later, and as I approach the playing area, I can hear a voice haranguing the crowd. The voice belongs to a presenter named Rob, and I last heard it a few hours earlier on a video clip. Rob was introducing the Masters contestants to a crowded arena, and his performance was a masterpiece of hyperbole. 'It's the Jester from Leicester. It's Mark Selby!' … 'He's from Hong Kong! He's full of Eastern Promise! He's Marco Fu!' … 'All hail the coming of a snooker legend! There was more than a rumble when this man was in the jungle! He's a Wembley champion! He's the People's Champion! He's your champion! Hold on to your hats. It's the Whirlwind! It's Jimmy White!' And so on. The players came stumbling out to meet their public, wading through a babble of exclamation marks, desperately trying to remember the poses they had practised. It was awful. Somebody, possibly an image consultant, has decided that snooker players must at all costs become 'characters'. It is a toe-curling mistake, but nobody has told Rob.

Today, he is attempting to generate some atmosphere from the small crowd. We are less than 5 minutes from transmission time, and the place has yet to start buzzing. There are empty seats in the front row, which suggests lack of interest and support. This is a cardinal sin. 'Please fill these seats here,' requests Rob. 'The director has asked me to ask you.' Then, shamelessly: 'If you sit here, we can guarantee you'll be on television.' It is the ultimate inducement; after all, who wouldn't want to be on television?

Soon, the players will be making their entrances. The public must react with appropriate frenzy. There must be a rehearsal. Rob insists on it. 'We do like to punch some energy down the lens,' he yells. 'The happier you look, the more likely you are to be on TV. Let's give it the big one!' He bawls a few introductory lines and the crowd breaks into a small cheer. Not good enough. I can't see Mrs Collins. I doubt that she's giving it the big one. There is another rehearsal, another tepid cheer. Rob seems dubious, but there's nothing to be done. The director is counting down; the players are ready and waiting. Rob launches his breathless, deathless spiel which concludes with the words: 'He is the

Pocket Dynamo! He is GRAEME DOTT!' As sporting introductions go, it falls a little short of: 'Next to bowl from the Nursery End, Shane Warne,' or 'From Brownsville, New York City, Ir-on! Mike! Ty-sonnnn!' The crowd cheers. Energy is punched.

A brief interview is in order: Rob – 'How's your Christmas been? Have you seen a practice table?' Pocket Dynamo – 'Not as much as I should have seen.' Applause. Graeme retreats as another welcome is prepared. Once more, Rob delivers a tour de force as he introduces – 'The Wizard of Wishaw … JOHN HIGGINS!' The interview is equally brief, although a touch more revealing. Rob – 'You haven't quite produced your best at Wembley in this tournament?' Wizard – 'No, I've lost nine times in the first round.' A small titter ripples through the crowd to acknowledge his honesty.

In fact, the honesty of Higgins had been the subject of some debate in snooker circles, after a newspaper 'sting' operation had accused him of being party to match-fixing. As he was then world champion, the charge represented a serious blow to the integrity of the game. An independent resolution service heard the case, and Higgins received a six-month ban and a fine of £75,000 when he admitted 'intentionally giving the impression' of agreeing to breach the betting rules. Charges of accepting bribes and corrupt conduct were withdrawn. Scarcely two months have passed since the ban ended, and he is still feeling his way back into the world of competitive snooker.

Higgins does not carry the aura of a champion, moving tentatively, looking anxiously into the audience as he sets to work. Dott, who lives at Larkhall, just three miles from Wishaw, is similarly nervous. Thin and frowning, he takes an age to play his shots. He prowls the table, studying angles, considering consequences. If Jonathan Trott were a snooker player, this is precisely how he would perform. There are endless longeurs, countless safety shots. Quite soon, the match starts to drag.

I find myself studying the programme, the one for which Mrs Collins has made her journey. It yields some nuggets. I had no idea that 'Rocket' Ronnie O'Sullivan – another 'genius', possibly flawed – had considered using a purple cue last year. 'If people can adapt to being in Guantanamo Bay and those conditions, I can surely adapt to a purple cue,' he remarked, with that keen sense of perspective for which he is justly celebrated. Similarly, I was unaware that John Virgo – 'One of snooker's best loved characters' – has appeared in no fewer than eight pantomimes alongside Jim Davidson. 'I loved working with Jim, he is the most generous person I have ever worked with,' says Virgo. The programme also features my favourite advertisement, the one which poses the show-stopping question: 'Ever wondered why 80 per cent of table owners choose Aramith Belgian Phenolic Billiard Balls all the time?' The publication is a glossy masterpiece, which richly repays the fiver it costs.

'If people can adapt to being in Guantanamo Bay ... I can surely adapt to a purple cue'

But if I am restless, then I am in a tiny minority. For the slower the match becomes, the harder the audience concentrates. Nobody seems to mind, nobody thinks it irritating or unusual. George Bernard Shaw's oft-quoted remark that 'The English, not being a spiritual people, invented cricket to give them some idea of eternity' could equally well apply to snooker. They are not merely observers, they are students, noting every nuance, inwardly agonising over every option. The cast seems largely unchanged from this afternoon and, looking around, I am starting to view them as old friends. The quintet who debated the university course are sitting shoulder to shoulder, eight rows back. Alice Cooper is in the front row, brazenly soliciting a glance from the camera, while the Liverpool and West Ham shirts have been joined by a boy of 12 or 13 in Newcastle's black and white. Nobody moves. And the silence is as deep as ever, broken only by the gruff intonation of the new referee, Eirian Williams. A bulky fellow with a military moustache, he spent 18 years policing the town of Llanelli. A solid citizen, our Eirian. If he were ever to find himself in Cleethorpes, I doubt he would oversleep.

At the close of the second frame, both won by the dilatory Dott, a young man arrives clutching pints of lager. He hands one to his friend, who has been saving his seat. 'What kept you, then?' asks the friend. 'Been a bit stupid,' comes the answer. 'I was early, so I stopped in Chancery Lane. Had one, then another. Read a book. Before I knew, I'd had four pints, and I still had to get the bloody train.' His friend nods, understandingly. Easily done. Everything about them, from the drawl to the hair to the unassailable confidence, screams public school. Yet they too are students of the game. 'Winner of this plays Mr Ding next up,' says Chancery Lane. 'He'll blow them away. Trust me.'

In the row behind me, a man tells his wife that he believes he has spotted Steve Davis. Within 20 seconds they are reminiscing about that night in 1985 when Davis played Dennis Taylor in 'the greatest match in snooker history'. I believe there is a little-known law which decrees that whenever two or three snooker fans are gathered together, the topic of Davis v Taylor must be raised. All of the boxes are dutifully ticked: '18½ million viewers … after midnight … all on the black … Dennis does that double-fisted thing with the cue … never see its like again.' Both participants are fully aware of the commercial value of nostalgia. On the 25th anniversary of the greatest match, they organised a tour of the corporate lunch circuit. In Bradford, Preston, Leeds, everywhere there was chardonnay to be sipped and chicken to be chewed, they answered the same questions, made the same jokes, divulged the same coy confidences. It was said to be a huge success.

But then they were recalling an era when snooker could do no wrong. It was in 1986, just 12 months after playing their celebrated match, that Taylor and Davis, along with two or three of their contemporaries, collaborated with the great Chas & Dave in a song called 'Snooker Loopy', the chorus of which went:

Snooker loopy nuts are we,
Me and him and them and me.
We'll show you what we can do,
With a load of balls and a snooker cue.

It reached no. 6 in the UK singles chart, which says a good deal about snooker, and perhaps even more about the state of British music in the Eighties.

Dott and Higgins resume their argument. Nobody ever asked them to make a record with Chas & Dave, and if they had, then few would have bought it. But they graft away, building their breaks and pursuing their strategies, and the evening crowd maintains the silence of the grave as they strive to understand the unfolding patterns. Dott leads by three frames to one. Higgins claws it back to 4–4, then Dott wins the last two frames for a 6–4 victory. And every shot, from first to last, is watched with studious respect. It isn't my game. I stand with the lady who says that it's 'Not what you'd call a sport. You don't get out of breath doing it.' But I am impressed by the skills of the people who play, and still more by the unfailing courtesy of those who observe those skills. In snooker, the actors occupy centre stage while the audience sits and watches from beyond the footlights. It is a simple distinction, which too many games have forgotten.

I walk out into the late evening, past the persistent fountains and through the shadows of the stadium. I imagine Mrs Patricia Collins returning home to Croxley Green, making herself a coffee and settling down with her glossy programme to watch the end of Dott versus Higgins. The tournament would be full of surprises, culminating in a final contested by Ding Junhui and Marco 'He's full of Eastern Promise!' Fu. Snooker sources would report that an audience of 100 million would watch Ding's ultimate victory. That is the usual figure when China is involved. It is merely a piece of propaganda skimmed from the top of a publicist's head. But it is satisfyingly round, it sounds a touch less fanciful than 200 million, and it will be used to argue that snooker is irresistibly evolving into a world game.

That isn't how it feels this evening, in the emptiness of the car park. But no matter, serious people have been enormously entertained by professionals like Higgins and Williams, Ding and Dott. I neither understand not appreciate their curious craft, but I know that they are astonishingly good at what they do. If only Ms Widdecombe and her friends could make a similar claim.

CHAPTER 13
THE CHELTENHAM FESTIVAL

Spring has come to the Cotswolds. It arrived this morning, an hour or so after breakfast, when a weak shaft of sunlight nudged through the sulky clouds and beamed down upon Brimpsfield, Birdlip and Bishop's Cleeve. As the day wore on, the beam grew broader, lighting the hills and villages and lifting winter-jaded spirits through the lanes and byways of Gloucestershire. The seasons turned, and all things were brighter and more beautiful.

That hopeful mood seems an age away as I sit in a traffic jam on Bouncer's Lane, close by Cheltenham Racecourse, while the engine mumbles and elderly ladies nod sympathetically as they stroll past on their way to the shops. A blackboard is propped on a garden wall. It is tilted to catch the eye of dawdling drivers, and it bears the chunkily chalked inscription: 'Compost – £10 for 3 sacks'. I find myself wondering about those impulsive souls who purchase compost on their way to the races. Is it really such a bargain? Could they not buy it as cheaply at home? How do they cram three sacks into a car boot? I have ample time to consider these questions because the traffic has been stationary for 10 minutes, and the prospects are not promising.

It is the first day of the National Hunt Festival, and I have allowed myself 2½ hours for the 30-mile journey to the course. This is what a wiser, more worldly colleague will later term 'a basic schoolboy error'. The Borough of Cheltenham has a population of 112,000. Today, that number will be swollen by 53,318 visitors. Logic dictates that nobody, save an elite corps of jockeys, will be moving very quickly. As well as encouraging contemplation of compost, the jam offers the chance to enjoy BBC Radio's preamble to the Festival. I am especially struck by the response of the racing correspondent Cornelius Lysaght, when asked for his selection of the day. 'Well,' he said, 'Quevega's going for a hat-trick [in the David Nicholson Mares' Hurdle]. She does look absolutely head and shoulders above the rest. If we had a printing press to print money, I think we couldn't do any better than lumping on Quevega.' Lysaght has always struck me as a rather cautious chap, but I've rarely heard any forecaster exude such boldly unqualified confidence. We shall see.

Another 10 minutes, another ten yards. The Cheltenham authorities are aware of the problems; indeed, they have been inventing resourceful ways of spreading the load. Their website makes an intriguing offer: 'We've got hundreds of free bowler hats to give away, so get here early. First come, first served.' Sadly, it hasn't worked. By the time I have reached the car park, handed over the £10 parking fee and assured a hectoring brigade of touts that I have no spare tickets, the bowlers have gone and the first race has been run.

This is my first visit to Cheltenham for some years, and the absurdly protracted journey reminds me of the inconvenience involved. The crowds are still far too big for the facilities. The attendance is perhaps 10,000 beyond what can reasonably be accommodated. And this is day one. On Friday, day four, they are expecting around 65,000 for the Gold Cup, which is clearly insane. Yet the organisers need the revenue and the bookmakers crave the custom, so they maintain their swollen numbers while persuading the punters that acute discomfort is all part of the Cheltenham Experience. It is a hazardous ploy that, for the moment, shows few signs of being rumbled.

And yet there is enormous fondness for both the place and the event, and the feeling is readily understood. For one thing, Cheltenham is extraordinarily beautiful; 350 sprawling acres in the lee of Cleeve Hill, with the crowds in their springtime colours fringing the green, undulating track with its trim hurdles and fearsome fences.

And the horses, my God, the horses! Lean, surging, sinuous beasts, ear-prickingly alert and blessed with blistering pace and a curious nobility that marks them as the main attractions. The former jockey Mick Fitzgerald describes it rather well: 'People go to Royal Ascot to be seen,' he says. 'But they come here to see the horses. There's something almost innocent and honest about the whole deal.' Racetracks are rarely regarded as the natural homes of innocence and honesty, but again we can understand the sentiments.

'People go to Royal Ascot to be seen,' he says. 'But they come here to see the horses...'

Then there is the power of tradition. Cheltenham has been staging its Festival since 1911; indeed, today has been dubbed Centenary Day. Stirring deeds have been done in the course of that century, and the names which linger most vividly are those of the equine champions: Golden Miller and Cottage Rake, Persian War and Istabraq, Dawn Run, Best Mate and the incomparable Arkle. Even those of us for whom horse racing is little more than a hugely entertaining mystery are familiar with their achievements. Each of these horses has a racecourse bar named in its honour, while Golden Miller, Best Mate, Dawn Run and Arkle all merit Cheltenham statues. For it was at Cheltenham that their legends were created.

In truth, today's punters are less concerned with history than with profit, and none more than the visitors from Ireland. Without the Irish, Cheltenham would be scarcely more than a West Country race meeting: large, of course, and adequately important, but with little of the colour, passion, whimsy and outrageous geniality that the Irish provide in such abundance. The official line is that the numbers travelling are as great as ever, despite the perilous state of the Irish economy. This version has gallant Paddy defying the culpable gang of felonious bankers and failed politicians by ignoring the depression, wrapping the green flag round him and taking on the combined forces of England's bookmakers. It is not only patronising, but largely untrue. Seasoned observers tell us that the Irish contingent is sharply reduced, that stern reality has detained many of the dreamers. Yet their presence remains significant, their voices have not been stilled, and their horses are working their annual wonders.

One of their champions rode the winner of the opening race. Ruby Walsh, from County Kildare, is an earnest man in his early thirties. He has ridden hundreds upon hundreds of winners these past 15 years and has enjoyed more success at Cheltenham than any jockey in history. Like so many of his breed, he wears his laurels lightly; you suffer a few falls, break a few bones and dismiss it as part of the game. When you win, you praise your horse; when you are beaten, you take the blame. It is an instinctive chivalry, bred in the bone, and men like Walsh, along with A.P. McCoy, Richard Johnson, Barry Geraghty and the rest, they all observe this admirable code. And the watchers recognise their qualities. In the wide world of sport, I struggle to think of one whose participants enjoy similar, unreserved affection from its public.

In fairness, not all of that public is actually watching at first hand, whatever Mick Fitzgerald says. The races are wickedly difficult to follow with the naked eye. Given the topography of the track, the angle of the stands and the pressures involved in accommodating so vast a crowd, races are followed by means of commentary and rumour: the first is difficult to decipher above the clamorous din, the second is impossible to trust. Many turn to the scores of television screens dotted around the various stands, many more to the large screens erected at busy junctions. So easy is it to watch this coverage that a huge number of fans choose to stand and shout at the images while the real thing is taking place just a few yards away, on the other side of a fence. Some, of course, much prefer the atmosphere to the actual racing. A man known to his friends as Mike the Millionaire has made the journey from Glenbeigh in County Kerry. He was given his name when he won a prize in the Lottery; not a million, nor anything like it, but enough to enjoy his regular Cheltenham trip without worrying too much about the bills. And Mike has his familiar ways, which involve installing himself in his favourite bar, observing events and enjoying the conviviality. A young member of his company, unaware of this routine, urged him outside to watch the opening race:

'Quick, Mike!' he said. 'They're under starter's orders.'

'And who would that be?' inquired Mike.

'The horses, of course,' said his friend. 'Come and look!'

The Millionaire was affronted. 'Horses!' he snorted. 'Horses! I've been coming to Cheltenham for 16, 17 years. And never seen a horse yet.'

A good many people share Mike's preferences. Cheltenham is not short of licensed bars; I count 31, and may have missed a few. It is said that around 220,000 pints of Guinness will be drunk in these four days, just as it is suggested that some £600 million will be gambled in the course of the meeting. I suspect that both statistics are the products of a public relations seminar, but no matter: even the true figures will be spectacular.

I wander down to the rails to watch the second race. An overstatement, in truth, since nobody really 'wanders' in such an assembly. Rather, I wait for openings, shuffle sideways, apologise for bumping, drift with the throng. There is a hum of speculation and scents of new-mown grass and stale beer, the sounds and the smells of Cheltenham. I find a few square feet of space near the top of the hill, and a new sound. Music drifts across from a clearing by the private boxes. A six-man jazz band is playing a trad version of 'Exactly Like You'. A pantomime drunk, carelessly swaying, is conducting them with a rolled up newspaper. On the balcony of a ground-floor box, a stout man in a Garrick Club tie, with a cigarette in one fist and a champagne flute in the other, attempts to sing along. He doesn't know the words, but he is not deterred. As the band crashes into the finale, he punches the air and shouts: 'Yeah!' Then, as if that were insufficient, he adds: 'Yeah, baby!' His female companion gives his cheek an indulgent kiss, and tops up his glass.

There is a hum of speculation and scents of new-mown grass and stale beer, the sounds and the smells of Cheltenham

A few hats take to the air, the odd free bowler among them, when Captain Chris wins the next race, the Arkle Chase. The official racecard (£3) had shown no great enthusiasm for the chances of the eventual winner: 'While it would be unwise to rule him out, may be vulnerable again'. It sounded like a timid civil servant advising a difficult minister. At 6–1, the Captain makes mock of such caution.

By now, the day has developed a rhythm for the Cheltenham multitude: race, inquest, join stampede for bar, begin contemplation of card, take decision, place bets, cross fingers. Some are aware of a wider picture: 'Seen anyone famous?' asks a lady on the walkway behind the grandstand.

'Not sure, but I think I saw Peter O'Toole,' says her friend, a touch implausibly.

There is a brief, intriguing collision near the Gold Cup restaurant. A large man, florid of face and wearing a loud tweed suit, is having his hand pumped by an acquaintance. The florid man is complimented on his tan.

He cackles: 'Tan? Nah! Blood pressure.'

His friend is concerned. 'Honest?' he says.

There is a pause, broken by another, louder, cackle. 'Nah! Barbados.'

There are benches dotted around the grounds; all are full. On one, a woman is lightly dozing, her hat slipping towards her left ear. On another, a man is deep asleep, his mouth hanging open, a copy of the *Racing Post* in his lap. The pace is beginning to tell, the discomfort is kicking in.

Some are more fortunate, of course. In the Panoramic Restaurant, on the fifth floor of the main grandstand, overlooking the winning post, guests are enjoying 'first-class cuisine, excellent table service and, of course, that spectacular view'. They have purchased a package which includes, according to the brochure: an admission ticket, car parking (one per two people), a table for the day, an official racecard, morning coffee and biscuits on arrival, a five-course meal, television racing coverage throughout the day, floral decorations, Tote betting service and 'a dedicated hospitality team to ensure the smooth running of your day'. At an initial cost of £550, plus VAT, per head. Strong drink is an optional extra, although many guests seem to think it desirable. The Glass Fronted Restaurant is one small step down from the Panoramic. From here, you can 'watch the action as the horses thunder towards the winning post'. This suggests, correctly, that it is situated a little way down the course. You may rely upon the racecard, the coffee, the floral decorations and the dedicated hospitality team, but instead of a five-course meal, you must make do with 'a superb four-course luncheon'. Prices start at £349 plus VAT, which is surely something of a snip. Certainly they have many satisfied customers, including one Mary

Jane Skeys, from what the brochure calls 'a Facebook fan page'. She is captivated by the Cheltenham Experience. It is, she says: 'the perfect racecourse with a fantastic backdrop. I've enjoyed many a race day accompanied by good food and drink (and even shopping). What more could a girl want?' What indeed, Mary Jane?

Like so many major sporting events, Cheltenham works hard at attracting the corporate market. There are a number of appropriately titled restaurants: Gold Cup, which is 'linked to the main grandstand by the Hall of Fame, our homage to some of the sights, sounds, heroes and heroines of Cheltenham's rich history', and boasts a complimentary bar, excluding champagne. There is the Horseshoe Pavilion, the Moscow Flyer. There is a Business Club and a Festival Club. There is a membership drive going on, with the subtly unspoken yet wholly bogus implication that the title of Cheltenham Member confers social cachet. Full membership, including the Festival, costs £310 plus £100 enrolment fee, and buys entry to the Club Enclosure as well as access to the Members' Marquee on the Tote terrace. Along with reserved seating (£299 for four days) and reserved parking (£165 for the meeting), it is apparently keenly sought.

For the vast bulk of the Cheltenham crowd, all this might be happening in a faraway country of which they know little. Their needs are more modest; a kind word from a stranger, a consoling drink from a friend, a handful of pounds from an obliging bookmaker. Some are more easily come by than others. Yet on they trudge with uncomplaining tenacity, and many of them find their way to the so-called Guinness Village, a teeming conglomeration of bars, betting tents and fast-food outlets. It is said that racing is a confraternity of snobs and slobs, and both are richly represented here. There are braying voices and faces full of unconfessed sins. There are green wellies from Wessex and white stilettos from Essex. There are staggering numbers of drunks, which is surprising when the day is still young and the weight of numbers makes drink so difficult to come by. Yet everything seems to be going rather well. Fish and chips cost £8.30, and the treat is attracting long and hungry queues. Guinness is gushing at £4.10 a pint, much of it being poured in the naffly named 'Craic Bar'. In the middle of the boozy melee, five middle-aged men, slightly the worse for drink, are

attempting to harmonise 'The Boxer': 'Ly la ly, ly la la-la, ly, la, ly...' Paul
Simon would not forgive them. But they press on, heads bowed, fingers
jabbing, words jumbling. I recall the ancient boast: 'There's more drink
spilled at Cheltenham than drunk at Royal Ascot.' There are no figures
to support that assertion, but I wouldn't doubt it for a moment.

Seeking sanity, I shuffle through the tangled gathering and walk
away from the masses to a small tent on the edge of the crowd. The
Arkle Bookshop caters for a limited clientele. There are signed copies
of Ruby Walsh's biography. There is the biography of A.P. McCoy.
There is Jilly Cooper's *Jump*. I scan the volumes, and then notice
a familiar face lurking beneath a brown trilby at the rear of the tent. At
the age of 93, Sir Peter O'Sullevan has driven himself to the course.
Now he is signing copies of his latest book and receiving respectful
compliments from members of a small queue. One man whispers
a brief tale. Sir Peter nods his interest. 'Thanks for listening. Very kind,'
says the man. And he adds: 'You're one of my true legends.' The true
legend inclines his head, and scribbles another autograph. Close by the
bookshop is the Cheltenham Superstore. It is offering 'Centenary' ties,
caps, teddy bears and tablemats. I do not linger. Instead, I hurry across
to the big screen to watch the next race.

As the horses thunder up the hill and a roar wells up from the
adjoining stand, a man in a green sweatshirt is jumping up and down.
His face is a disturbing shade of scarlet and he seems to be screaming
louder than the rest. 'Go'rn, Daryl! Go'rn, Daryl!' he shrieks. And
then, mysteriously: 'Double 'andful! Double 'andful!' The racecard
indicates that his favoured horse is Reve de Sivola, which is ridden
by Daryl Jacob. It is a 9–1 chance and it appears to be hanging on for
third place. I conclude that my man in the sweatshirt has backed it
each-way. It is his passion, bordering on desperation, which intrigues
me. What makes him scream so urgently? Is it something as basic as
money? Surely not, since at best he can only double his stake; scarcely
a life-changing amount. Is he pleading for the vindication of his own
judgement? Nothing so trivial, I fancy. Is he simply carried away by the
thrill of fine sport? Possibly, but that kind of emotion usually springs
from a loyalty to a team or an individual. It is likely that this gentleman
has never before set eyes on the horse, and is quite unacquainted with

the owner or the trainer, or even with Daryl, whose name he yells with such ferocity. No, his only link with Reve de Sivola and the jockey on his back is the fact that he has selected them from a field of 19, he has invested in his hunch and he now suspects that bawling advice at a large screen might somehow bring the process to a successful conclusion. It is a line of reasoning which only a gambler may truly understand.

Barriers are lowered to hold back the crowds as the runners leave the course. The horses, sweating and snorting, regard their audience with haughty indifference. The trainers are equally haughty, equally indifferent, like men who know the secrets of the universe and have no intention of sharing them. The owners and part owners tend to lack that kind of assurance. They walk with self-conscious strides, pretending they haven't noticed the public staring at them as they follow in the wake of their animals. Finally, there are lots of vets in green jackets. Intense characters of some authority, they are important figures at the Festival.

The overwhelming impression is of tweed, thousands of yards of tweed, tailored to create overcoats, jackets and suits for both sexes

The barriers rise, the crowds converge. The overwhelming impression is of tweed, thousands of yards of tweed, tailored to create overcoats, jackets and suits for both sexes. Most of it is in green; sage green, asparagus green, pea green, camouflage green. Much of it is intersected by a windowpane check, with russet being the favoured colour. For countrymen and women, it represents a uniform: his and hers, perfectly natural, possibly compulsory. Townies tend to wonder where on earth they sell those clothes.

The answer is tucked away beside the Guinness Village, a row of trade stands where discerning shoppers might equip themselves for the next ten Cheltenhams. They carry the promise of 'country clothing with style and performance': Royals of Leyburn, Wizzer and Whitehead, Bredon Hill Shooting School. John Betjeman would have dashed off three fizzing verses before the last race with such names to hand. I watch a couple, in their late forties, as they examine the various delights. The man, in tan trousers, is studying a green gilet. He is approached by a young fogey in green fitted overcoat with velvet collar. 'Need any help, sir?' inquires the fogey. The shopper shoots him a mirthless smile and carries on studying. He tries his luck with the woman, square and hefty, who is assessing a ladies' shooting coat, also in green and featuring a map pocket and two cartridge pockets. 'Madam...' he begins. She stuns him with a glance. I long to tell her that a few yards away at Timothy Foxx they are selling tweed hot pants. But my courage fails.

There is more than a touch of eccentricity about the Cheltenham retail experience. In the course of a long Festival day, the diligent shopper may pause at Graham McCartney Millinery: 'Purveyor of fine vintage top hats'. Or look in at Silver Editions, 'luxury for less', where they offer, among other treasures, jars of Marmite with silver-plated lids. This is clearly one of those gifts you either love or hate. A personal favourite is Stevenson Brothers: 'Rocking horses made to commission'. I imagine the man in tan trousers remarking to his square and hefty soulmate: 'That reminds me, old thing. We need a new rocking horse.' And she grunting her derision: 'How, pray, are you intending to get it home? We've got three sacks of your bloody compost in the boot. Remember?'

I make my way to the rails to watch the Champion Hurdle, or rather, the Stan James Champion Hurdle, since it is being sponsored by the bookmaker. The reasons for the sponsorship have nothing to do with advertising or brand awareness or forcing a name in front of the nation. They are wholly altruistic. As the chief executive explains, perhaps with a lump in his throat: 'Stan James benefits from racing, and we felt we had to give something back.'

There are rumours of a major Irish gamble on this one, with most of the action involving Hurricane Fly, the mount of Ruby Walsh. A week earlier at Naas, while easing his way back following a badly broken leg, he fell from his mount and was buried beneath another horse. As the animal rolled away, Ruby was heavily trampled by a third horse. A couple of hours ago, I heard him interviewed. 'How are you, Ruby?' came the opening question. 'I'm grand,' he replied. There was never a chance of his missing the Champion Hurdle, and today, bold, brave and undaunted, he sits aboard the favourite. Those who truly understand National Hunt racing will speak of the rider's sensitive touch, his nerveless judgement of pace. I see little more than a busy man in blue silks with green diamonds lifting a hulking bay gelding up the hill to hustle him home by a length and a quarter.

You can hear the brogue in the Cheltenham roar, a noise that tells of a race won and a project completed. The losing jockeys come bobbing across to congratulate Walsh; generous characters, they understand his suffering and acknowledge his triumph. They are the best of friends, the best of men. Then they retreat, crestfallen, while Ruby is interviewed by a woman in a curious hat. He brings Hurricane Fly along the front of the grandstand while the applause flows down in sumptuous waves. The punters wave their winning tickets at him, and he punches the air, a great grin on his anxious face. He springs from the saddle in the winners' enclosure as people jostle to slap the horse. A bucket of water is produced, and Hurricane drinks nonchalantly. A green winners' blanket is thrown across his back. Lots of people pose for pictures, they are known as 'the connections'. The air is bubbling and there is a feeling that we have just witnessed something rather wonderful. But two men in front of me turn away with shoulders slumped.

The losing jockeys come bobbing across to congratulate Walsh; generous characters, they understand his suffering and acknowledge his triumph

'Good position, but he couldn't find a thing,' says one of his own fallible fancy.

'Not a thing,' says his friend.

'Flat, he was,' mutters the first man.

'Flat,' agrees his friend. For every winner...

While the Hibernian visitors count their cash, we are told that the owners of Hurricane Fly have won £161,246. In 1911, a two-day meeting, the total prize money was £3,310. This year, £3,375,000 will be distributed over the four days, an average of around £125,000 per race. Over by the press room, I meet a bored tabloid news reporter.

'I'm looking for celebs,' he says. 'You seen any?'

I say I've heard that Zara Phillips is around. 'Very helpful,' he says. 'Every other woman in this place looks like Zara Phillips.'

I make an excuse and leave to watch the next race, a cross-country steeplechase.

This time I choose the ring as my vantage point, partly because most of the action is taking place a long way off, and partly because I want to watch the bookies. They are an unremarkable group: conservative jackets, sober ties. Any one of them could join an identity parade without fear of the tap on the shoulder. By the time I arrive, the bulk of their business has been done. They stand at their pitches, six together, as a distant voice barks: 'And they're away!' Not one of them watches the race, either on screen or in reality. Instead, they swap small jokes, clear away the clutter of the recent activity, swig at water bottles to clear the head.

Their clients, by contrast, are becoming agitated.

'One Cool Cookie has run out,' booms the race commentator.

'Good!' grunts an elderly man, staring at his card. 'I ain't bothered about that one,' he adds, ruthlessly.

After almost four arduous miles and an immoderate number of fences, home comes a horse named Sizing Australia, trained in Knockeen, County Waterford. It is a good result for the Irish and, at 13–2, a decent result for the bookies. They show not a sliver of emotion, unlike the paunchy gentleman with a three-day beard, grubby trainers, elderly jeans and a red woollen hat. As the horse crosses the line, he holds both arms to the skies, swears very loudly and makes his intentions crystal clear by yelling: 'Right! Which way's the champagne bar?'

Weariness is setting in, and the opening day is not yet done. Even for a non-combatant, there is something strangely draining about the crush of the crowd, with all its conflicting emotions: joy and elation, disappointment and despair. I meet an Irish friend, a man of robust constitution, who is making plans for his annual visit to the Punchestown Festival for five days in May.

'What's that like?' I ask.

He searches for the *mot juste*. 'Lively,' he says.

My ailing spirits are lifted by the prospect of the next race, the David Nicholson Mares' Hurdle, and the appearance of the horse that will carry not only Ruby Walsh but also the professional reputation of Cornelius Lysaght.

All afternoon I have been quoting Lysaght's unreserved recommendation: 'Quevega ... head and shoulders above the rest ...

printing press to print money'. Nobody actually scoffed, but many were agnostic. One prominent racing person confided that such immoderate confidence was the reason why bookmakers lived in extremely large houses. I think of him as Quevega takes up the running at the second-last hurdle and appears to be yawning at the ease of it all. She stretches her legs, languidly accelerates and comes trotting up the hill to win by ten lengths at odds of 5–6. Ruby has his third winner and the indomitable Irishry are enjoying the day of days.

I retreat from the contest. Past the Guinness Village, where the singing is louder and still more discordant. Past the parade ring and the winners' enclosure. Past the weighing room and the Arkle statue and a cashpoint at which 13 people are queuing: shuffling forward, jabbing in their pin numbers, wincing as they make their demand. The last time I was here there was frost in the ground, and snow was dusting the slope of Cleeve Hill. Today, the air is mild and the sun is lingering into late afternoon. A bitterly protracted winter has finally relented. Optimism abounds; life is good. Spring has come to the Cotswolds.

EPILOGUE
Looking Back: Marvellous Memories (and a Meat Pie)

A dictionary definition of the term 'sport' tells us it is 'an activity involving physical exertion and skill, in which an individual or team competes against another or others for entertainment.' Nothing could be more simple, nor more splendid. That word 'entertainment' places it in its true perspective. Sport is a diversion, an amusement, an activity designed to give pleasure to both players and watchers. It demands exceptional dedication and sacrifice from those who aspire to its highest levels, but it becomes dangerous only when it loses that essential perspective.

One of the most pleasing discoveries of my journey was the way in which the passions of all the various fans fell comfortably short of fanaticism. Of course the result is important: if it wasn't, then why keep the score? But the games, all the games, are played for reasons that far surpass cold statistics. An especially agreeable revelation was the BBC Radio football phone-in. Naturally, a number of partisan points were paraded, but the really effective contributors were those who argued a principled case and rejected the pragmatism which prizes destinations far above journeys.

Courage was another recurring virtue, one that is not always appreciated from the relatively insulated press box. There is the physical courage to be found at the looming fences of the point-to-point, or on the first hazardous bend as the speeding bikes converge. And there is the daunting combination of physical and mental fortitude that attends the opening over of a Test match, or those moments in the Ryder Cup when short putts must be buried and drives must find the fairway. The fans revealed an instant, heartening recognition of this central quality of competitive sport.

Mention of speeding bikes prompts another warming reflection. When it comes to sport, I thought I knew what I liked. I love Canterbury and Twickenham and I suspected, of course, that the Ryder Cup, the Adelaide Test and the football World Cup would be stunning. And so I set out eagerly for those events, while others were calls of duty, undertaken to fulfil a schedule. Well, as it happened, the point-to-point was wonderful, the speedway was genuinely thrilling and Crayford dogs was a terrific night out, superbly organised by hard-working people. Still more surprising was the transformation of Wimbledon. The sport is truly sublime, but it has become a venue which actively welcomes its public, and that was probably the single most gratifying discovery of my tour.

The snooker was distinguished by the intensity of its audience; studiously silent and patently knowledgeable, they brought an air of sober sanity to a rackety old game. The darts fans were rather different. Like Wimbledon, I hadn't visited a darts tournament for many years. Unlike Wimbledon, it hasn't changed a scrap. Alexandra Palace was packed with people who seemed to be having a night off from football. Their songs, jokes, gestures and attitudes were all taken from the grandstands and terraces of the nation's winter game. I cannot regard darts as authentic sport, indeed, that phrase in the dictionary definition – 'an activity involving physical exertion' – would seem to settle the matter. There is also the fact that, on the night I attended, many of the customers appeared to be drunk, and most of the drunks seemed intent on verbal confrontation with imaginary enemies.

And yet I concede that the whole affair has acquired a kind of laddish cachet. A day or two after my visit, I heard two BBC radio broadcasters discussing their night out at the Palace. They were much taken with the process by which a witless slogan is scrawled upon a placard and flaunted before the television cameras in the hope of being picked up. 'Did your table's slogan get read out?' earnestly inquired one presenter. 'No,' said his colleague. 'We tried, but it's not easy. You know how it is.' On reflection, 'laddish' may be far too kind.

The notion of appearing on television retains a curious appeal. The darts crowd would sell their grandmothers for five seconds of screen time, likewise a chunk of the Wimbledon patrons. At the Wembley Arena, the snooker director actually appealed for fans to fill the front row seats, with a guaranteed place on television as the reward. Andy Warhol spoke slightingly of 15 minutes of fame. What might he have made of five seconds?

Drink plays a major part in the spectator experience; at the darts obviously, but also, in moderation, at the dogs. Rugby and booze have been propping each other up since Prince Obolensky revealed a nifty outside break at Thirties Twickenham, and detailed research reveals that the alliance is as firm as ever. England's World Cup watchers guzzled their fill, but mercifully declined to use the excuse to wipe out Cape Town. The Cheltenham Festival has elevated drinking to the level of a four-day event. And, in the heat of a critical Test match, the lawns of the South Australian Cricket Association were engagingly awash with booze and bonhomie.

Food receives rather less attention. Suffice to say that Crayford dogs offers a bargain, that corporate Twickenham costs roughly the same as a second-hand Ford Fiesta, that Wembley Arena is both reasonable and excellent, and that Alexandra Palace is dreadful beyond words. A speedway 'salad burger' won no friends, but my stomach, not especially sensitive, still rebels at the memory of a noxiously grisly Ally Pally meat pie. On balance, the fans are not well served by the available fare.

And yet they return, again and again, because they adore the experience, they relish the entertainment on offer, and because they seek the Holy Grail, when extraordinary achievement unfolds before their eyes and when pride and pleasure coalesce in a memory to endure down the years. In short, they yearn for another Ryder Cup. The mud and the din and the glory of that day in South Wales represented the ultimate spectator experience. It was the pinnacle of my gleeful journey.

ACKNOWLEDGEMENTS

I should like to thank all those who have so generously helped in the preparation of this book. Not only my amazing wife and wonderfully supportive family, but also Malcolm Vallerius, (Sports Editor, *Mail on Sunday*), Tim Phillips (Wimbledon), Hannah Grisell (point-to-point), Russell Lanning (speedway), Ed Delaney (Test cricket), Jo Tongue and Dan Garvey (BBC Radio), Mark Pennell (Kent cricket), Ian Bland and Barry Stanton (greyhounds), Trevor Geer and Chris Macdonald (speedway). And Matthew Engel, whose judgement is greatly valued and whose editorial sympathy is enormously appreciated.

INDEX